The Free Women of Petersburg

Anne Scott
The Southern Lady

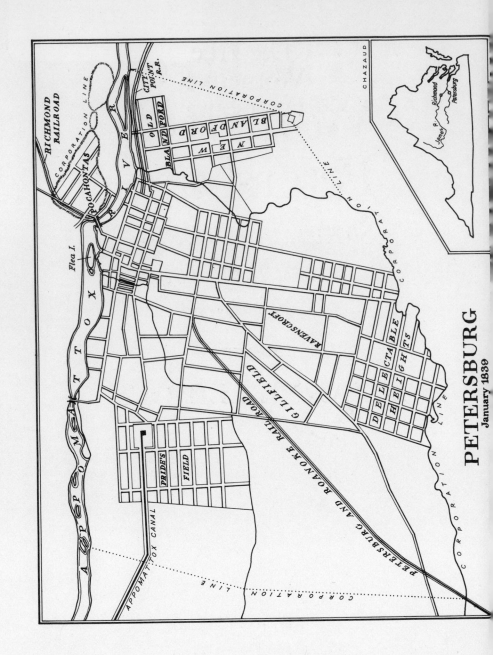

PETERSBURG
January 1839

The Free Women of Petersburg

Status and Culture in a Southern Town, 1784–1860

SUZANNE LEBSOCK

W·W·Norton & Company

New York   London

First published as a Norton paperback in 1985

Published simultaneously in Canada by
Penguin Books Canada Ltd,
2801 John Street, Markham, Ontario L3R 1B4.
Printed in the United States of America.

The text of this book is composed in Bembo, with
display type set in Baskerville. Composition and
manufacturing by the Maple-Vail Book Manufacturing Group
Book design by Bernard Klein

Library of Congress Cataloging in Publication Data
Lebsock, Suzanne.
The free women of Petersburg.
Bibliography: p. 250
Includes index.
1. Women—Virginia—Petersburg—History—19th century.
2. Women—Virginia—Petersburg—Social conditions.
3. Women—Virginia—Petersburg—Economic conditions.
4. Afro-American women—Virginia—Petersburg—History—
19th century. 5. Petersburg (Va.)—History—19th
century. I. Title.
HQ1423.L39 1984   305.4′2′09755581   83–8065

ISBN 0-393-95264-9

W. W. Norton & Company, Inc.,
500 Fifth Avenue, New York, N.Y. 10110
W. W. Norton & Company Ltd.,
37 Great Russell Street, London WC1B 3NU

2 3 4 5 6 7 8 9 0

In memory of
Mary Eisenach Lebsock
and
Lois Sommers Wells

Contents

Acknowledgments

I am part of a lucky generation. We were born too soon for formal courses and graduate programs in the history of women, but we came of age just in time to benefit from a remarkable range of activities already in progress. My first debt is to the historians who formed feminist pressure groups in the professional associations, who wrote the pioneering articles and books, who produced newsletters, who organized conferences and founded journals, and who took special pains to welcome newcomers. My more particular debts are many. At Carleton College, Kirk Jeffrey introduced me to the study of women's history in 1970. Investigating the legal status of southern women was Willie Lee Rose's idea; along with methodological clues from social history, the paper I wrote in her seminar at the University of Virginia was the germ of this book. My greater debt to Willie Rose arises from her knowing the importance of direct encouragement: "I want you to be a Scholar," she said. I wasn't sure exactly what being a capital-S scholar might mean, but I got help from a timely appointment as the student member of the American Historical Association's Committee on Women Historians. On the committee, Linda K. Kerber, Jane deHart Mathews, and the late Joan Kelly let me pester them with questions and by example taught me a great deal about scholarship, professionalism, and engagement.

From the time it was only an idea for a dissertation, Anne Firor Scott has supported this project in numerous ways. "Are you writing?" came a postcard. "If not, why not?" Joseph F. Kett saw it through as a dissertation and has remained at the ready with encouragement and good advice. Elaine Hobby, Phyllis Mack, Richard L. McCormick, Anne Firor Scott, Kathryn Kish Sklar, Ronald G. Walters, and Joan G. Zimmerman all read and critiqued the entire manuscript. So did Robert E. Kehoe, my editor at W. W. Norton, who has been helpful in every respect. Paul Clemens, Roberta Clemens, Mary Hartman, Martha Howell, Charles McCurdy, James Reed, Catherine Swatek, Warren Susman, Judy Walkowitz, and Virginia Yans offered beneficial suggestions at various stages. Veronica Yarus's diligent typing helped me meet an urgent deadline. Many of those already named were my friends long before they were called upon to be my critics, and I want to thank them for their friendship. I also want to thank other friends and family members who provided moral support: Kenneth Lebsock, Maxine Lebsock, Tessa Bridal, Randall Lebsock, Louise Kilpatrick, Pat Kilpatrick, Larissa Brown, Jim Jubak, Dee Garrison, Peggy Darrow, Ellen Mappen, Evelyn Hu, Midge Quandt, Barbara Tucker, Jane Fremon, and Tory Mack.

In Virginia, Brent Tarter, Jon Kukla, Jeanette Kukla, Sandra Gioia Treadway, and John Treadway provided unlimited hospitality, good humor, and logistical assistance. I owe them a special debt. I also want to convey thanks to William D. Henderson for helping me become more familiar with the sights and sources of Petersburg.

I am indebted to the librarians and archivists of the following institutions: The College of William and Mary, Duke University, the Harvard University Graduate School of Business Administration, the North Carolina Division of Archives and History, the Petersburg Public Library, Princeton University, Rutgers University, the University of North Carolina—Chapel Hill, the University of Virginia, the Virginia Baptist Historical Society, the Virginia Historical Society, and the Virginia State Library. Financial assistance was granted by the Colonial Williamsburg Foundation, a Woodrow Wilson National Fellowship Foundation Doctoral Dissertation Fellowship in Women's Studies, and the American Council of Learned Societies. The Rutgers University Research Council granted summer research funds and, more important, a leave when I needed time to write.

Rutgers has proved to be an unusually supportive place for the study of women. Now we do have a formal graduate program in women's history, and time and again our graduate students have demonstrated how intellectually valuable such programs can be. The students in the Rutgers graduate seminar in the history of women—Polly Beals, Rachel Bernstein, Anna Clark, Claudia Clark, Adrienne Scerbak, Carolyn Strange, and Laura Tabili—continue to explore what it means to be feminists, scholars, and professionals, and I thank them for keeping the question alive. Together with Dick McCormick, they have made the past year one of adventure and depth.

Suzanne Lebsock
New Brunswick, New Jersey
May 1983

Introduction

The women of Petersburg would have been surprised at the suggestion that someone might want to write their history. Not one of them was famous in her own time. Most of them centered their lives on making a home, some of them on making a living—not the stuff history was made of then. Could they have known that their historian would base their story on the humdrum details that the court clerk wrote into the public record books, they probably would have been more surprised. One hopes they would also have been at least a little bit curious.

This book grows out of two major concerns. One is women's status—how it changed, and why. The other is the search for a women's culture, an attempt to find out whether women acted from a set of attitudes and values different from those held by men. Both concerns are central to the history of women, and on both counts, intensive study of local records can tell us things we could learn in no other way. This study is based on a reading of almost every extant document written in or about Petersburg, Virginia, from 1784, when the town record books were begun, to 1860. It is only one community, but the records of a single community can change the way we understand women in the past. In so doing, they can change the way we look at history itself.

Our understanding of history has already changed a good deal in the past generation, of course, and for this the increasing centrality of social history is largely responsible. Social history has many faces, as readers familiar with recent scholarship will agree, but among its central features is the conviction that we cannot develop a comprehensive vision of the past unless we study the lives of ordinary people. Most people, however, did not make it easy for historians to learn about them—they did not leave diaries or letters or autobiographies—and that helps to account for a second central feature of social history, innovation in method. Social historians have culled all kinds of new sources—city directories, probate records, the house-by-house jottings of census takers—amassing countless fragments of information in order to construct a meaningful past for groups who could not speak for themselves.

Despite the democratic impulse behind their enterprise, social historians did not at first pay very much attention to women. In the social historians' defense, it should be said that including women does pose special research problems. Accumulating evidence about ordinary men is never painless or quick; tracking women is more difficult still. Women did change their names, as many as three or four times among the chronic remarriers, and as long as the husband lived, the wife made few, if any, appearances in the local record books.

Local records are nonetheless rich sources for the recovery of the female past, so rich that historians who do community studies in the future will have to think twice before using source limitations as a rationale for excluding women. In Petersburg, women surface in every kind of source. They surface in the sources of "traditional" history—letters, diaries, institutional records, and newspapers. They surface, too, in the sources first mined by social historians—wills, deeds, court minutes, census schedules, city directories, and tax lists. These sources make it possible to describe some aspects of women's status with considerable precision, and better still, they allow us to measure and plot change over time. A major aim of this book, then, is to bring the patient methods of social history to the study of the female past.[1]

When this project was first begun, the prevailing interpretation in the history of nineteenth-century American women was the thesis of decline. The most influential work was Elisabeth Anthony Dexter's *Colonial Women of Affairs,* first published in 1924. Dexter found colonial women engaged in every imaginable trade and enterprise, and she concluded by proposing that women's economic opportunities contracted in the decades following the American Revolution. Although Dexter herself reversed that decision in a later study, her initial thesis of decline was quickly established as conventional wisdom when the rebirth of feminism in the 1960s gave rise to a new wave of historical writing on women. This made sense, given what we were learning about the nineteenth century's ideas about woman's proper place; with the cult of true womanhood, as Barbara Welter named it, women were told, more stridently and more frequently than ever before, to stay home.[2] Putting Dexter and Welter together, it was easy to imagine a female variation on the Rip Van Winkle theme: In 1750, a busy, brassy woman pauses from setting type for her newspaper to catch a few winks and wakes up blinking in 1850, becorseted and a prisoner in her own house.

Subsequent research has made it plain that no such easy scheme will do, and the evidence from Petersburg affirms that the experience of women in the nineteenth century cannot be readily classified as either decline or progress. In one respect, however, there was development in a nearly straight line: Women in Petersburg experienced increasing autonomy, autonomy in the sense of freedom from utter dependence on particular men. Relatively speaking, fewer women were married, more women found work for wages, and more married women acquired separate estates, that is, property that their husbands could not touch.

This is about as straight as any line we will be looking at. When we explore how this new autonomy was acquired and what changes it inspired in turn, the line curves in intriguing ways. To cite the clearest example, women acquired separate estates, not because anyone thought women deserved more independence, but because of the nineteenth century's sudden panics and severe economic depressions. A separate estate was a means of keeping property in the family when times were hard and families stood to lose everything because of the husband's indebtedness. It did not take organized feminism to bring about positive change in the status of women. Petersburg provides a case study of how the condition of women could change for the better in a nonfeminist, even antifeminist culture.

This is also a study in the limits of such change. Petersburg's women were not able to translate what they gained at home into bolder action in the public sphere. The 1850s, in fact, saw a sharp turn in the direction of less autonomy for women in the public sphere, as men co-opted causes formerly championed only by women, while the new organizations open to women, organizations devoted to temperance, agricultural progress, and the local library, were all auxiliaries to organizations run by men. It was as though the women were required to pay for their private gains with some visible, public currency.

Meanwhile, important areas were left out of the Petersburg records. These subjects therefore receive less attention in this book than they deserve. The widest blind spot concerns sexuality and fertility. No one wrote about sex, not the clerk of the court (the local authorities made next to no effort to regulate sexual behavior), not private citizens. Even about pregnancy, Petersburg women wrote very little. These were women who could describe vomiting or bowel diseases in gruesome detail, but pregnancies brought down a veil of modesty. In 1811, Mary Cumming announced her first pregnancy thus: "My health, my dearest Margaret, since I left England has been far from good, but do not be alarmed, it is not the climate that has any effect on me, there are other reasons which you can guess." Anna Campbell, pregnant in 1856 with her third child, crept up on the subject in a paragraph on the prospect of summer travel. "I suppose in the *natural course of things* I must expect every *two years* to be in a situation not very favourable to travelling which is the case at present."[3] A good set of vital records could help us break through this steadfast reticence, but no such records are to be had; most of the period under study fell in the gap between the parish recordkeeping of the eighteenth century and the science-inspired birth and death registers begun in the middle 1850s. In the chapters that follow, information on factors such as age, family size, and length of marriage is patched together from diverse sources to help explain the behavior of various groups. But no calculations on long-term demographic trends have been attempted.

Petersburg's records are also deficient in that they carry a class bias similar to that inherent in letters and diaries. The records are mainly about property, and although they sometimes concern only small amounts, they nonetheless tell us more about middling to rich people than they do about those with little property or none. Much of what follows is therefore about the relatively privileged. Moreover, property records do not provide the materials for distinguishing how different groups of women were affected by their class position. Property records do tell us a great deal about gender, as we compare how women and men disposed of what they owned. Property records also tell us something about race, as we compare what free blacks and whites were able to achieve. But they offer no basis for comparing the behavior of poor women with that of the well-to-do. For this reason, no general theory of women's relation to the class structure is hazarded here. At the same time, opportunities for direct comparison are seized when they do arise. The wills, for example, show that the wife of a poor man was far more likely to be named her husband's executor than was the wife of a rich man. This is one of several indicators that women were most likely to exercise control over resources when the stakes were small.

None of this should be taken to mean that women had no part in determining their own status or that they readily accepted whatever was handed them. Some women did make choices, and the greatest virtue of local records is that they permit us to see what some of those choices were. The first thing we see is an implicit critique of the fundamental constraints imposed on nineteenth-century women. This implicit criticism was leveled first of all at marriage: Free black women frequently opted not to marry the men in their lives, and an analysis of the remarriage patterns of widows shows that widows did not generally marry a second time if they were wealthy enough to remain single. The fact that the women who refused to marry again most often belonged to the upper middle class is particularly significant, for these were the women who allegedly benefited most from the new "companionate" style of marriage.

Petersburg women also made telling choices concerning work and responsibility. Antebellum women were not supposed to want careers, and they presumably did not seek gainful employment unless driven to it by stark necessity. But in Petersburg, the milliners, who were the elite among female entrepreneurs, carried on their businesses year in and year out, marrying and raising children along the way. The moral, it seems, is that women were perfectly willing to combine family and career when it was possible and when it paid. To cite one last example, it appears that well-to-do women dissented from the notion that they should be sheltered from financial responsibility. The evidence here comes from decisions on whether the wife would take charge of the husband's estate after he died. When husbands made the decision, the wives were usually sheltered. When the wives had the chance to decide for themselves, they often decided to take up the challenge.

Some women, to repeat, were able to make some choices, and when we compare their choices to those made by men, the results are arresting. The comparison, it should be said, takes place mainly on economic ground. In a place committed to capitalism and to minimal government, local public records were largely devoted to keeping track of who owned what—and, until 1865, who owned whom. Deed by deed, this makes dull reading. But the transmission of property can provide a surprisingly clear window on human values. When we compare what women and men did with what they had, we find the outlines of a distinctive women's value system or culture.[4]

At the center of this culture was personalism, a tendency to respond to the particular needs and merits of individuals. When women wrote wills, for example, they tended to pick and choose among their potential heirs, rewarding personal loyalty and taking note of special economic need. Women were also more likely than men to reward the exceptional slave with emanicipation. They were more likely than men to grant separate estates to their daughters, thus placing a particular woman's need for economic security above the general principle of male dominance in the family. Altogether, women as a group were more personalistic, more attuned to the needs and interests of other women, more concerned with economic security, more supportive of organized charity, and more serious about the spiritual life than were men. This is not to say that no woman ever committed a greedy or evil deed or that the sexes shared no values. It is to say that women at times behaved according to standards of their own. With local records we can find out what some of these standards were.

This is of critical significance to the continuing development of women's history as a distinct field of inquiry. Much of what has been written on the history of women is, to use Gerda Lerner's term, "contribution history."[5] That is, the scholar marks off some endeavor that has traditionally been regarded as important and proceeds to outline women's previously unacknowledged contributions to it. One result is a relatively large literature on organized feminism and social reform, areas in which women were extremely active and in which traditional scholarly neglect is proportionally inexcusable. This is the kind of women's history that is now appearing in textbooks, as well it should.

The problem with the contribution approach is that it does not challenge traditional assumptions about what matters in history. It takes men as the measure; it allows women into history only when they thought as men thought, achieved what men achieved, or fought for what men had already won. With contribution history, we are forever testing how women measured up on a masculine scale of achievement.

But if we believe that women all along created cultures of their own, our approach to the past is different. With enough imaginative research, it should be possible to reconstruct women's cultures. We could then busy ourselves with testing how men measured up—not a very high-minded approach, but one with enormous therapeutic potential. Better yet, we can learn more about what women and men shared and where they diverged, about how women and men experienced change, and about the ways in which gender influenced their choices as active agents in history. The reward lies not only in giving women their due, but also in recognizing that in all societies the range of human values and aspirations was greater than we had allowed. But one society at a time: Here are some particulars about Petersburg.

The Free
Women of
Petersburg

1

Petersburg:
The Setting

"This is the most dirty place I ever saw." So declared Josiah
Flagg in 1786. Even by eighteenth-century Virginia standards, Petersburg was a grubby place, and to a New
England Yankee like Flagg, it was outrageous. "Nine
months of the year the mud is half leg deep," he griped;
"it is a very Sickly place owing in a great measure to its
Situation, the Streets are very Irregular, and not a Respectable Building in the Borough. . . . Agues, and fevers of
Every kind prevail." Flagg's perception of his hosts was
equally unflattering. "The Virginians as a people are given
to Luxury and Dissipation of every kind, and are supported in their Extravagance by Afric's sable sons, who
they consign to the most Abject Slavery." While Flagg
bowed to local custom and indulged in a bit of dissipation
himself, he knew that was not what drew people to Petersburg and bade them stay on. "What is the Reason that so
many merchants are induced to Establish Houses there and
sacrifice their Health? why their own private emolument.
As it is in the heart of a rich Countrey, where Remittances
may be easily made to their Correspondents."[1]

Why study a place like Petersburg? One answer is, and
it is not as frivolous as it may sound: Why not? No case

can be made for any one place having been typical of the whole nation; Josiah Flagg's dismay at life among the Virginians underscores the fact that the country was too diverse. That being so, what matters is that the location be, in important ways, interesting. Petersburg was interesting, "the most interesting city in America," according to one of its fond historians, Arthur Kyle Davis.[2] Davis had in mind Petersburg's connections to the legendary events of American history dating back to the beginning of European and African settlement. The town claimed Pocahontas as its earliest noteworthy resident, and from the skirmishes of the Revolution to the crippling siege of 1864–65, Petersburg found its place in the wars that in most minds punctuate historical time.

For the social historian, Petersburg's interest lies closer to the features observed by Josiah Flagg. Petersburg was a slave city, of course, and it attracted a large (and largely female) population of free blacks. While the high proportion of free blacks itself made Petersburg atypical, it also offers a rare chance to study white and black women together. Meanwhile, there was much that Petersburg shared with towns to the north and west. Petersburg, like other towns, experienced religious revivals and the proliferation of all kinds of voluntary associations. Like other towns, Petersburg developed a highly volatile commercial economy, and beginning in the late 1820s, it developed an industrial sector as well. It was not, perhaps, the best of both worlds, but Petersburg did mix important elements of northern with southern life.

When Josiah Flagg found the mud sucking at his boots in 1786, Petersburg, as a self-governing corporation, was but two years old. As a settlement, however, its history went back more than a century. At first, it was Fort Henry, one of several frontier forts erected to protect colonists from the Indians who resisted the theft of their lands. For decades, the tiny settlement was little more than a trading post and a jumping-off place for expeditions into unknown territory. By about 1730, Petersburg—it was allegedly named for Peter Jones, who married the trading post proprietor's daughter—was showing its first signs of future promise as a commercial center. Located just below the falls of the Appomattox River (the Appomattox was navigable to the James, and the James to the sea), Petersburg was the natural exchange point for the planters who were rapidly carving out farms to the south and west. The first tobacco inspection was established in 1730 at Robert Bolling's warehouse, and five years later, the vestrymen of Bristol Parish thought settlement near the falls sufficiently dense to authorize the building of a new brick church in Blandford, just to the east of Petersburg proper. By 1750, Petersburg was beginning to look like a town, and over the thirty years that followed, its residents gradually acquired some of the accoutrements of urban living—a bridge across the river to the village called Pocahontas, a Masonic lodge, a racetrack, stage connections to other towns, and a post office. The expansion hinged on the burgeoning tobacco trade, which now reached into North Carolina. By the time of the Revolution, the town could boast six tobacco warehouses, and the flour milling business was becoming important as well.[3]

In 1784, the general assembly of Virginia recognized the importance of the cluster of settlements on the Appomattox with an act making Petersburg, Blandford, and Pocahontas (each of which lay in a different county) into a single corporation under the name of Petersburg. While the statute marked the beginning of a new political era, the town itself did not undergo any immediate, dramatic changes. For close to thirty years, Petersburg retained much of the rough-and-ready flavor of its commercial frontier origins. Petersburg was a magnet for young merchants and artisans, and the sex ratio among white people was therefore acutely unbalanced; the men outnumbered the women three to two.[4] The physical layout of the town, meanwhile, bespoke the unplanned nature of its growth. There was no real center. A few narrow, muddy streets meandered along the low ground parallel to the river, lined by small, mostly wooden houses, here clustered, there spaced around the sloughs. As in other eighteenth-century towns, homes and shops were interspersed with stables, butchers' blocks, tanyards, and hogpens, the surviving inhabitants of which mingled freely in the streets with their two-legged owners.[5]

Altogether, it was an unhealthy place; "rather unhealthy," according to one source; "very unhealthy," remarked another; "extremely unhealthy," said a third.[6] The season from late summer to the first frost could be deadly, and those who could afford it left town for the duration. "My family are all in tolerable good health at present," printer William Prentis wrote to his cousin in July 1800, "but how long this may continue so, unless I can carry them in the country, is uncertain: A change of air in the fall I have for several years found advantageous, and have generally left town for a few weeks in that season. . . ." If the autumn was difficult for native Virginians like Prentis, it was a crisis for newcomers. "This is a sad unhealthy climate," Mary Cumming told her family in County Antrim, having spent her first Virginia fall bedridden. At times, she managed to joke about her frequent bouts with illness; a near treatise on her enlarged spleen was capped by banter: "How very learned this trip to America will make me! Do you not think so? What if I begin to study anatomy??" Mary Cumming eventually managed to escape Petersburg during the "sickly season," but she escaped too late.[7] She died on the return journey, not yet thirty years old.

Perhaps it was the uncertainty of life that encouraged the townspeople to live high while they had the chance. In any case, what Petersburg lacked in sanitation it made up in recreation. Neither piety nor the ascetic life held much attraction for its residents. The Methodists had managed to maintain a small meeting since 1773, while the Anglicans straggled along, half starving their rector and at times unable to dispatch routine business. Noah Webster phrased it well after passing through Petersburg in 1785: "It seems to be the taste of the Virginian[s] to fix their churches as far as possible from town & their play houses in the center." Between sermons and horse racing, there was no contest. In April and October, the town was jammed for the running of the New Market races. Stuffed in a garret of Mrs. Armistead's tavern with seven other gentlemen ("Their different merits of snoring I could descant upon at great length . . ."), Benjamin Latrobe discovered the full depth of the local passion for racing: "Everybody here is so engaged in talking of Lamplighter, the Shark mare, the Carolina horse, etc., that I am as much at a loss for conversation as if I were among the Hottentots. There indeed I should be much better off, for I could talk to the women without knowing their language. But the case is desperate in an house occupied by seventy men in leather breeches."[8] The races were not for sportsmen only, however. "The ladies" attended as well, although by the early years of the nineteenth century, they were expected to remain on New Market Hill above the "promiscuous crowd." On the field below, people of all colors and classes placed bets, tilted flasks, and argued the merits of their favorite horses and (black) jockeys.[9]

During the races, the theatre was open every night. But whatever the season, traveling troupes could count on enthusiastic audiences when they arrived in Petersburg.[10] Other, more occasional visitors provided entertainment, too. "A LIVE ELEPHANT Has just arrived," the Republican announced in 1805, and soon after, the townspeople were tantalized by a description of the forthcoming feats of Mr. Church, a tightrope walker: "After which he will do a trick called WHIRLY PURLY. With a number of other performances equally pleasing. The whole to conclude with A SPANISH FANDANGO, danced blindfolded over thirteen eggs."[11] Who could resist? Other popular pastimes were cockfights, card games ("some of the ladies are great Gamblers," a visiting schoolgirl reported), dancing, and drinking. The sole citizen to have the misfortune of being arrested for lack of sobriety was one Robert Lloyd, who was presented by the grand jury in 1791 "for Practicing Solitary Drunkenness." Getting drunk with friends, however, was another matter, and the Fourth of July provided a patriotic opportunity. Everyone took the day off to parade, to hear again the story of '76, and to toast a long list of heroes and principles of the Revolution. The day ended "with a universal uproarious jollification."[12]

On the Fourth, the Declaration of Independence was taken seriously; people of every rank celebrated elbow to elbow in "a perfect leveling of all distinctions of caste and society. . . ."[13] In a town so sharply stratified as Petersburg, that took some doing. Petersburg was Virginia's third largest town in 1790, numbering close to three thousand souls. Nearly half the people were slaves. Another 10 percent were black and free. Among the whites, there was some diversity of origin. There were Yankees as well as Virginians among the native born, and immigrants represented every part of northern Europe. A small group of men from France via the Caribbean brought a touch of New Orleans to Petersburg by their open intimacy with black women; the vast majority of the immigrants, meanwhile, were Scottish, Scotch-Irish, and English. Among the white ethnic groups, there were visible, audible differences in manners and speech, and the differences were not lost on Mary Cumming, who found a "complete national character"—and some relief from her homesickness—in the person of Mary Moore:

> She has resided twenty years in America, but she is completely Irish in her manners, which I like very much. She is a great, large, fat, bouncing-looking woman, appears to be perfectly good-natured, and extremely obliging to me indeed, but I come from Ireland, and that is my recommendation with Mrs. Moore. When she came to see me she shook hands, and welcomed me to Petersburg in the true Irish mode of hospitality.[14]

The ethnic differences were not barriers, however; Mary Cumming made friends with immigrants and natives alike. The significant divisions in Petersburg were those of class, color, and sex.

At the very top was town matriarch Mary Marshall

Bolling. Heir to much of the land on which Petersburg was built, not to mention an immense portion of Amelia County, she was the town's largest proprietor in 1790. Among her Petersburg holdings were thirty-eight slaves, thirty-three of the town's most valuable lots, and four of the eight tobacco warehouses, amounting to more than 10 percent of the total taxable wealth. No one else came close to that figure. The top 10 percent of Petersburg's 372 taxpayers, however, together controlled over half the town's taxable property; the upper 50 percent claimed more than 90 percent of the taxable wealth.[15]

Over the next twenty years, the rich stayed rich while the poor grew more numerous. Among white men, property ownership became much less commonplace. From 1790 to 1810, the number of white males above sixteen years of age increased by 53.7 percent while the number of male taxpayers increased by only 9.3 percent.[16] The most spectacular growth rate, meanwhile, was registered by free blacks, who more than tripled their numbers during the two decades. In that time, some 170 Petersburg slaves gained their freedom, and they were joined by hundreds of newly manumitted, mainly poor women and men from the countryside. By 1810, there were more than a thousand free blacks in Petersburg. Altogether there were about thirty-five hundred free people in Petersburg, and nearly a third of them were black.

Then in 1806, the Virginia legislature put a virtual halt to slave emancipations. For Petersburg's free blacks, this was a pivotal event. Not only was there a sudden slowdown in population growth, but the 1806 law also signalled the beginning of a long-term policy of increasing legal debasement. What gains free blacks were able to make in the antebellum period—and they did make some progress in property holding—they made against formidable odds.

In fact, all of Petersburg's people were experiencing change in the nineteenth century's early years. The dating of the transition is necessarily imprecise, but in the years from about 1805 to 1820, Petersburg lost much of its frontier character, and in its place gained more complexity, greater gentility, and a more straitlaced morality.

In architecture, things were looking up, although much of the improvement was the result of the great fire of 1815. The loss was enormous, initially estimated at three million dollars, but the townspeople evidently saw in it a silver lining. The fire, one of them explained, "in one short July night obliterated more eye sores, and abated more nuisance than the proprietors of real estate would have done in half a generation." In place of the old eyesores rose "buildings that would stand an examination with the best constructed mercantile houses in Baltimore, Philadelphia or New-York," and that, as the *Republican*'s editor hastened to point out, was confirmation of his original prediction "that the town would be *benefited* by the *disaster.*"[17]

Even before the fire, however, Petersburg had begun cleaning up. Paving of the main streets began in 1813, and negligent property owners like Adam Naustadter found themselves answering to the court for such offenses as "Suffering & permitting a quantity of Dirt & filth highly offensive & injurious to the publick health to remain in a hole upon a lot of Back Street." After the fire, influential citizens were more vocal than ever on matters of trash and mud. One, fearing that country customers might take their business elsewhere, wrote the *Republican* to ask whether proprietors whose new buildings were complete should not be encouraged to clean up the surrounding rubbish:

> . . . in case of refusal, I leave it with the proper authority, whether compulsion ought not to be resorted to. My opinion is,
>
> TOUCH 'EM
> N.B. I touch U again.

"Touch 'Em" did repeat the complaint, and a new ordinance was put into effect within the week. The battle against filth seems to have done some good. Petersburg, like most antebellum cities, would have its bouts with cholera and other epidemic diseases, but the town lost its reputation for exceptional unhealthiness by about 1830.[18]

The cleansing process was moral and spiritual as well. From the early years of the century, there was evidence of growing vitality among the Protestant sects. The black Baptists formed a congregation in 1803 and by 1817 were strong enough to contribute money to the white Baptists, who were having a harder time of it. The Anglicans built a new church nearer the center of town in about 1808. The town's first Presbyterian congregation was established five years later, and the gathering of an interdenominational Bible Society in 1814 marked the beginnings of organized religious benevolence. Church membership skyrocketed after 1821–22, when Petersburg surrendered to its first full-scale religious revival.[19] Meanwhile, a few voices sounded a new tone of moral rectitude. In 1809–10, for example, the grand jury launched its first concerted antigambling campaign, and schoolteachers began to promise moral as well as academic results. All the while, Petersburg's favorite amusements flourished, with as much drunkenness as ever, and as late as 1821, it was still possible to get away with publishing a story whose heroine was the victim of repeated gang rape and the perpetrator of mass murder.[20] Zion was not reached in a day.

The economy was volatile. Petersburg, like other American communities, experienced extraordinary booms, devastating crashes, and long, disheartening depressions. For Virginians, the 1820s were lackluster years, and by 1828, merchant Samuel Mordecai was very discouraged. Mordecai had just returned from a journey north, where all appeared to be tidiness and efficiency, ". . . and then to come to Petersburg the coach traces breaking before we arrive – the roads in ruts – the fields uncultivated – the houses tumbling down, groups of free negroes mullatoes and whites lounging around a grog shop – the town half depopulated, while nature has been more bountiful than to the thriving country I had left." Mordecai's sister Ellen urged him to light out for the West. "If I were a man I would go where the lands are rich," she wrote, and, indeed, a great many young men seem to have done that very thing.[21] By 1830, there were for the first time roughly equal numbers of white men and white women in Petersburg, and this remained the case through 1860.

Even as the Mordecais wrote, however, Petersburg was showing some of its potential for industrial growth. In good times, enthusiasm and funding could be raised for almost any internal improvement scheme. Petersburg promoters founded a canal company to dig a waterway around the falls of the Appomattox; they had the river dredged to allow bigger boats to dock at their wharves; and they obtained charters for turnpikes, plank roads, and railroads—especially railroads. The first call for subscriptions to build a railroad came early, in 1830, and the response was a booster's dream: "By night," William S. Simpson exclaimed, "nearly a hundred thousand dollars were down!!!" The railroad was in full operation by 1833. The same spirit of exuberant capitalism infused the growth of a manufacturing sector. In 1833, *Niles' Weekly Register* reported the opening of a stock subscription for a new cotton mill: "The whole amount [was] readily made up in the course of two hours."[22] Altogether in the 1830s, Petersburg entrepreneurs obtained corporate charters for twelve cotton mills. Some of their plans were scratched after the panics of the late 1830s. But by 1850, six mills were actually operating, and they employed more than thirteen hundred hands, almost all of them white, many of them women. More important was tobacco, another industry that employed female hands. A few Petersburg proprietors had begun tobacco manufacturing on a small scale in the late eighteenth century. In the antebellum decades, the manufacture of tobacco became big business. By 1860, there were twenty tobacco factories in Petersburg, employing on the average more than a hundred slave and free black hands each. In 1860, the federal census ranked American cities according to the value of their manufactures. Petersburg just made the top fifty.[23]

The profits, not surprisingly, went into the hands of those who were already doing well. This is not to say that people of the propertied classes were guaranteed any sort of economic security, for there were plenty of individual riches-to-rags stories. It is to say that by 1860, wealth was apparently more concentrated than ever. The top tenth of taxpayers paid a full 65 percent of the taxes (in 1820, the figure had been 59.6 percent; in 1790, it was 51.7 percent). It is also to say that poverty was more visible than ever. Mary Cumming, fresh from the north of Ireland, had reported the scene to her father in 1813. "The people of this country certainly enjoy many blessings," she wrote; "provisions of all kinds are so plenty that you seldom or never see a beggar."[24] By the 1850s, a financial panic meant that hundreds of factory workers could be laid off in a trice, and no government agency would step in to assist them. Newspaper editors wrote as though beggars and vagrants belonged to the urban landscape as a matter of course.

Petersburg by 1860 had more than eighteen thousand residents. Half of them were black, and about a third of the blacks were free. Petersburg by this time was Virginia's second largest city, and it was, to use a hackneyed but apt phrase, a city of contrasts, a city in which features of modern urban life existed right alongside what contemporaries might have called "relics" of the past. On the side of modernity, there was a substantial degree of residential segregation. The white poor were concentrated in West Ward, near the mills. Free blacks were sufficiently clustered to inspire whites to give their neighborhoods names like "Niggertown" and "Little Africa." Still, there were times when blacks and whites came together in the curious kinds of intimacy engendered by the slave system. Petersburg's little boys invented a game they called "Harpers Ferry," a game based on John Brown's 1859 attempt to touch off a slave rebellion by raiding the federal arsenal at Harpers Ferry, Virginia. The white boy who took the part of Brown and the black boys who played his confederates always had the good grace to let themselves be vanquished.[25]

In the physical environment, old problems detracted somewhat from the splendor of new accomplishments. Some fine buildings were constructed in the 1840s and

1850s, and the quality of life was considerably enhanced with the introduction of gas lights in 1851 and the completion of new waterworks in 1857. The streets were a perennial problem, though, and while standards might have gone up since Josiah Flagg's time, muck and mire still prevailed. The mud on Washington Street, one editor hyperbolized in 1853, was "deep enough to float an Ohio steamboat." That was fine with the local livestock, which still drank from the gutters and grazed at the streets' edges. An exasperated editor demanded in 1858: "Is there no law, Messrs. Councilmen from East Ward, to prohibit persons from feeding their cattle upon, and making a barn-yard of our principal streets?"[26]

The editors who agitated for passable streets and tighter cattle pens had cultural concerns, too. The *South-Side Democrat* in 1853 pointed out that five of the last six road shows to visit Petersburg had been minstrel performances. That, the editor hoped, was a consequence of the lack of an adequate concert hall, and not proof of the lowbrow taste of the community. As for religious institutions, the editors found more to applaud. There was still a vigorous lowlife in the Petersburg of the 1850s, but there was also a thriving temperance movement, and there were thirteen churches. "If the morals of a city are to be judged by the number of church edifices which it contains," the *Intelligencer* pronounced in 1859, "then Petersburg must be regarded as one of the most unexceptionable and well ordered communities in the country. . . ."[27] Be that as it may, Protestant hegemony was firmly established. The new challenge was toleration of other religious groups, and here the number of steps forward about equaled the number of steps back. When Petersburg's first Young Men's Christian Association was organized, some members wanted to exclude Roman Catholics on the grounds that Catholics were not Christians. On the other hand, a fundraising campaign of 1853 to repair the twelve-year-old Catholic church building elicited generous contributions from people of all faiths, and the Catholic congregation took out a newspaper ad to convey their thanks. Petersburg's Jews did not yet have a synagogue, but they were able to hold services, and local editors sometimes took it upon themselves to educate their readers as to the significance of Jewish holy days. Others were quick to stereotype. The agents hired to report on the creditworthiness of Petersburg businesses persistently typed Jewish storekeepers as shady and secretive.[28]

Possibilities for a more cosmopolitan outlook also derived from the new and swift rail connections to other cities. The railroads ran special trains to allow Petersburgers to attend big events—religious conventions, political gatherings, militia musters, conclaves of volunteer firemen, and performances by celebrated lecturers and artists—and horizons expanded accordingly. By the same token, however, Petersburg increasingly became a satellite of Richmond. Travelers' accounts were an index to the change. In the early national period, professional travelers, usually from the North, came to Petersburg on ship or by stage, and they often stayed on for several days before proceeding south. In the 1850s, travelers arrived by train and were gone again within a matter of hours. If they commented on Petersburg, it was to grouse at the fact that they were required to disembark on one side of town, take an omnibus to the other side of town, and then board another train. "As this trip was peculiarly barren of incident," one writer remarked,

> it may gratify the reader to be informed, that in the confusion of shifting from one station to the other I lost my best and only hat. I hope this simple record will be received as conclusive evidence of the monotony and dulness of the journey. I do not mention it to excite sympathy, for I am happy to say that I have since purchased a new and a better one; and in case my old one is found, I hereby will and bequeath the same to the mayor of Peterborough, his heirs and successors, hoping that they may wear no other until a railroad round or through the town connects the termini.[29]

It seems unfair that Petersburg should have been given such unseeing treatment when it was just reaching its liveliest phase. But it was a sadly appropriate harbinger of what was to come, of the eclipse that would occur after the Civil War.

And where were the women in all this? Our trusty curmudgeon Josiah Flagg provides a starting point. "A Young Lady is not valu'd here for her Accomplishments or personal Charms," he observed in 1786, "but for the number of Negroes and plantations she possesses."[30] Marriage, as far as Flagg could tell, was for money. That is where the next chapter begins.

2

The Political Economy of Marriage

To the literate people of Petersburg, marriage was as much a matter of financial calculation as of romance. That, at least, was the message of the didactic tales printed in the local newspapers at the beginning of the nineteenth century. "The Triumph of Patience and Virtue," pirated for the benefit of the *Republican's* readers in 1801, was in its outline a typical deserted-wife story. The marriage in question was a mismatch from the start, Mrs. Harwood being "serious, of simple manners, and fond of a domestic and retired life," while her husband was "gay, luxurious and dissipated." True to his character, Mr. Harwood abandoned wife and child in favor of a "mistress of gaiety." Mrs. Harwood, having failed in her best-of-faith efforts to work a reconciliation, retired to the country and endured. After two years of the riotous life, Mr. Harwood repented, hastened to his wife, and fell at her feet in a silent plea for forgiveness. She forgave him without a second's hesitation, and they lived happily enough ever after.[1]

The remarkable quality of "The Triumph of Patience and Virtue" was the manner in which the plot turned on financial details; behind every heartthrob lay a commercial transaction. In the first place, when Mr. Harwood left his wife, he left her "to live on her own fortune, which had been secured to her as a jointure, and produced about three hundred pounds a year." Our heroine, in other words, was neatly provided for by means of a separate estate, a fund unaffected by the debts of her wayward spouse. She could afford to be patient. Mr. Harwood, meanwhile, could afford nothing but a reconciliation. Half his property, the author itemized, was mortgaged to cover his gambling debts and his mistress's "profuse" expenditures, and much of the rest was assigned to assorted tradesmen. It was only when his mistress absconded with his remaining capital that Mr. Harwood realized his folly and flew to his wife. The final sentence of the story concluded the cost-benefit analysis: ". . . the prudence and economy of Mrs. Harwood contributed greatly to relieve the embarrassed affairs of her husband, and at length restored to him nearly the whole of that estate which his extravagance had so wantonly dissipated."

It was a fitting story for the new century and for a culture undergoing a transition in its marriage ideal. The standard formula for successful marriage had once concentrated on concrete, calculable assets—property, earning capacity, social standing. But by the early nineteenth century, romantic love competed for first billing. Of course, the romantic love ideal would eventually prevail; the workings of money and power would thereby be obscured, and concern with such mundane matters would be reclassified as vulgar. In the meantime, however, in the first half of the nineteenth century, middle-class Americans were frankly intrigued by the sources and uses of power within marriage. They explored the theme in a voluminous and none too subtle literature, and in the process, they betrayed a good deal of anxiety, particularly over the roles of women. The author of "The Triumph of Patience and Virtue," for example, tried to reassure his (her?) readers on two counts. The story assured women that they indeed had power, moral power strong enough to outlast the worst male dissipation. The husband, meanwhile, was told that the power of the wife would not be turned against him.

Mrs. Harwood had the wherewithal to leave her husband or to punish and humiliate him. Instead, she stood by her man and on his return slipped quietly into the conventional role of helpmeet.

In the decades that followed, oceans of ink were devoted to the celebration of "woman's influence," to telling women that their duties as wives and mothers gave them all the power they could want. The problem is that with the recent revival of the study of intimacy and power, some historians have come dangerously close to saying the same thing. The key concept is "<u>companionate marriage</u>." Companionate marriage is a term used by some historians of the family to describe a new marriage pattern that allegedly took hold in the eighteenth and nineteenth centuries, primarily in the middle classes. Marriage partners had once been chosen by parents, whose main considerations were wealth, prestige, and political power. Companionate marriage, however, was for love, something that could be decided only by the young people themselves. With companionate marriage, in other words, emotion moved to the center; mutual affection and respect replaced the call of duty and pressure from the community as the main ties that year in and year out bound husbands and wives together. Finally, in companionate marriage, the old habit of male command was replaced by shared activities and joint decision making. The result for women was enhanced status—greater power, greater autonomy, and a strong, even equal voice in family affairs.[2]

Women who at this moment find themselves on the short end of either love or power in marriage will find it odd to hear historians pronouncing the problem solved more than a hundred years ago. The historians, in turn, might well take refuge in qualification: Companionate marriage only describes the general direction in which marriages were moving; it was an ideal that influenced behavior, but as with all ideals, it was often difficult for real people to achieve. This might do for characterizing change over a period of several centuries. But if we are to understand the experience of women in a given time and place, we need to know just how fast marriages were moving toward the ideal and by how much they fell short.

The evidence from Petersburg suggests that marriage was fundamentally asymmetrical. Men retained the upper hand in almost every aspect of marriage; mixed with the new ideal of mutual affection and respect were substantial elements of male dominance and coercion. Many marriages were still financially motivated. It is doubtful that the majority of Petersburg's wives would have classified their own marriages as companionate. Moreover, to the extent that companionate marriage prevailed as an ideal, it brought problems of its own. The more emotional richness women expected from marriage, the more profoundly they could be disappointed. And the more they believed in their right to make domestic decisions, the greater the potential for serious combat with their husbands. The closer we look, then, the more complicated marriage appears. We begin here with the topic of marrying for money. This was a game played by both sexes, but women played for special stakes.

In the letters written by the people of Petersburg, marriage was a leading topic. The subject of who might marry whom captured the interest of both sexes and almost all ages and was an inexhaustible source of speculation, reportage, and the sharp remark. "I cannot help thinking that there is a fine girl thrown away upon a stupid preacher," Eliza K. Myers muttered on the marriage of a friend in 1830, and when a second friend announced her engagement a month later, Myers was ready with more derogatory words for the groom: "The ugliest, most cross-eyed ungainly Scotchman I ever saw—" she wrote, "simple & chicken-hearted to boot – but young & pious – Davie Dunlop ycleped." Young women were equally inclined to make fun of suitors of their own. Maria Antoinette Morton reported her progress in the Petersburg marriage market in 1841: "I have not caught but one beau since I came to Petersburg and he is so old and infirm that I am affraid that he cant possibly live through the Winter. . . . I believe he is about *80 years old* an *old widower* too *with great grand-children* but enough of my foolishness."[3]

A joke here, an insult there—both served to establish a little distance from what was, after all, a momentous decision. The marriage choice was all important, and not only because it meant a lifelong commitment. Marriage was a material investment with material consequences. Whatever inroads were made by the ideal of romantic love, the people of Petersburg—at least those people who left letters—remained obstinately aware of the economic dimensions of matrimony. They seem to have agreed on two propositions. First, money helped make a marriage. And second, marriage was an honorable means of making money.

The first proposition—that an adequate income was essential to a happy marriage—was usually visited upon the younger generation by worried elders. Eliza Selden went husband hunting in Richmond in 1791. If she was pained by her initial lack of success, she disguised it in dry commentary: " . . . I have not one suitor though they say I have been admired. the gentlemen's minds are I believe occupyed chiefly with speculating in paper money certificates &c which they find more profitable than wives." Within a few weeks, however, Eliza found her suitor and returned to her mother's home in Petersburg. She soon found that not everyone was as taken as she was with her prospective husband. Robert Fitzgerald, a kinsman from Nottoway County, was quick to offer his somewhat garbled reservations:

> . . . from what I learn, his circumstances in life, his age, his connections in business &c, all tend to make it an imprudent match on your side—you should consider that you have been brought up under the indulgent hand of an affectionate mother, you have been accustomed to genteel company, and to walk in that sphere of life which would be humiliating and mortifying to one of your sensibility and delicacy to be under the necessity of departing from and knowing at the same time that it is your misfortune to be possest of a slender fortune yourself

should make you more circumspect and consider this matter
with more serious attention, for on your present choice
depends not only your own welfare for life; but the happiness
I may say in a great measure of all your friends. . . .

Eliza's reply went straight to the point; "want of fortune
is his only fault," she claimed, but she conceded it was a
serious objection. She promised Fitzgerald she would not
go through with the wedding until her betrothed could
support her. Meantime, she oiled the waters with some
teasing flattery:

> . . . I am convinced when you come to be acquainted with
> him from the great degree of simmalarity in your sentiments
> & dispositions that you will admire him as much as I doo you
> indeed I believe that a supposed likeness to your self was one
> of the first inducement[s] to my admiring him at all now should
> it prove unpropitious blame yourself & not me.[4]

Many decades later, Fanny Bernard gave some homely
advice to her grandson, urging him to postpone going
courting: "A living must be made first, as love comes in at
the door, & soon hops out of the window do you not think
so without a support. . . ." She then summed up the problem in seven words: "Love will not make the pot boile."[5]
No one seemed to worry that love might be sullied by
crass materialism. Marrying was a routine and respectable
way to improve one's financial condition, and this was as
true at the end of the antebellum period as it had been earlier. A credit report of 1858, for example, counted marital
prospects as business assets. Samuel H. Marks had recently
failed in his confection business, but he was still regarded
as a good risk. "His children are all married off," the report
explained, "& he has now no expence but his own to
encounter, & I think he will marry & make a rise, as he is
a brisk widower." The report, as it turned out, was right.
Fifteen years later, the word on Marks was: "Has succeeded well in the business which is chiefly managed by
his wife. . . ."[6]

Given the fact that making money was a legitimate object of marriage, the trick was to distinguish between marrying up, which was honorable and prudent, and fortune hunting, which was despicable. The difference seems to have been a matter of whether or not the marriage was for wealth alone. In 1854, Ann Eliza Pleasants pressed her uncle Thomas E. Massie to pursue her friend Betty Organ. "She is a sweet, lovely girl with 30,000 and large expectations," Pleasants wrote, and when she learned a few weeks later that Massie had been jilted by some other young woman, she intensified her campaign. "She has most *excellent* sense, very fine manners, untiring energy, affectionate disposition, *high proverbially* high principles, religion, good looks & an independent fortune." So numerous were Betty Organ's selling points that Massie would probably not have been accused of fortune hunting, even though his income was paltry beside hers. A more suspicious case was the marriage of William P. Russell to Eliza Caldwell. William S. Simpson told the story:

> He came to Petersburg during the Fall of last year as a Professor of Languages. . . . Well, the said Mr. Russell settles himself and three children down here to board with Mrs. Caldwell, and in the course of five or six months, *when we may naturally suppose his Bill had grown to something considerable,* he woos and marries her. The Honeymoon is scarcely past than, thinking he does not meet with sufficient encouragement here, he determines to look out for some other sphere of operation, and forthwith starts off with his own 3 children upon an exploring expedition, first of all, however, having induced her to break up housekeeping and sell her Furniture in order to raise the needful for his travelling expences! In the meantime she has gone with her two boys into the Country to live quietly until he comes back for her. And there she may wait long enough methinks ere she sees her Gentleman again.[7]

Just how often people married for money, in either the honorable sense or the dishonorable one, is something we will never know. Surviving correspondence suggests that it happened often enough to keep tongues clacking and pens scratching.[8] And it happened often enough to be a source of bitter frustration for women and men who believed themselves spurned for lack of funds. "As to my having any sweethearts that is not thought of," a young woman told her brother in 1808. "Money is too much preferred, for us poor Girls to be much caressed," she went on, submitting as evidence her recent experience at the wedding of a friend. Of all the young women in the room, the ugliest and dullest was a certain Miss Hicks. But she was also the richest and was therefore "universally followed and courted." Men felt the sting as well. Herbert Gregory, scrambling for a loan to see his business through a crisis in 1831, wrote a short, cross essay on the prevalence of human greed:

> The Christians & good people may say what they will – but I may be damned if the money don't carry the day with all & every class of people in *this* world – What it may do in the *next* I cannot tell—Were I rich do you not think that I could marry some rich lady? Yes, for I know several now who would be damned anxious to get any man so he had the change.

Gregory then cursed all women and asked his brother to appeal to their aunt for a loan.[9]

As Gregory's outburst suggests, women could be as money-conscious as men when it came to sizing up potential partners. And yet marrying for money had a different meaning for women than it did for men. The law, first of all, made a critical difference. When a woman married, the law stripped her of her property rights and vested them in her husband. The woman who married money thus acquired a higher standard of living and greater social prestige. The man who married money, however, acquired not only income and prestige, but almost unlimited power over his wife's assets as well. Differences in earning capacity were also critical. Most men could earn a living outside of marriage, but most women could not, and the result for women was pressure, sometimes desperate pressure, to marry. For men, to put it bluntly, marrying for money meant power. For women, it was more often a matter of survival.

The law for Virginia women was the English common law, lifted from the mother country in colonial times and retained without substantial revision until after the Civil War. Under the common law, marriage was a pivotal event. So long as a woman remained unmarried, she was subject to no special restrictions; single women and widows could own and control property on the same terms as men. For married women, the story was entirely different. Marriage brought an automatic transfer of the woman's property rights to her husband. The husband assumed absolute ownership of his wife's personal property, and for all practical purposes, he owned her real estate as well.[10] The husband also owned his wife's services. If she were gainfully employed, he owned her wages. The logic of the law went on: Because the wife owned nothing, she could perform no transactions. Although she was entitled to act in her husband's stead under some circumstances—the wife could enter a store and charge groceries to her husband's account, for example—she had no standing as an independent economic agent. She could make no contracts; she could not sue or be sued in her own name; she could not execute a valid will; she could neither purchase nor emancipate a slave. And since she had no legal capacity to transact business for herself, she certainly had no capacity to transact for others. The married woman was not eligible to serve as a trustee, executor, administrator, or legal guardian. The summary term for this list of disabilities was, appropriately, "civil death."

There were loopholes and there were some benefits. Equity was a second system of English jurisprudence, a system that had developed alongside the common law, and some married women were, like our fictional friend Mrs. Harwood, able to use equity to retain control of their property and earnings. As time went on, increasing numbers of Petersburg's women took advantage of equity, and that is the subject of the next chapter. The majority of women, meanwhile, took their chances under the common law.

The long list of common-law disabilities was offset in part by a short list of benefits. First, the husband was obliged to pay any debts the wife had brought to the marriage; since the wife had no legal control of money or property, she could hardly be expected to discharge debts. Second, the husband was obligated to support his wife and minor children according to his means. The third benefit was dower. This was important and should not be confused with dowry, a term which had no meaning under the common law. The law of dower was designed to see to it that the husband's estate would provide some support for his wife after he died. As a byproduct, it gave the wife her one check on her husband's power. Every widow had a right to her dower, that is, to one-third of her deceased husband's personal property and the use of one-third of his real estate and slaves. (If the couple was childless, the wife's portion was increased to one-half.) To defend this right, the law gave the wife one weapon to be used while the husband was still alive. This was the power to block conveyances. Whenever a man acquired real estate, his wife acquired a dower right in it. No subsequent conveyance of that real estate (sale, mortgage, or gift) was complete until the wife relinquished her dower right. The "privy examination" ostensibly protected the wife from coercion; the wife could sign away her dower right only after she swore to a commission, in her husband's absence, that she acted voluntarily.

Or she could refuse. This sliver of power was all that was available to married women under the common law, and, as will be discussed later, in the antebellum period, some women began to use it to considerable advantage. Otherwise, the married woman was legally passive, powerless, and thoroughly dependent on her husband.

This basic structural inequality was compounded by women's lesser capacity to earn money on their own. Making a living for oneself was challenge enough, but many women also had families to look after—children, parents, sisters, or brothers. Kate Devereaux Beckwith's story was the classic tale of the dutiful daughter who married to pay off the mortgage. Kate Beckwith first met Henry Spaulding in New Jersey in 1848. He was thirty-five, a New Yorker, and rich; she was an accomplished young southern lady of twenty. They were introduced by mutual friends, and Henry thought he had found a wife. Kate, however, was in no hurry to get married, not to Henry Spaulding anyhow, and so she rejected him and went back to Petersburg and her family. More than eight years went by before Kate and Henry met again; the second time she was in no position to dismiss his advances. Kate's father, Dr. John Beckwith, had been accused of quackery by the assembled regular physicians of Petersburg. The charges touched off a ferocious dispute (a dispute that will surface again in the next chapter). Dr. Beckwith soon tired of fighting, and he retired from the practice of medicine, leaving his large family with very little income. Into the breach stepped the Beckwith women. Kate's mother tried taking in boarders, but had to give it up "as her old fashion-open-house-entertaining was not money-making." Kate, for her part, tried to get some cash out of her accomplishments. She opened a school for young ladies in which she taught piano, guitar, voice, and drawing, and she was apparently a popular teacher. But she, too, failed to make enough to solve her family's continual financial problems. Then in 1856, who should reappear but Henry Spaulding. Spaulding had experienced changes of his own over the eight years past; he had married, fathered three children, and been widowed. But he was still rich. Kate, as her niece later phrased it, "accepted the situation." Kate and Henry were married early in 1857. Henry literally paid off the mortgage, and Kate began a new life in New York, homesick but determined to do her best for her new family.[11]

Variations on Kate Beckwith's story must have been legion. Motivation is always a difficult subject, but the numerical evidence suggests that for women, economic motives for marriage were central. The numbers come from an analysis of the remarriage patterns of Petersburg's widows. What is particularly interesting about widows is the fact that they were free, in ways that single women were not, to choose or reject marriage. For the single, white woman, socialization and social pressure were relentless: Marriage was a must. (The greater tendency of free black women to remain unmarried is discussed in Chapter 4.) But she had to marry only once. With marriage, she acquired her identity as an adult and a woman, and she acknowledged her willingness to do what her society asked of her. Even if her husband dropped dead two weeks after the wedding, she had already been made respectable for life, and she would be under no special pressure to marry again. Widowhood was an honorable state; as a widow, she could opt for or against remarriage according to her individual opportunities, judgment, and needs.

The widows of Petersburg made some telling choices. The wealthier the widow, the less likely she was to remarry; widows generally did not remarry if they could afford to remain as they were. This is not to say that wealth was the only factor. Age was extremely important, and it should come as no surprise that the younger women were more likely to remarry. Exact ages are known for ninety of the women widowed in Petersburg from 1784 to 1850. Among the women widowed when they were thirty or younger, 55.6 percent remarried (15 / 27). The remarriage rate fell significantly for women widowed in their thirties; of the women widowed between the ages of thirty-one and forty, only 30 percent (9 / 30) married again. For widows over forty, meanwhile, remarriage was a rarity; only 9.1 percent (3 / 33) would settle down with new husbands.[12]

When we look at age and wealth together, the numbers become quite small, but far more suggestive. While there is no way to determine exactly how rich or poor each widow was, rough categories can be established, based on the amount of bond the court required of the executor or administrator of the deceased husband's estate. (Bonds were usually set at approximately double the value of the total assets of the deceased.) Confining our count to those women who were widowed at forty or younger, the progression is almost too neat to be true. The poorest group (bonds set at two thousand dollars or less) had the highest remarriage rate; 72.7 percent (8 / 11) married again. In the middling group (bonds of twenty-five hundred to nine thousand dollars), exactly half of the widows (3 / 6) married again. Among the wealthiest widows, however (bonds of ten thousand dollars or more), only 28.6 percent (6 / 21) committed themselves to new marriages.[13] Petersburg's most eligible widows—women who were well-to-do and still young—were the least likely to marry again.

In other words, the widow who had the best chance of finding a new husband usually did not want one. There are at least two ways to read these numbers. One is a straightforward economic reading: Poorer widows needed the money, so they remarried when they could. A second interpretation admits the possibility that there were important cultural differences between wealthier women and women of the artisan and laboring classes. It may have been that there was more in the experience of poorer women to dispose them toward marriage, a more exuberant sexuality, perhaps, or less psychological ease with whatever degree of autonomy widowhood afforded. But either way (and both could have been true) the fact remains that the widows with the most options usually did not opt for remarriage. This is curious, for these were the women who should have experienced marriage at its nineteenth-century best. It was the urban, upper middle class, after all, who presumably invented companionate marriage—marriage based on affection, mutual respect, and enhanced power for women. We need to take a closer look at the experience of marriage in the nineteenth century.

If the women of Petersburg had been polled on how they felt about their marriages, their responses would undoubtedly have run the gamut. As it is, the women who left diaries and letters divided into three roughly equal groups. There were those who were satisfied, even joyful, in their marriages. There were those who were miserable. And there were those who wrote as though their husbands lived on some other planet. This range is exactly what we should expect from an institution as dependent on the vagaries of human personality as marriage. And yet the remarriage patterns of Petersburg's widows suggest that some sort of generalization is called for; the reluctance of wealthier widows to marry again suggests that in the eyes of women themselves, something had gone wrong with marriage.

Or perhaps it is more accurate to say that standards were running far ahead of performance. The new standard was companionate marriage, a partnership based on mutual devotion and respect. The ideal marriage hummed along on sharing and consensus; the ideal home was a serene, nurturing retreat from the rough-and-tumble world outside. The problems with companionate marriage were apparently two. First, it was simply not easy to achieve. Consensus and mutual respect did not come easily when the law, the economy, custom, and nature still conspired to make husbands vastly more powerful than their wives. Second, to the extent that couples tried to reach the companionate ideal, they opened themselves up to new risks. Once husbands and wives thought they had a right to be loved, the potential for feelings of rejection and betrayal grew. Once the wife was allowed to voice opinions, the opportunities for overt conflict multiplied. The companionate ideal, in short, raised the emotional stakes in marriage. The rewards could be great, but the potential for disappointment had never been greater.

The ideal of companionate marriage drew strength from the fact that it worked for some people. The letters of Mary Cumming described just how well it worked for her. Mary Cumming had been brought up in the north of Ireland. She was brought to Petersburg in 1811 by her new husband William, who had already established himself there as a commission merchant. Mary was not happy with the move to America—she hated being separated from her family—but her marriage never caused her a moment's regret. "My dear William looks and is perfectly well," she wrote a few months after their marriage; "the longer I know him I love and esteem him more, he is everything to me my heart could wish for." And again: "What keeps my spirits up is the constant attention and kindness of my dear William, he has without exception the best temper of anyone I ever knew, months fly away and still find us happy with each other. . . . You know I am not given to boasting, this I assure you is how I feel, and I have no doubt of its continuation."[14]

Mary and William Cumming appreciated one another's company, and they spent a great deal of time together. They shared leisure time—they read to each other on chilly evenings, and they went to dinner parties and card parties together. They also interested themselves in one another's work. William helped with the care of their first child; he was an "excellent nurse," said Mary. When the War of 1812 brought William's business to a near standstill, Mary taught him to garden, and he took it up with a will. Mary, meanwhile, had learned a good deal about William's business, and before the war disrupted trans-Atlantic trade, she had intended to dabble in it herself. "We have three cows," she explained; "I intend vealing all my calves this year, and laying out my money in the purchase of tobacco, which I will have shipped off the first opportunity, so you see I mean to become merchant." The war evidently checked her plan (it was, as she predicted, "a terrible thing for *us merchants*"), but she revived it as soon as rumors of peace began to fly early in 1814. "Do you know I am going to commence tobacco merchant? William gave me for my Christmas gift a quantity which I intend shipping off when peace takes place. If I succeed in my first attempt I shall go on in the same manner till I return to Ireland." It is not clear whether Mary Cumming was ever able to launch her commercial venture. In 1814, she suffered a stillbirth and became gravely ill. In 1815, she wrote her last letter. This one was to William.

> You have ever been the most affectionate, kind, attentive friend and husband to me that it was possible to be. Let this console you that it was always your study to make me happy. If I ever

offended you, forgive me for it; but, alas! why need I say so?
We were almost too happy with one another.

Go to our beloved native country, there you will find peace.
Talk to my beloved friends of me. Tell them we will all meet
in a better world. If I can I will hover round and bless you
wherever you go.[15]

Companionate marriage, when it worked, worked
wonderfully well. When it failed, it was almost unspeak-
ably painful. Anna Campbell recorded the degeneration of
her marriage in sporadic, impassioned, sometimes cryptic
diary entries. In 1850, Anna Burdsall was married to
Charles Campbell, a teacher, historian, and writer, and at
first they were radiant with the good fortune of having
found each other. Anna described how they basked in loving silliness in the evenings. At twilight, she wrote, they
climbed into the rocking chair,

> *it* holding C.C. & he holding me, sometimes we amuse our-
> selves, & edify all within hearing, by singing duets in the most
> scientific manner of course, little 'Bo peep,' being a great
> favorite second only to 'Cats in the cream pot' I generally feel
> very loving about this time & kiss my husband until he tells
> me to stop such foolishness.

A few weeks later, an old friend asked Anna how marriage
compared with the single life. "It did me good to say with
my *whole heart,*" Anna proclaimed, "That I never had
been happier than since my marriage." And on returning
from a visit to the country, Anna recorded her feelings in
phrases that could have been published in any of the ladies'
magazines of the day. "Home is always more pleasant after
an absence even of short duration . . . what a happy part
of our nature is *the love for home!* the disposition to find
there, in that *one spot, all to make* us as *happy as we can be in
this world!*"[16]

Anna Campbell's diary entries soon lost their publish-
able quality. In 1854, she poured out her grievances on
pages no one would be likely to find, pages in the middle
of an old diary from the 1840s.

Oh, strangely is woman formed, her nature is indeed to suffer
& to endure, for strive as we may, endure we must, while
man has no comprehension of our capacity for suffering. we
conceal or stifle our griefs & learn to be hypocrites in very self
defence. a kind word would melt us to tears, & move in us all
the impulses of our better nature, while harshness or coldness
freezes up the very heart's blood & rouses in us that spirit
which is a destroyer to us only, for it cannot affect the strong
man in his armor of indifference stronger than steel itself.[17]

It is not certain what turned Charles and Anna Campbell
against one another, though money was clearly a major
point of irritation. Charles Campbell was a talented man
but an erratic provider. Since early adulthood, he had been
plagued by violent headaches that made him irascible and
caused him to doubt his own capacity for sustained labor.
He had trained for the law, but could not bring himself to
practice it. He had the confidence of his fellow citizens,
who offered him the post of principal of the Anderson
Seminary, but he had to be nearly dragooned into accept-
ing the position, and he resigned it after a few years. His
fallback vocation was operating a day school for boys, but
this he found irksome. Anna, meanwhile, worried over the
expenses of their growing family and pitched in when she
could by teaching school herself. She also pushed Charles
to accept the positions offered him, to exert himself more.
Sometimes he ignored her, sometimes he lashed back. In
time, both of them became skilled contestants in battles of
will. Their newborn daughter went for months without a
name, because Charles and Anna could not agree on what
to call her.[18]

The conflict between the Campbells, as Anna recognized, was partly the product of a personal mismatch; "my
nature is not adapted to his," she reasoned.[19] But it was
also a product of companionate marriage itself. Anna
Campbell believed that she had the right to name her
baby—a right her great-grandmothers would probably not
have claimed—and therein lay the material for a fight. Once
it was conceded that women were to share in decision
making, occasions for overt conflict between husbands and

wives became far more numerous than before. Moreover, as the nineteenth century progressed, there were simply more decisions to be made. Deciding where to send a child to school, for example, became a complicated affair as the number of local schools multiplied and as a swifter transportation network brought more distant schools within reach. More options meant more decisions. More decisions, in all likelihood, meant greater potential for open conflict.

Companionate marriage also increased the likelihood that the wife would encroach too far on her husband's sphere. One of the reasons the Campbells fought so much was that they shared so much. Anna, like Charles, was a teacher, and when she could get adequate child care, she helped Charles in his school. This arrangement seemed to satisfy both of them. Then Anna made plans to open a school of her own. She carefully composed a short newspaper advertisement to announce the opening of her school—this was routine procedure for schoolteachers—and handed it with pride to Charles for his approval. Charles was livid. He would let her have her school, but under no circumstances would he let her advertise it. Anna felt as though she had been slapped. When companionship verged on something like real (and public) equality, there were fireworks.

Companionate marriage, one gathers, was rather like the companionship between a seven-year-old and a ten-year-old: They may have the best of times together, but everyone knows who is in charge. Marriage in the companionate style required a certain delicacy from both sides. The wife, for her part, had to let her wishes be known, while taking care not to trespass on male prerogatives. The husband, meanwhile, had to exercise enormous restraint. As late as 1860, the power was still almost all on the side of men. The maintenance of a companionate marriage therefore depended on the voluntary compliance of the husband, on his willingness to refrain from using the many clubs his society handed him.

There was, first of all, the common law. As we have

seen, the law granted the husband almost unlimited authority over his wife's property and labor. The law also gave the husband sole authority to decide where the pair would live, and it vested in the husband all legal authority over children. When a child was apprenticed, for example, it was up to the father to make the decision and sign the papers; the mother's wishes were legally irrelevant, and her signature had no legal force.

The husband's dominance with regard to the law was reinforced daily by the economic system. The occupational options open to men were far more numerous than those available to women, and the earning capacity of men was far greater. There were always exceptional women, of course, wives who contrived to support themselves, their children, and ne'er-do-well husbands to boot. But most women needed their husbands' earnings to live, and if their husbands abandoned them, they were in desperate trouble. Superior earning capacity transformed the husbands' legal authority into actual power.

As though the law and the economy were not enough, at least three other factors contributed to the stark imbalance of power between husband and wife. One of these was age. Men were almost always older than their wives; among the merchants and professionals of Petersburg, the average gap between husband and wife was nearly seven years. Men of the merchant and professional group did not usually marry before they reached their late twenties (their average age was twenty-eight). Their brides, on the average, were only twenty-one, and the gap must have fostered patterns of dominance and deference that were not easily altered as marriages matured. Among artisans and laborers, the gap was not so wide, and some men went so far as to marry women older than themselves. Still, the typical artisan was from three to five years older than his wife.[20]

The authority that came with age must have been fortified by men's greater knowledge of the world outside the home, knowledge that came not only from their work, but also from higher literacy rates and greater freedom of movement. The census schedules for 1860 reported equal numbers of white girls and boys attending school (free black children were not allowed to go to school after 1831), but this appears to have been a very recent development; among white adults, illiteracy rates were higher for women than for men.[21] For white women of the middle and upper classes, meanwhile, freedom of movement was, by the 1850s, restricted by both clothing and custom. Women who dressed fashionably were cinched up in corsets and weighted down by voluminous skirts (think of Virginia in the haze and heat of July). They were not to go out by day when the weather was foul. They were not to go out at night without escorts.[22] Men, of course, ventured out at will.

Finally, there was sheer superior physical force. The surviving sources do not tell us how commonplace wife beating was. They do tell us that wife beating infected all classes and both races, that some men beat their wives repeatedly, and that a few men behaved with extraordinary cruelty. William Robinson was jailed for beating his wife "with a stick"; Thomas Ferguson used a "large stick"; Frederick Miller was hauled to court for "beating his wife in the streets in a brutal manner with a cowhide"; James Ellis broke a chair over his wife's head and then had at her with an iron bar.[23]

For the woman victimized by beating, divorce was hardly ever the way out. Divorces, as the next chapter makes clear, were infrequently sought and even less frequently granted. The main legal recourse for the battered wife was the filing of a breach of the peace complaint. A breach of peace proceeding provided no remedy for damage already done, but it did get the husband out of the house until he cooled off or sobered up, and it gave him financial incentive to restrain himself in the future. The husband was not released from jail until he posted bond for his good behavior during a stipulated number of months (the wealthier the man, the higher the bond). If he assaulted his wife again, he forfeited the money.

In some cases, the deterrent seems to have been effective. David Bissett was brought before the court on a wife-beating charge in November 1844. In this first instance, the case was dismissed. A few months later, however, Bissett appeared again for "beating his wife Catharine unmercifully. . . ." This time Bissett was compelled to post $250 bond. He did not appear before the court again. "Jesus Be Merciful To Him," his epitaph later read.[24] Other men proved less tractable. William Costigan (whose wife eventually did divorce him) was hauled in twice, Thomas Prosser three times, James Ellis and Matthew Scroggins five times each. Scroggins, in particular, was incorrigible, in his wife's words, "of no earthly benefit to her in any way." Scroggins drank hard, gambled freely, interfered with his wife's efforts to support their four children, and from time to time beat her up. Each time Rosena Scroggins had her husband taken to court, the court imposed on him a higher bond; at first it was $50, then $150, then $200. But the escalating costs never restrained him for long, and neither did public humiliation. One local newspaper, after a breach of the peace proceeding of 1855, refrained from naming names so as not to embarrass Scroggins's "respectable" family, but a rival paper printed the names of all concerned and presented the case as a cautionary tale on the dangers of strong drink. Scroggins was back in court within the year. A few years later he died at the age of forty-one of what was called "dropsy."[25]

Marriage, in sum, was only as companionate as the husband allowed it to be, and there was very little to stop him from lapsing into authoritarian behavior—very little, that is, except genuine respect for his wife's feelings and judgment. That being the case, we need all the more to find out how much regard nineteenth-century husbands had for the capacities of their wives. Evidence for a systematic exploration of this question lies in the wills.

Many men did not write their wills until they were deathly ill. From the wording of the wills themselves, however, one would never know what the men were suffering, for only rarely did a testator let himself write with feeling. William Meikle, married just two months, was one of the few who did. "Jane is one of the most amiable and best of women," he wrote with terse eloquence. "She is dearer to me than life."[26] Ordinarily, the language of wills was businesslike and thin; the testator would say no more than "my beloved wife," and this was so much a convention that it conveyed no profound emotion. On the matter of emotional bonds between husband and wife, the wills simply do not tell us much.

What the wills do tell about is respect for the wife's capacity to manage property in an intelligent, responsible way. When the testator nominated his executors or when he nominated a guardian for his children, he made a declaration as to his wife's capacity to manage property for others. When the testator stipulated the specific terms of his wife's legacy, he determined her future capacity to manage for herself. While there are problems of interpretation, the terms of wills are nonetheless among our best measures of long-term changes (or lack of change) in the attitudes of men toward their wives.

The wills left by the men of Petersburg deliver a mixed message. On the one hand were some subtle changes. In the beginning, there was a clear relationship between wealth and the amount of discretion granted the wife: The wealthier the testator, the more likely he was to fix his widow in a position of passivity and continued dependence. Poorer men, by contrast, usually expected their wives to assume active control. After 1830, this neat pattern began to dissolve, and the relationship between class and female activism blurred somewhat. At the same time, there was remarkable stability. In the aggregate, the terms of men's wills were much the same in the 1850s as they had been in the 1780s. The implication is that men's attitudes did not change enough to make any dramatic differences in the fortunes of women as a group.

Both features, both the subtle shifts and the continuity overall, were visible in the nomination of executors. Executors were important persons. Whatever the unfinished business of the deceased, the executor was obliged to carry it through. Business partnerships had to be dissolved and settled. Debts had to be paid, and here a sale of property was often necessary to raise the requisite cash. Debtors of the deceased had to be located, hounded, and if necessary, taken to court to force them to pay their bills. If the deceased was himself serving as someone else's executor at the time of his death, then his executor in turn took over the charge. (This last obligation, however, was removed by the legislature in a statute passed during the session of 1824–25.[27]) It was up to the executor, too, to distribute the estate to the proper heirs. The final distribution was sometimes delayed for years, and in the meantime, the executor was to manage the estate, to maintain or hire out slaves, to rent out and repair buildings, and to pay the taxes. The person who undertook all this was not expected to do so out of any charitable feelings. The executor was reimbursed for expenses incurred and took a commission, usually 5 percent, on the estate's income. In some cases, this was a handsomely profitable enterprise. In any case, it was no job for the innocent, the dishonorable, or the impatient.

In Petersburg, just over half of the men who left wills trusted their wives to serve as executors. This percentage did not change over time. From 1784 to 1830, the proportion of married male testators who nominated their wives as executors was 54.5 percent (42 / 77). From 1831 to 1860, the proportion was an astonishingly close 53.9 percent (42 / 78)[28]. What did change was the relationship between wealth and female activism. Until about 1830, the clear preference of well-to-do testators was to isolate their wives from any active control over their estates. The numbers, as shown in Table 2.1, were again almost too tidy to be believed. While a full 80 percent of the poorer testators named their wives their executors, only about a third of the wealthiest did so. And while three-fifths of the poorer testators nominated the wife sole executor, not one of the wealthiest testators did so.

The typical well-to-do testator believed executorship to be either beneath his wife or beyond her, or perhaps both

Table 2.1

TESTATORS' WEALTH AND ROLES OF WIVES AS EXECUTORS,
1784–1830

Amount of bond	Number of wives named sole executor	Number of wives named coexecutor	Number of wives excluded
$2,000 or less	16 (59.3%)	6 (22.2%)	5 (18.5%)
$2,500 to $9,000	3 (25.0%)	3 (25.0%)	6 (50.0%)
$10,000 or more	0	14 (36.8%)	24 (63.2%)

at once. There was, first of all, an ethic of female gentility. Men of means apparently believed it degrading for a lady to concern herself with commerce, with property, or with litigation. (The ladies themselves seem to have had other ideas, a topic to be taken up in Chapter 5.) There were more practical considerations as well. While poorer testators tended to have local business interests with relatively simple accounts, the wealthier testators were for the most part merchants, men likely to be engaged in international trade, to have accumulated lengthy lists of debts and credits. It should come as no surprise that the wealthier husbands less often thought their wives competent to untangle and safeguard their interests. In this connection, it is worth pointing out that the women least likely to be named executors were not only relatively wealthy, but also relatively young. Precise ages are known for only a few of these widows, but the information that is available suggests that women over thirty were more likely to be named executors than were women widowed in their twenties.[29] It seems logical enough that testators would want to protect their estates from what they perceived as youthful inexperience. More to the point, perhaps, they wanted to protect their estates from the men their young widows might marry. The more property men accumulated, the more anxious they became to preserve it and pass it intact through the generations. Given the particulars of Virginia law, a man with dynastic ambitions had to think twice before naming his wife sole executor, for if she remarried, the new husband became executor "in right of his wife." The estate might thus be given into the hands of a stranger who could then manipulate it for purposes of his own.

The result, in any case, was a situation all too familiar to students of the history of women. Men were most willing to place women in positions of authority when the stakes were small. When the stakes were higher—when there was enough property to make its management a source of considerable power in the family and perhaps beyond it as well—the wife was ordinarily left on the sidelines; the best she could hope for was a position as coexecutor, serving jointly with one or more male executors.

The pattern blurred somewhat after 1830. The changes were not heralded by verbal flourishes on the part of testators, for the language of wills remained matter-of-fact. But change was detectable in the numbers. After 1830, more of Petersburg's wealthiest testators—exactly half—nominated their wives as executors. And for the first time, some of Petersburg's wealthiest testators—a full third (16 / 46)—named the wife sole executor. It is not clear how much this was due to a change in consciousness and how much due to a change of law. In its session of 1824–25, the Virginia legislature removed remarriage as an obstacle to the nomination of the wife. The new law stipulated that a widow's powers as executor were extinguished upon her remarriage and that a court must appoint a new executor in her place.[30] So long as one trusted the court to make a wise appointment, the new law quieted fears of what might happen if one's widow remarried, and it probably played a significant part in increasing the number of well-to-do testators who did nominate their wives.

Curiously enough, the law had no impact on the decisions of poor to middling testators. After 1830, in fact, these men were less likely to nominate their wives than they had been earlier.[31] Two possible explanations present themselves. One is that men who were artisans or small businessmen were beginning to adopt the ideal of female gentility at the same time that wealthier men were beginning to abandon it. The other is that men of all classes were behaving less according to formula and more according to individual circumstances. It may have been that the class pattern began to dissolve when husbands actually began to ask their wives whether the wives themselves wanted to serve as executors.

Meanwhile, the class pattern did not dissolve completely. After 1830, as before, a well-to-do woman was less likely to be named an executor than was her poorer sister.[32] The same was true with legal guardianship. In this century, we ordinarily think of a legal guardian as a substitute parent, someone who has the custody and care of the child, as well as the legal responsibility. In the nineteenth century, this was far less the case. The guardian often had nothing to do with nurture, discipline, or policy decisions. Rather, the legal guardian was, like an executor, a financial steward; the guardian's duty was to manage the child's inheritance until the child (or "ward") came of age. Like an executor, the guardian was to keep accounts. Like an executor, the guardian was entitled to take a commission on income. And like an executor, the guardian was subject to a certain amount of court supervision. A guardian could not sell land or spend the principal without obtaining special permission from the court.

The nineteenth-century guardian, in short, was more a financial officer than a parent, and this helps account for the rather hit-and-miss appearance of guardianship appointments. Only occasionally was a guardian assigned immediately after the death of a parent. In some instances, a guardian was assigned while both parents were still alive; this usually occurred when a child received an inheritance from an aunt or uncle or grandparent. After one parent died, the child stood in no immediate need of a legal guardian. The surviving parent would take charge of the child's person; the child's property, meanwhile, was handled by the executor. It was only when the estate was settled, when the executor closed the books and distributed the legacies to each of the individual heirs, that the assignment of a guardian became essential. In many cases, the estate was not settled at all until the youngest child had reached adulthood, and the need for a guardian was thus obviated altogether. Most testators, therefore, did not concern themselves with finding guardians for their children. In Petersburg, only a sixth of the married men who wrote wills and who left minor children (16/97) used their wills to nominate legal guardians.[33] The rest apparently trusted the court to select a competent guardian, should the need for one happen to arise.

The fact that guardianship was primarily a matter of managing money also meant that when the father died, the mother had no special claim to the guardianship of her own children. The court did want to make sure that the guardian had the child's best interests at heart, but beyond this, the mother's demonstrated devotion to her children was simply beside the point. The point, once again, was to locate an able manager. That being the case, it is on first sight heartening to learn that in Petersburg, the mother's chances of being assigned guardian did improve over time. Before the 1840s, the mother had an even chance. In twenty-eight cases, the mother was appointed. In twenty-nine other cases, the mother was not appointed, even though she was documentably living and legally eligible for the job. From 1841 to 1860, the mother's chances improved to better than two to one (twenty-nine to thirteen, to be precise). The change was particularly dramatic in the 1850s, when mothers were assigned in eighteen out of twenty-one cases.

On second sight, the change is less impressive. When we sort out guardianship assignments by wealth, three facts emerge. The first is that for women, guardianship, like executorship, was largely conditioned by wealth: A mother was most likely to be assigned guardian when her child's inheritance was relatively small. (Here the amount of bond required of the guardian provides the base for establishing rough categories of wealth.) For the entire period 1784 to 1860, the mother whose child had only a modest inheritance (bond two thousand dollars or less) stood a very good chance of being assigned her child's guardian, a three-in-four chance, in fact (34 / 46). In more prosperous families (bond more than two thousand dollars), the mother's chances were substantially less, about three in seven (22 / 50). The second fact is that there was some improvement within this wealthier group. As with the nomination of executors, men became somewhat less nervous about permitting women to manage relatively large estates, and this helps account for the increase in maternal guardianship after 1840.[34] The third fact, however, is that most of what the mothers gained was due to a change in probate policy. As time went on, and especially after 1850, the court simply appointed guardians for more children of modest means. (This, it appears, was part of a larger campaign to settle estates quickly and thus to increase the fluidity of capital. Instead of waiting until the youngest child turned twenty-one to distribute the estate, guardians were more often appointed for minor children; the mother and her grown children were then free to possess, sell, or invest their individual portions.)[35] The increase in maternal guardianship did not, therefore, bespeak any major shift in men's estimates of women's managerial capacities. Like husbands, the justices of the court were most likely to grant authority to women when the stakes were low.

The husbands, meanwhile, made one last collective statement about female competence when they decided how many strings they would attach to the legacies they granted their wives, and here again the story was one of offsets and small changes. The husband was required by law to give his wife at least a third of his estate (one-half if they had no children), but he could give her more if he chose, and it was also up to him to determine the nature of her control over whatever he gave her. He could, if he chose, give her only a "life estate." This meant she could use the property or draw its income, but she had no ultimate authority over it—she could not sell it, for example. When she died, the property would pass to the testator's children or to other heirs named in the will. On the other hand, the testator could choose to give his wife a "fee simple" or "absolute" estate. This empowered her to do exactly as she liked with her inheritance. So long as she remained a widow, she could keep it, improve it, sell it, mortgage it, will it, or give it away. Martha Douglas, for example, was authorized to exercise unfettered control over her legacy, a point her husband made with emphasis and at length in bequeathing her part of his real estate:

> I not only give to my wife full & compleat Control over all the said lots and lands, but also ample & unrestrained power and authority to sell and dispose of the same, whenever she may deem it juditious & advantageous to do so, and I strongly recommend to her, as prudent & beneficial to sell my lots & houses in town as well as my other lands herein before mentioned on a long credit of several annual instalments, bearing interest from the date, and I hope and doubt not, she will Consult and advise with my Executors in the propriety thereof—but this is merely recommendatory, not obligatory, if she should deem a sale unadvisable.[36]

It was also possible to mix life and fee simple estates, and as a result the terms of the wife's inheritance could become quite complex. The will of cabinetmaker John McCloud is a good example. When he wrote his will in 1795, McCloud entrusted his wife with most of his property, but each segment of the estate came on different terms. Isabella McCloud received both of her husband's town lots, but while his shop was hers for life, the house where they lived was to be turned over to their son when he reached the age of twenty-one. The greater part of John McCloud's personal property went to Isabella, too, but again on variable terms. His one slave was Isabella's for life, his cattle and furniture were hers in fee simple, and the proceeds from the sale of his shop tools and materials were to be handled as a kind of trust for the children; the money was to "remain at the disposal of my Wife for the purpose of Educating our children in the fear of the Lord, which God grant."[37]

For the wives of Petersburg, the trend over the long term was an increased incidence of fee simple inheritance. Although the terms of the wills were sometimes complex, they can be distilled into answers to two key questions. How often did the husband give the wife her entire inheritance in fee simple? And how often did the husband give the wife at least a part of her inheritance in fee simple? As we might expect, the men most likely to give their wives fee simple estates were those who had no children. Among childless men, more than 90 percent (57/61) gave their wives some property in fee, and three-quarters of the childless men (46/61) gave the wife her entire inheritance in fee.[38] This pattern did not change over time.

There was some change, however, among testators who did have children, and the change was once again most pronounced among men in the upper income bracket (executor's bond ten thousand dollars or more), who after 1830 were more likely than before to bequeath property in fee simple. In the beginning, it was the wealthy testator who was least likely to give his wife property in fee simple. This is curious. One would think that the wealthy man would be most inclined to give his wife at least a small part of his estate in fee simple; if the widow was unwise in the management of her share, or if she lost it through remarriage, there would still be plenty left for the children. By the same reasoning, the testator with nothing to spare would opt for a life estate for his wife in order to guarantee each child the greatest possible share in his property. This was not, however, the reasoning of the testators of Petersburg, at least not before 1830. While the wife of a poor to middling testator had a fifty-fifty chance of receiving at least a part of her inheritance in fee simple, the wife of a wealthy testator was more likely than not to have to settle for a life estate only. Greater wealth, it seems, only generated greater conservatism. After 1830 this changed. High-income men were more likely than not to give their wives some property in fee simple, and it was this shift that accounted for the overall increase in fee simple inheritance. Before the 1830s, the wife's chance of receiving a part of her legacy in fee was 42.5 percent (31 / 73); after 1830, her chances rose to 55.8 percent (48 / 86). The chance that the wife would receive her entire inheritance in fee simple likewise grew, from 21.9 percent before the 1830s (16 / 73) to 34.9 percent (30 / 86) after 1830.

The increase in fee simple inheritance spelled a modest increase in power and in options for Petersburg's widows. This gain, however, was offset at least in part by losses of other kinds. For one thing, more testators inserted remarriage clauses, stipulating that the wife, if she remarried, would have her portion cut. It also appears that as time went on, fewer testators were willing to grant their wives more property than the law required.[39]

There remains a question of emphasis. The terms of the wills did undergo some changes, but there was considerable continuity as well, and it is not immediately obvious which deserves the greater attention. When we pool our numbers on executorship and fee simple inheritance, however, continuity prevails: The terms of the wills were remarkably stable over time. This judgment comes from the construction of a discretion spectrum. (This device allows us to rank the women according to how much discretion they were granted in their husbands' wills; it takes into account both the woman's status as an executor and the character of her inheritance.) At one end of the spectrum were women like Eliza Ritchie, whose husband named her sole executor and gave her her entire inheritance in fee simple. At the other end were women like Martha Trokes, who would never have to lift a finger. Her husband instructed his executors (Martha was not among them) to sell all his property and invest one-third of the proceeds to provide Martha with an income as long as she lived. After her death, her share would pass automatically to their children.[40] Most of the widows, of course, ranged somewhere between Ritchie and Trokes, and Table 2.2 shows their distribution on a descending scale of authority.

All in all, about four-fifths of the widows were granted discretion of some kind, and roughly 30 percent were

Table 2.2

A Discretion Spectrum: Terms of Wives' Inheritance

Status as executor		Nature of inheritance	Number of widows 1784–1830		Number of widows 1831–60	
Sole executor	and	Entire inheritance in fee	16	Major discretion 30.7%	23	Major discretion 28.8%
Sole executor	and	Part inheritance in fee	2		1	
Coexecutor	and	Entire inheritance in fee	10		4	
Coexecutor	and	Part inheritance in fee	7		2	
Sole executor	but	Inheritance for life only	6	Partial discretion 47.4%	13	Partial discretion 51.0%
Coexecutor	but	Inheritance for life only	14		1	
Excluded	but	Part inheritance in fee	11		19	
Excluded	but	Entire inheritance in fee	12		14	
None named	but	Entire inheritance in fee	9		2	
None named	but	Part inheritance in fee	2		4	
Excluded	and	Inheritance for life only	22	No discretion 21.9%	17	No discretion 20.1%
None named	and	Inheritance for life only	3		4	

granted major discretion. Whether these figures are high, low, or average for an urban community will not be known until comparable figures are gathered for other locations. What is clear is that in Petersburg time brought no change. If the character of marriage in fact changed in any significant way, there is nothing in the wills to suggest that the attitudes of men were on the cutting edge.

The attitudes of women, however, were changing: As time went on, women were less willing to accept whatever was offered them. As Virginia law had it, the widow was not obligated to accept the terms of her husband's will. If the husband left her less than her legal third, if he directed the sale or emancipation of slaves she wanted to keep, or if for some other reason she found her provision inequitable, she could renounce the will and apply to the court for a redivision of her husband's estate. From the behavior of Petersburg's widows in the early days, one would hardly know such a law existed. From 1784 to 1820, only one widow (of ninety) renounced her husband's will, though there were several widows with clear cause for protest. After 1820, the practice began to catch on. The clerks seem to have regarded will renunciation as rather irregular. (With uncharacteristic indecision, the clerks could not fix on a place to record them; some renunciations appear in the will books, others in the minute books, and others in the deed books.) But some of the women pressed their rights. From 1821 to 1860, one will in ten was renounced by the widow.

In some of these cases, the widow had been utterly cheated. Samuel Stevens was a partner in Petersburg's largest tanning and leather goods firm, and when he died at fifty-five, he was certainly comfortable. To his wife, however, he left nothing. Stevens bequeathed his entire estate to his three children, "and I particularly enjoin them to take care of their mother which belongs to a dutifull child and who has a prior Interest to any of them in the property." Elizabeth Stevens, not wishing to live at the mercy of her children, renounced the will.[41] So did Maria Matthews, a free black who had been pushed aside in favor of a daughter. Richard Matthews's estate consisted of a house and lot in Pocahontas, and this he left to his daughter Sarah Ann. To his widow he allotted half the furniture. She renounced the will the day it was brought into court. Other cases were more ambiguous. Nathaniel Lee ordered the sale of both land and slaves and granted his wife Sarah whatever was left over for her life. Sarah's protest may have been intended to give her a larger share of the estate, or to block the sales, or both. Ann L. Pace, to cite one last example, seems to have rejected her husband's will in order to defeat the provision that his debts be paid first and her portion taken out of the remainder.[42] Pace probably calculated that she would do better if her dower were allotted first and the debts paid from the remainder.

Ann L. Pace did not marry again. Nor, so far as it can be documented, did Sarah Lee, Maria Matthews, or Eliza Stevens. Once women were well out of marriage, they tended to stay out. This is arresting commentary on the character of nineteenth-century marriage. It also raises questions about how we should view women's changing status over the long sweep of American history. For historians in search of an overarching interpretation of women's past, locating the place of women in the family is a crucial enterprise. Before taking a second look at marriage among the people of Petersburg, here is a brief review of the controversy among historians.

When feminism was reborn in the late 1960s, historians were quick to resuscitate the study of the female past. They were equally quick to adopt a thesis of decline as the standard interpretation of the history of American women. In briefest terms, the thesis of decline holds that the colonial period was a kind of golden age and that after the Revolution the status of women deteriorated badly. Deterioration provoked protest in the form of organized feminism in the mid-nineteenth century; by the dawn of the twentieth century, woman's rights activists had succeeded in starting women on their long and still unfinished march toward equality.[43]

In its earliest versions, the thesis of decline rested on relatively few props. The case for a colonial golden age was based on three main considerations, the first of which was the sex ratio. Women's scarcity, it was reasoned, increased their value and strengthened their position in the marriage market. Second, in a preindustrial economy, the home was the center of economic production. Both men and women worked at home, therefore, and women's labor was as important as men's in the production of basic goods. Third, there was a certain apparent fluidity about sex roles. The literature of the seventeenth and eighteenth centuries was not much concerned with establishing firm boundaries between the activities of men and those of women, and in the world of work, women did in fact cross boundaries; at least a few women were to be found in almost every imaginable trade or occupation.

It would be a long time before women again had it so good, or so the argument continued. The case for decline in the nineteenth century was built mainly from two historic developments. The first was industrialization. When economic production moved out of the home, men moved with it, leaving their women at home, unpaid, dependent, and no longer producing society's most basic goods. The second was the meteoric rise of the cult of true womanhood (also called the cult of domesticity), an ideology that tried to make a virtue out of women's confinement to the home. According to the popular literature, both female nature and the needs of the country demanded that women stay within their special domestic sphere. "The world" was meanwhile staked off for men. Never before had differences between the sexes been pressed with such urgency and persistence.

The thesis of decline has drawn fire from a number of critics. For the colonial period, Mary Beth Norton and Lyle Koehler, among others, have identified weaknesses in the case for a golden age, and they have shown that some of the evidence indeed suggests an age of oppression.[44] For the nineteenth century, the most sweeping rejection of the thesis of decline comes from the combined work of Daniel

Scott Smith and Carl N. Degler.[45] Where some historians saw decline, Smith and Degler see progress, and from their point of view, women's changing status in marriage was pivotal. Smith and Degler, in other words, shift the ground of the argument. Where the thesis of decline stressed the economic aspects of women's status, particularly productivity and employment, Smith and Degler refocus on sexuality, affection, and family relationships. Where the thesis of decline emphasized public roles—gainful occupations and the democratic mission of organized feminism—Smith and Degler concentrate on the internal dynamics of the nuclear family.

This shift of ground is of enormous importance, for it is loaded with judgment on what mattered most and on how change was achieved. Smith and Degler argue that to the typical American woman, the family mattered most. Through most of American history, Smith points out, the great majority of women married, and after they married, they only rarely worked outside the home. The family was thus the main site of female activity, and it was within the family that women's great gains in power and autonomy were won. The main evidence for gains lies in statistics on marital fertility. At the beginning of the nineteenth century, the typical white woman could expect to bear seven or eight children. Thereafter the numbers declined steadily, until by 1900 the typical white woman gave birth to only three or four children. Given the limitations of nineteenth-century birth control technology, such a marked decline could only have been accomplished with the cooperation of husbands in withdrawal or abstinence, or, as Degler adds, by a high incidence of abortion. Either way, to Smith and Degler the fall in the fertility rate was a major manifestation of enhanced power and autonomy for women.

Where did the power come from? Smith and Degler are properly cautious about ultimate causes, but they do suggest that ideology and intimate relationships were important power sources. Both authors give a charitable reading to the cult of true womanhood. However sexist the doctrine of separate spheres may look from this distance, it can nonetheless be regarded as an improvement over the sex-role ideology of the colonial period, an ideology that held women to be inferior in every way. Nineteenth-century Americans believed women were at least the moral superiors of men, and this was a first. The glorification of domesticity and child nurture can also be seen as a step up: Better glorified than taken for granted. The assignment of greater social prestige to women's traditional roles, Smith and Degler conclude, was another plus for the women of the nineteenth century. Smith goes so far as to assert that once woman's sphere was valued more highly, women themselves chose to stay within it.

Where else might the power have come from? Smith proposes that wives bargained with the only commodity they had: sex. Degler suggests that marriage and motherhood became sources of power. Families had fewer children than before, but those children were the recipients of intense interest and care. Since work drew fathers more and more away from home, childrearing was left almost exclusively to the women, and separate spheres of activity thus became the rule for husbands and wives. The relations between women and their husbands were nevertheless "companionate," based increasingly on affection and mutual respect. To Degler, this was so much clear gain for women. Because women were in charge of children at a time when childrearing was assigned great social importance, motherhood became a source of power. So did companionate marriage. Affection, Degler believes, gave wives leverage, the power of "extracting concessions" from their husbands.[46]

Finally, the Smith-Degler thesis minimizes the significance of organized feminism. This is not to say that women are portrayed as passive, for both Smith and Degler attribute much of the improvement in the status of women to the agency of women themselves. Smith in fact uses the term "domestic feminism" to describe the drive for autonomy within the family. Degler steers clear of so provocative a term, but refers repeatedly to assertiveness, individualism, and the recognition and pursuit of self-interest. The implication is that nineteenth-century women did not really need a feminist movement. With Degler, this is only an implication; he suggests, for example, that although by public definition men had most of the power within marriage, the question of who actually wielded the most power was ultimately a matter of individual personalities. With Smith, the trivialization of organized feminism is explicit. Organized feminism was limited in its appeal, he suggests, because it misguidedly attacked "arbitrary male authority," a phenomenon that was "nearly obsolete."[47]

The feminist reader blinks. The enduring contribution of Daniel Scott Smith and Carl Degler is their insistence that we give full weight to roles within the family whenever we hazard any generalizations about long-term changes in the status of women. The rest is destined to be controversial. As it happens, there is much in the chapters that follow to sustain the Smith-Degler thesis. In Petersburg, women did gain power within the family, and they did become more assertive, and this demonstrates that women's status could indeed improve without the assistance of organized feminism. But the Petersburg case also points up the need for better evidence and more analytical precision as we continue to probe the links between intimacy and power.

The Petersburg evidence will not support the idea that for nineteenth-century women the story was progress alone.[48] Leaving aside for the moment the question of whether women's overall condition got better or worse (subsequent chapters suggest that this can be argued either way), the question of what became of women within marriage is still open. Major social changes usually come at a price. They generate anxiety or resistance; they produce unanticipated consequences and complications. If this chapter is right, this was as true of marriage as of anything else. Whatever benefits the companionate ideal brought to women, it also seems to have brought a good deal of conflict and disappointment.

Meanwhile, there is very little evidence that companionate marriage brought women actual power. There are really two points here. One is that we need more persuasive evidence that women were in fact gaining power. Smith and Degler's evidence—the declining fertility rate—can be explained away as the product of male self-interest, as Smith himself concedes; in the nineteenth century, children got to be expensive, so men began to restrain themselves. Second, if it can be demonstrated that women were indeed gaining power, we need stronger evidence that love, sex, or affection had something to do with it. In Degler's portrayal, affection in marriage, freedom for women, and power for women all rose together. But love and power do not necessarily rise and fall together; they are analytically and historically distinct from one another, and they may affect one another in a variety of ways. It could be argued, for example, that the romantic love ideal in the nineteenth century was a means of maintaining male dominance at a time when it was no longer acceptable to demand submission for submission's sake. (The seventeenth-century wife made sacrifices out of duty. The nineteenth-century wife made them for love, but she, too, sacrificed.) The Petersburg evidence will not settle these issues once and for all, but it does suggest that there was no simple relationship between love and power. In wills, as we have seen, the amount of power men gave their wives had more to do with class than with feeling. The love of men, it appears, was no guarantee of power for women.

The gains made by Petersburg's women had quite another source. The next chapter takes up separate estates, and here the evidence of growing power for women in marriage is indisputable. Through separate estates, women gained power, not because men changed their minds or even their hearts, but as the result of an attempt to escape the terrible uncertainty of the nineteenth-century economy.

3

Loopholes: Separate Estates

Of all the early studies of the history of women, the most provocative and perhaps the most important was Mary R. Beard's _Woman as Force in History._ _Woman as Force_ was a complex and in places indignant assault on the idea that women throughout history had been mere passive victims of male tyranny. It was also an indirect assertion of the importance of law as an indicator of the status of women in the past. While Beard ranged over enormous stretches of time and ground, she devoted more than a third of her book to the Anglo-American law of married women's property. Here she portrayed a dramatic struggle between two major systems of jurisprudence, between the common law on the one hand and equity on the other. To Beard's mind, the development of equity was proof that English and American women had achieved a substantial degree of freedom.

Equity did indeed have more to offer women than did the common law. Under the common law, as we have seen, married women had next to no property rights. Equity, however, was more flexible. Equity was an alternative system of justice that had developed over the centuries alongside the common law and was brought to

America along with the common law. Where courts of law ruled according to precedent and fixed principles, courts of equity (these were called courts of chancery, and the judges were called chancellors) were expected to rule according to the inherent justice of the case.

In time, equity acquired precedents and principles of its own, but for married women it offered loopholes by which they could escape some of their common-law disabilities. Under equity, a married woman could acquire a separate estate. This was property set aside for her benefit; over this property the husband was not allowed to exercise his usual common-law rights. The amount of control the woman was allowed to exercise over her separate estate was, as will soon be clear, highly variable. But it was enough for Mary Beard. By 1830, she claimed, equity "had emancipated millions of women from the rigidities of the Common Law." From the particulars of law it was but a short hop to the sweeping statement on the long-term condition of women: "It seems perfectly plain that the dogma of woman's complete historic subjection to man must be rated as one of the most fantastic myths ever created by the human mind."[1]

Woman as Force in History first appeared in 1946, and equity has hardly been touched by historians since. Despite the present exuberant revival of research in women's history and despite considerable interest in Mary Beard herself, Beard's enthusiasm for the study of equity has proved to be distinctly noncontagious. Where equity has attracted notice, its significance has generally been downplayed. It has been pointed out, for example, that separate estates were neither as commonplace as Beard claimed nor as liberating as she implied.[2] This criticism is just. Yet equity deserves better, and so does Mary Beard.

For the historian, the great virtue of equity is that in some states, Virginia among them, it generated an extraordinary set of documents. Each time a married woman acquired a separate estate, a written conveyance was required. The conveyance typically stipulated what assets were covered and where they had come from. What is more, the wording of the conveyance determined the powers the woman could legally exercise. She might be given the same rights as a man, she might be granted some powers and denied others, or she might be given no active powers at all.

Taken together, the terms of these conveyances provide an unusually sensitive index to the changing status of women of the propertied classes, and they speak to some of the most important issues in the history of women. They speak on the timing and nature of changes in women's status. They speak on the question of what motivated change, on the riddle of why women's status changed for the better in an antifeminist culture. And they speak on the character of female agency in history.

In order to bring each of these issues into better focus, it will help to take one more look at the status of married women under the common law. Under the common law, as the previous chapter spelled out, the married woman was economically passive, nearly powerless, and thoroughly dependent on her husband. What needs emphasis here is that she was also extremely vulnerable. The law presumed that the husband would use his powers wisely for the couple's joint benefit. If he abused his power, there was simply no remedy available at law. It was therefore open season on the property and earnings of the wife. It was perfectly legal for a husband to collect his wife's wages directly from her employer and to spend the money however he chose. The husband could confiscate his wife's savings; he could pawn her most treasured possessions; he could gamble away her inheritance in a poker game. The possibilities for evil were almost limitless.

Most men were not deliberately malicious, but if they were incompetent or even unlucky, they could do just as much damage. When a man fell into debt, his creditors had every right to take the wife's property in payment. As early credit ratings reveal, creditors were very much aware of this option. Beginning in the 1840s, R. G. Dun & Company hired agents to file regular reports on the habits and assets of owners of local businesses. The notations were brief and very much to the point: "Was poor himself but has within 2 years married a Lady with good Estate"; " . . . just married the daughter of a wealthy planter . . ."; " . . . married a lady worth $20,000"; "his wife is sole heiress of a rich father"; "his wife I believe has some value."[3] The hard fact was that under the common law the wife's property was fair game for husbands and creditors alike.

Men knew this and on the whole seem to have approved. Ancient as the common law was, its provisions on married women's property dovetailed neatly with the nineteenth century's ideas about separate spheres; both law and literature called for a radical division between the sexes, with economic responsibility and economic authority vested in men alone. This was a powerful and durable ideal. In Petersburg, the one instance of editorial dissent came in 1859. "There are hard working wives in every community whose unceasing efforts to support themselves and their children in respectability are constantly thwarted by lazy, profligate and drunken husbands. Is this just?" the *Intelligencer* asked. "Is it right?" The editorial then pressed for legislation that would give "industrious women who have worthless husbands" the legal powers they needed to support and protect themselves.[4]

The law did not change in Virginia until 1877, and neither did the ideology. There was, however, an increasing willingness to resort to separate estates to protect the property of individual women from disaster at the hands of husbands and husbands' creditors. In Petersburg, separate estates were rare until about 1820. In the antebellum period, the use of separate estates increased markedly, and this was a major improvement in the condition of women of the middle and upper classes. Mary Beard would have been pleased.

There was a catch, however. Although the number of separate estates mushroomed in the antebellum period, there was no corresponding growth in the number of women who exercised unrestricted control over property. Here intentions were central. While some separate estates were unequivocal instruments of power, in the majority of cases empowering the woman was not the intention. Instead, the main object was to keep property in the family—to achieve some measure of economic security when times were hard, husbands failed, and creditors closed in. Under these circumstances, the woman was not likely to be given active power over her separate estate, for if she had power over it, she could lose it, and no one wanted to risk any further losses. Moreover, since the goal was ordinarily to protect property rather than to free the woman, separate estates were fertile ground for confusing, complicated, and expensive litigation. For all that, the rise of separate estates did advance the condition of women overall. Separate estates make it clear that the status of women could improve without the help of overt feminism. They are also a study in the limits of such improvements.

Finally, separate estates supply the first link in a chain of evidence concerning the operation of a women's value system. In Petersburg, women were extremely active—relatively speaking, more active than were men—in establishing separate estates for other women. This would seem to indicate a measurably greater concern on women's part for the welfare of other women and for economic security.

In *Woman as Force in History*, Mary Beard tended to cast women as passive beneficiaries of equity. But she also called for a new history, a history that would give women their due as active agents, that would stop taking men as the measure of what counted in the past, and that would consider the possibility that women have all along contributed to civilization in distinctively humane ways.[5] Equity, where women exerted more "force" than Mary Beard knew, was a good place to begin.

Every time a woman acquired a separate estate, her husband relinquished power or had it wrested from him. Dr. James T. Hubard expressed best the humiliation of a man who found his wife's means placed beyond his reach. When Hubard brought his bride to Petersburg in 1805, he had anticipated a financial lift. "At the time that I married," he recalled, "I certainly had a right to expect pecuniary or money assistance. Susan was wealthy and her funds quite sufficient." But Dr. Hubard had signed a marriage contract, and within the year it became clear that his wife's mother intended to retain control of Susan's separate property. Hubard gave his mother-in-law notice that he would never accept her authority: "No earthly power can ever make me so far degrade myself, unless I have so stupidly committed myself in your marriage contract as to make me a slave—which I know I have not done. . . . I cannot submit to be trampled on and to be made a subject of general talk & laughter to oblige any one on the face of the globe." The doctor's final paragraph showed more composure. "You have it perfectly in your power to manage your own concerns. I wish to manage the concerns of my wife."[6]

In his huffy assertion of male prerogative, Hubard spoke for his generation and for subsequent generations as well. The husband alone was generally expected to control his family's finances; the man who did less was, at least by implication, an incompetent, a weakling, or a fool. And yet as the nineteenth century progressed, the numbers of men who did do less increased dramatically, for every decade brought substantial growth in the numbers of women who acquired separate estates. People do not ordinarily give up power lightly. The question is, why should men have given it up at all?

The best answer is that some men were willing to give up power and some had it taken from them, but both for the sake of economic security. The ideal of male financial dominance was deeply held, but it could be undercut by the desire to minimize risks in the nineteenth century's highly volatile economy. It was the counterpoint between the two—between the stubborn commitment to male dominance in marriage and the search for economic security—that patterned the development of the majority of separate estates.

Establishing a separate estate was a fairly simple procedure. It did not require the assistance of a lawyer, and it could be done even when the property in question was not worth very much; in Petersburg, roughly one-half to two-thirds of white couples and perhaps one-fifth of free black couples had enough property to make a separate estate worth thinking about. A separate estate could be established before the wedding by marriage contract (also called a prenuptial agreement), or it could be done by separation agreement after the honeymoon was over. It could also be done by will, deed of gift, or deed of sale. In each case, the essential element was the written conveyance of property or property rights to a trustee, charging the trustee to hold the property for the separate use of a particular married woman.[7]

That much accomplished, the powers of the trustee and the powers of the woman hinged on the precise wording of the conveyance. The trustee was a man or a single woman who technically held the property, performed conveyances, and if necessary stood in for the wife in court. In practice, the trustee's role was highly variable, ranging from exclusive management and control to no involvement whatsoever. The role of the married woman was likewise variable. She, too, might be granted exclusive dominion over her property; some conveyances included a blanket grant of all the powers ordinarily exercised by a single woman or a man. At the other extreme, she might be left passive. In some cases, the wife and the trustee divided powers between them; in other cases, they exercised power jointly; and in still other cases, neither the wife nor the trustee was granted any explicit powers. In the last instance, the sole function of the trust was to exempt the wife's property from liability for the husband's debts.[8]

In Petersburg, that was the dominant motive, and it apparently grew more urgent with time. Before about 1810, separate estates were almost unheard of. Only thirteen of them were established in Petersburg from 1784 to 1810, and only twenty-three more were added in the decade that ended in 1820. Thereafter the numbers grew impressively. From 1821 to 1860, nearly six hundred separate estates were set up in Petersburg.[9]

The prototypical sequence ran like this. The man and woman were married without any kind of equitable settlement; to demand a separate estate at the outset was to insult the groom and deprive him of working capital. (Only a fifth of the women who held separate estates in Petersburg did so by virtue of marriage contracts.) It was only after the husband had demonstrated his inability to stay out of debt that a separate estate was created: Better to settle property on the wife than to see it sold off to pay the husband's creditors. The wife would not be granted much discretion over her new estate, for if she had active power over it, she, too, might lose it in paying off debts of her own contracting. The growth of separate estates constituted a major advance for women of the middle and upper classes, but it began in expediency, a response to the failures of scores of individual men.

Examples are legion. Most readily documented is the tragic and acrimonious Ruffin-Beckwith feud.[10] Edmund Ruffin is best known as a champion of agricultural reform and as an early and passionate advocate of southern secession. In family affairs, he was equally partisan and just as vehement, and no one could top him at nursing grudges. The object of Ruffin's particular disapproval was T. Stanly Beckwith, a Petersburg physician who had married Ruffin's daughter Agnes in 1838. Ruffin always had at least one unkind word for his son-in-law—"spendthrift & worthless," "wasteful & spendthrift," "lazy & heedless of the future," Ruffin grumbled. It was true that Beckwith was forever in debt and that he had a talent for antagonizing those he depended upon. In 1846, Beckwith and his father (a newcomer to Petersburg and also a doctor) engaged in a suicidal dispute with the Petersburg Medical Faculty, a group of regular physicians who, like physicians elsewhere, had recently organized to define and combat quackery. High on the Medical Faculty's new list of unethical practices was the promotion of "secret nostrums." The Beckwiths meantime had made a considerable investment in the production and sale of Beckwith's Antidyspeptic Pills, and they saw the Medical Faculty's code of ethics as a mere pretext for driving out competitors. The Beckwiths stood their ground and took the dreary consequences. Consultations were refused, and patients grew fainthearted. Creditors closed in, and the Beckwiths' furniture—evidently a gift from Edmund Ruffin—was sacrificed to pay them.

Over the years it got no easier. Agnes continued to bear children, thirteen in all. Stanly assumed part of the burden of his aging parents' support. Ruffin let them live on one of his farms; he also contributed loans, gifts, advice, and censure, perpetually miffed that his contributions elicited neither gratitude nor compliance with his wishes. In 1857, finally, he closed the books. Having decided to retire from active life as a planter, Ruffin divided his property and deeded portions to each of his children. It went without saying that Agnes's share would be made a separate estate. Agnes was given no active powers over it, however, Ruffin doubtless fearing she would fall prey to her "despicable" husband's influence. The property—the farm on which they were living, ten slaves, household furnishings, and railroad stock—was instead conveyed in trust to Agnes's brother Julian, who was to manage it for her benefit, as he saw fit.

No sooner was the ink dry on the deed than T. Stanly Beckwith moved off the farm to make another try at a medical practice in Petersburg. Agnes followed him after a few months. Edmund Ruffin had always been hurt by his daughter's implacable loyalty to her husband, and this was too much. Ruffin swore off further communication with all Beckwiths, even avoiding visits to Petersburg lest he bump into one of them. And he stuck to his resolve, even in wartime. Early in 1863, Agnes begged her father to make peace; the death of her sister had left Agnes as Ruffin's sole surviving daughter. Ruffin's reply was swift. "It is not my disposition, nor in my nature, to put off & put on love, according to my changes of temper, or expediency," he wrote. "I have *no daughter* left alive." Agnes still hoped for a reunion when the war was over, and in July 1865, she thought she would have her chance. Weak and sick after months of refugee life in North Carolina, Agnes headed for home, sustained by a fantasy of reconciliation. In Petersburg, the news was out: Edmund Ruffin had committed suicide, gone down with his beloved Confederacy. Agnes Beckwith never recovered from that last blow. She died in November 1865.

The creation of Agnes Beckwith's separate estate was only one event in a long and painful story. In most cases, we do not know the whole story, but it is clear that a great many separate estates were established only after the husband had proved himself a loser. Harriet Rushmore acquired her separate estate in 1856, the year after her husband, a carpenter, was "completely skinned."[11] Elizabeth McIndoe received her separate estate, a house and a woman slave, after her husband Charles went under for the second time. McIndoe had done well enough in the dry goods business, but that, as a friend explained in 1828, "did not satisfy Charley—he must also be a Shipper of Produce to Europe, & in the end Tobacco & Cotton have completely swamped him." Nathaniel Harris also went in for credit in the grand style, and he, too, would have been swamped, had it not been for the intervention of his wife's brother in 1812. Harris had registered a string of five loans and four defaults stretching back to 1803, and the final default destined his house slaves and household furnishings for the auction block. Attorney Benjamin Watkins Leigh came to the rescue, bidding for seven of the slaves and some of the furniture. These he conveyed to trustees for the use of his sister Elizabeth Harris, "seperate from and free of all control of or by her present or any future husband." The Harrises were reduced to taking in boarders and teaching school, but Elizabeth's separate estate cushioned them from poverty.[12]

More hard luck stories were encapsulated in the preambles of the deeds by which separate estates were established: "Unfortunate in business," "stript of all his property," "somewhat embarrassed," "without a house or home," and "much embarrassed," said the deeds. As failures and the fear of failure grew, so too did the numbers of separate estates. It takes some imagining to appreciate the violent uncertainty of the economic lives of middle-class people in the nineteenth century. Economic conditions fluctuated wildly. With sudden booms followed by spectacular crashes and long, dull depressions, it was a challenge for the most conscientious provider to stay ahead of the game. Many failed, their difficulties compounded by the depersonalization of business. Banks, for example, began to replace family and friends as sources of credit. Dry goods merchant Samuel D. Morton lectured his partner on the difference: "You must recollect that the debt is due to the Bank, not to an individual, and we cannot get indulgence by promising to pay it tomorrow or next week, but it must be paid on the day on which it is due, or our credit must be ruined." Educator Mary L. Simpson put the problem very succinctly: " 'Tis Diamond cut Diamond," she wrote, "all over town."[13]

There was no relief from government either, no unemployment insurance, no social security, no welfare payments. In Virginia, there was not even a bankruptcy law. Some men, desperate to stay ahead of their creditors, mortgaged everything they owned. In 1839, George Mountjoy mortgaged every bit of his personal property, including "2 large Dolls – belongs to my child." Had Mountjoy failed to pay his creditors, the dolls along with everything else would have been sold. As the hard times of the late 1830s intensified, Samuel Morton recorded his grimmest vision: "I have in imagination seen all my property taken and sold for almost nothing – my family turned out of doors, without a shelter or a bed, without the necessaries of life or the means of procuring them – destitute and friendless."[14]

It could happen to almost anyone. A trace of the financial biographies of a small group of upper-middle-class women suggests that serious reverses were the norm. In 1811, forty-six Petersburg women founded the Female Orphan Asylum, the town's first charitable organization. Their work as organizers will be discussed in Chapter 7. Their collective economic history, meanwhile, is a surprisingly dismal one. Nine of the women cannot be traced, and ten either died or moved away before 1819. Of the remaining twenty-seven, ten were married to men who were ruined in the panic of 1819, and three more were married to men who lived long enough to fail in the panic of 1837. Six other women eventually found themselves scraping—taking in sewing, boarders, and schoolchildren. Only eight of the women lived out their lives in apparent uninterrupted comfort.

The pressure on men was, of course, enormous, and a few of them cracked. Richard Rambaut, a French refugee from the revolution in Saint-Domingue (Haiti), worked for years to make up his earlier losses. The hard times that followed the panic of 1819, however, stripped him once again of everything he had gained. Rambaut poisoned himself in 1827. "He left a long letter to his wife," a friend explained, "& said it was owing to his pecuniary embarrassments that he killed himself." The town was electrified a few months later, when banker and model citizen Nathaniel Snelson embezzled forty-two thousand dollars and fled to England. No one had even known that Snelson was in trouble.[15]

A separate estate could help relieve the pressure. Even a hopelessly insolvent man could settle separate property on his wife under certain circumstances. If property was owed to the wife (say, a legacy that had not yet been delivered) and the husband had laid no claim to it, then he could set it aside for her as a separate estate. If he failed to do so, then the court might intervene; when the husband initiated legal action in order to recover the wife's forthcoming property, the court itself could demand that that property be protected from the depredations of the husband's creditors. "He who seeks equity," the saying went, "must do equity."[16] Samuel R. Caldwell, a cabinetmaker, was among the first in Petersburg to learn how the law worked. In 1817, Caldwell blithely mortgaged the forthcoming inheritance of his wife Pewniffe to secure a debt of $423. A week later, Caldwell revised the deed, the wiser for some legal advice. Caldwell, fearing his wife might "soon be cast upon the world needy and penniless," and "taking into mind the affection & regard which he bears toward his said wife," and being "bound by the dictates of humanity & natural justice," and, finally, recognizing that "such an act would be required of him" in any case, conveyed the forthcoming inheritance, minus the $423 already committed, to a trustee for the support of Pewniffe and their children.[17]

The man who was clear of debt was free to settle separate property on his wife at any time—or as was commonly the case, to renounce some of his rights in property she had brought to the marriage in the first place. This was a sacrifice, for the husband relinquished his absolute control of the property (how much control he lost varied with the wording of the deed), and he could no longer use it to obtain credit. But come indebtedness and disaster, no one could take that property away from his family. After the panic of 1819 and more frequently after the panics of the late 1830s, Petersburg's most cautious businessmen sheltered themselves and their families from "the chances and dangers of commerce" and "the casualties and hazards of Trade" by granting separate property to their wives.[18] So, of course, did Petersburg's most devious businessmen. Equity always dangled temptation before the harried debtor, who might try to foil his creditors by making an eleventh-hour transfer of assets to his wife. Even if the transaction were eventually voided by a court, it might still give the husband enough time to scramble out of the immediate crisis. To quiet all doubts about their intentions toward their creditors, a few of the men who conveyed separate property to their wives (23 / 141) declared the property liable for any of their present debts. For the rest, prudence cannot be distinguished from attempted fraud.

The distinction is of little consequence, for honor and guile both worked toward the same end. The object was not to liberate the woman, but to keep property in the family, and the woman as a result was usually left passive. In Petersburg, from 1784 to 1860, husbands, friends, and relatives granted a total of 398 separate estates by deed and will. Only a quarter of them (100 / 398) gave the woman power to sell her property. Even on her deathbed, the wife would not ordinarily have the capacity to dispose of her property. The majority of conveyances (224 / 398) gave specific directions for the distribution of the estate after the wife's death, and less than a fifth (73 / 398) empowered the wife to make a will.

Still, no matter how little legal power it brought the wife, a separate estate was better than nothing. It was certainly better for slaves. Slaves who were held in trust for married women could not be sold for the husbands' debts (some could not be sold for any reason) and were thus more likely to be spared chattel slavery's loneliest ordeal—the public auction, the trader, the sale to who-knew-where. In Petersburg, well over a thousand slaves were made the separate, relatively secure property of married women.[19]

For the married women also, any separate estate was preferable to none, as the local disaster stories made clear. In the winter of 1845, for example, a Mrs. Parker took up residence in a Petersburg boardinghouse. All her furniture had just been sold to meet her husband's obligations, and not just for the first time, but for the third or fourth. "What a miserable life has her's been," wrote a sympathetic observer, "and how different might it have been had Col. P. possessed sobriety, with his talents, [and] good feelings—I cannot add prudence."[20] Mrs. Parker could have used a separate estate. Better protected and passive under equity than vulnerable and passive under the common law.

Better still to have been protected from male irresponsibility but free to make some decisions of one's own. In the antebellum years, this happier combination appeared with somewhat greater frequency. While the old pattern of passivity remained dominant, there were countertrends in separate estates. As time went on, they came on better terms, and more and more often, they came at the behest of women themselves.

No one had a more immediate interest in unraveling the economic bonds of matrimony than the woman whose marriage had become a nightmare. It was the wife, after all, who was left economically vulnerable by a fractured marriage. Responsible, in fact, for her own livelihood, she had at law no right to her own earnings, to credit, or to property. The double standard sharpened her predicament. A wife who ran off with another man forfeited both dower and her right to be maintained by her husband.[21] The husband who ran off, with or without another woman, forfeited nothing. He could return at will to scoop off whatever assets his wife had accumulated on her own, and so, with the proper court order, could his creditors.

The most resourceful among Petersburg's unhappily married women thus sought legal separations, the best available escape from their common-law bind. Divorce would have been simpler, had Virginia lawmakers chosen to make divorce simple. Before the 1850s, however, complete divorces were almost impossible to obtain. Until 1827, it took a special act of the legislature to secure a divorce, and the legislature was not easily moved. The *Intelligencer* remarked on the prospects in 1811:

> In the House of Delegates of this state, the Committee for Courts of Justice have reported on some petitions for Divorces, in which the most flagrant breaches of fidelity in the marriage state were exhibited; notwithstanding which they recommended the *rejection* of every one of them, and in this advice the House concurred. So it will be needless hereafter to attempt (thro' Legislative interposition) to sever the yoke of matrimony, let it be ever so *galling!*[22]

Only three Petersburg residents even attempted to procure legislative divorces, and the petitions of the two who succeeded offered further testimony to the fact that Virginians did not grant divorces lightly. In 1809, James G. Trotter asked for a divorce from his wife Elizabeth, who, Trotter believed, had tried to poison him, who did abandon him and their children, and who "at this moment . . . lives the life of a common and notorious prostitute in this very City." Janet Hunter's recital of misery had still more chapters. Samuel Hunter frequented brothels—"the most common stews in Town"—and boasted of it despite the fact that he contracted "loathesome diseases" in the process. He drank heavily and called Janet names "most grating to the ear of a virtuous woman." He beat her, he threw her out of the house, and he took what money she had and then refused to support her. "If there be a man in this State whose reformation in this life is utterly hopeless," Janet declared, "it is Samuel G. Hunter."[23]

Luckily for Petersburg's most embattled couples, the courts recognized the validity of separation agreements. A separation agreement was a kind of do-it-yourself divorce. While the pair remained legally married (neither was permitted to marry again), they pledged to treat one another as though no marriage had ever taken place, the wife surrendering her few claims on her husband, the husband renouncing his numerous rights to his wife's property and person. Her property was technically vested in a trustee; active control over the property was ordinarily vested in the wife herself. Thus was established a separate estate, and it rendered the wife as free as a married woman legally could be.

In 1827, the general assembly opened one more route to legal separation, an important addition for the woman whose husband would not consent to a separation agreement. The new law authorized the superior courts to grant divorces *a mensa et thoro*—"from bed and board"—on grounds of adultery, cruelty, and fear of bodily harm. These bed-and-board decrees had much the same effect as separation agreements; marital obligations were suspended, but the parties were not allowed to marry again. Complete divorces, in which remarriage was permitted, were to be granted only in cases of impotence at the time of marriage, bigamy, and "idiocy."[24]

Eventually, in statutes of 1848 and 1853, the legislature relented and made adultery, desertion, and a number of other causes grounds for complete divorces.[25] On the face of it, this was a major improvement in the legal condition of Virginia women. Its immediate effect, however, was to make men as active as women in seeking divorce. Before 1848, when the best most plaintiffs could hope for was a bed-and-board decree, men could profit little by going to court. There were only five court-ordered divorces in Petersburg before 1848, and in every case, the plaintiff was the wife. When the law in 1848 gave the injured party the right to remarry, men for the first time had real incentive to file for divorce. From 1848 to 1860, nearly half of Petersburg's successful plaintiffs in divorce cases (9/19) were men.

Women had had incentive all along, of course; since women sacrificed so many legal rights by marrying, they had more to recover via divorce. The women who sought legal separations and divorces were not, however, Petersburg's most defenseless wives. Rather, the majority were women with property or trades or businesses. Among all the town's miserably married women, the propertied had the most to gain by terminating their marriages and the best chance of doing so.[26]

Some women literally bought their way out. Eleanor Linch had come into two town lots in 1794 by the will of her husband Henry Linch. The two of them had kept a tavern on the river's edge, a business Eleanor continued in her widowhood. A few months after Henry's death, Eleanor married William Roberts, who seems to have had no property of his own. The marriage was stormy from the beginning. On three separate occasions, Eleanor hauled William before the hustings court on breach of the peace complaints—she was afraid, in other words, of being beaten. By 1798, they had had enough and filed their agreement "to divide the property which they possess, and to live and act hereafter with respect to each other, and each others property and affairs as if they had never been married." The property they divided was (or had been) Eleanor's. William emerged from the separation with half the lots and buildings that had once belonged to Henry Linch. For Eleanor, the separation came none too soon. She died before the year was out, but had recovered half her property in time to bequeath it to her niece and two nephews.[27]

For Elizabeth Clements, it was a similar story twenty years later. Elizabeth's first husband was Benjamin King, one of Petersburg's early tobacco manufacturers. When Benjamin died in 1816, he left the factory to Elizabeth, along with a valuable lot and several slaves. Two years later, Elizabeth married Benjamin Clements, who proceeded to reduce part of the King real estate to his possession by selling it for seven thousand dollars one week and buying it back for the same price the next. That move gave him absolute title to the property, and Elizabeth evidently did not like it. Whatever the precise causes of conflict, Elizabeth and Benjamin Clements were separated within six months of their marriage. Benjamin retained half of the original King estate, which was not bad for six months' work, and the other half, including the factory, was placed in trust for Elizabeth, who was empowered to receive its profits, make conveyances, and write a will. Although nothing was said about it in the separation agreement, Elizabeth took back the King name as well.[28]

In other instances, it was a trade or business that gave the wife the wherewithal to terminate her marriage. The ranks of the legally separated and divorced women of Petersburg included a "doctress," two milliners, three grocers, and three dressmakers and seamstresses. The outstanding example was Amintia D. Williams, who endured fifteen years of "profligate and unfeeling conduct" on the part of her husband before securing a bed-and-board divorce in 1835. It was no mean feat to support her three young daughters, but Williams was no mean businesswoman. She had opened a millinery and dressmaking shop before her marriage; she expanded her business during her marriage; and she continued it, with more orders than she could handle, until her death in 1852. "She is quite a business man," read her credit report, ". . . sell her all you can."[29]

Equity was a flexible tradition. As separation agreements made clear, an equitable settlement could be an un-equivocal instrument of power. Yet legal separations were very rare. In seventy-five years, only twenty-five women signed separation agreements or won divorces from the courts.[30] That being the case, it was well for the women of Petersburg that there were other means of limiting their legal vulnerability.

Marriage contracts were always relatively rare; from 1784 to 1860, only ninety-five of them were recorded in Peters-burg. Their frequency rose a little in the antebellum period, however, and this was an important indicator of increased leverage for some middle- and upper-class women. Mar-riage contracts were drawn up and signed before the wed-ding, and they did not ordinarily give the husband a chance to try his managerial hand. Rather, the convention of male command was shoved aside for the sake of the security of the wife's property. (And it *was* the wife's property: In only four of the ninety-five cases did the groom contribute any of the property covered by the contract.) Moreover, marriage contracts showed that the protection of the wife's property need not sentence her to passivity. Marriage con-tracts were empowering documents on the whole, and their terms grew more liberal with time. Finally, as time went on, marriage contracts were democratized somewhat, as the parties to them became a more ordinary group.

From 1784 to 1810, marriage contracts were distin-guished by their scarcity, for only one marriage in sixty-two (7/433) was regulated by a publicly recorded agree-ment.[31] The parties to these novel arrangements belonged to two groups. Four were women of affairs—women who were not about to let marriage interfere with the economic independence to which they had become accustomed. The others were members of Petersburg's first families, young women with a great deal of property to protect.

Margaret Falkner kept tavern in Petersburg and owned a two hundred–acre plantation in neighboring Chesterfield County as well, the latter a legacy from her first husband, who died in 1787. She remarried within the year, and the agreement she made with James Bromly not only cemented her control over the Chesterfield estate, but also prevented the marriage from cramping her commercial style:

And it is hereby declared to be the true intent, and meaning of them, and of this Indenture, that in case the said Margaret (notwithstanding her coverture) shall be minded, at any time, to carry on any Trade in the way of Merchandise, or Shop-keeping, as a Sole-trader, that she shall be at liberty so to do, without the Controul of the said James Bromly, and that neither her Stock in Trade, nor the produce thereof, or any money arising thereby, or therefrom, shall be at the disposal of the said James Bromly, nor shall he in any manner interfere therewith, or receive, or intermeddle with the same, or grant receipts, or acquittances therefor or if he should grant such receipts, or acquittances that the same shall be nul and void.

The deed went on for pages, piling noun on noun and verb on verb. Margaret was to "have, hold, Occupy, possess, and enjoy" all the estate in which she had any "right, title, Interest, Use, Trust, Property, Profit, Claim or Demand," exempt from the "interference, interruption, [illegible], hindrance, [or] participation" of either James Bromly or any "after taken husband." Margaret went on to keep her tavern in Petersburg. After James Bromly died in 1806, Margaret returned to her Chesterfield plantation and resumed the Falkner name. When she died in 1814, she founded by will the Falkner School, Chesterfield's first school for the children of the poor.[32]

Ann Swail was also accustomed to financial responsibility. Before her marriage in 1810, Swail lived with her mother, Elizabeth Swail, and between the two of them, they engaged in three of the standard women's occupations. Elizabeth was a midwife, Ann a grocer, and together they took in boarders. When William Dyer married Ann, he married into her grocery store, but a marriage contract limited his control. William was entitled to the profits from Ann's property (minus an annuity for Ann's aging mother), but Ann retained title to her house, lot, and slave, and she retained the power to will them to whomever she pleased. As it turned out, she never got the chance. On a late summer day some two years after they were married, the Dyers became embroiled in a drunken quarrel (Ann was drunk). The fight ended abruptly when William throttled Ann and threw her down the stairs. Ann died instantly, William was sent to the penitentiary, and the estate was committed to the sergeant of the town for safekeeping.[33]

Mary Dunn, to cite one last example, operated in a more genteel fashion. Dunn was a twenty-seven-year-old spinster engaged in some unnamed enterprise in the north of Ireland. In 1810, she entered into a marriage contract with Joseph Fleming, a Petersburg merchant. The Flemings had barely reached Petersburg when Joseph died. Mary had retained full disposal over her own property, and that, along with the income from Joseph's estate, made Mary Fleming, "otherwise Dunn," a moderately rich woman. She was not ready to retire, however. Her first move was an attempt to swell the size of her inheritance by initiating a lawsuit over a debt due her deceased husband's estate. (She eventually submitted to arbitration.) Her second move was to go into business with Thomas Dunn—doubtless a relative, but she referred to him only as "my Copartner in Trade"—putting up better than half the capital for their trans-Atlantic trading house. The partnership was dissolved by Mary Fleming's death in 1815. She had made a will, leaving to Thomas Dunn her share of the firm's inventory, provided he paid for it at its assessed value, and distributing most of the rest of her estate among kin and friends still in Ireland.[34]

The other little group of women who signed marriage contracts was made up of brides too young to have had much experience of worldly affairs; none of the three was over twenty years of age, and the contracts were probably the work of their elders. Mary Burton Augusta Bolling was a member of Petersburg's wealthiest family. In 1797, when Mary was only eight, her father Robert Bolling secured to her an enormous estate, the property that Mary's deceased mother had brought to her marriage with Robert. Ten years later, Mary was engaged to John Munro Banister, and a contract was drawn up to adjust the terms of the earlier settlement. Half the estate was to be paid to John outright. The disposition of the other half revealed the essentially dynastic motives of the deed's authors. Mary was given no explicit powers over her property, not even the power to make a will. Instead, the contract guaranteed the descent of the property to Mary's heirs upon her death and in the meantime directed her trustee to invest the property for the joint benefit of Mary, her husband, and their children.[35]

Nancy Vaughan was granted more discretion in a 1798 marriage contract that suggested bargaining if not bribery. Vaughan's husband-to-be, the Reverend William Harrison, pledged several town lots and a hundred rural acres to the support of Nancy and their as yet unborn children. In addition, William promised Nancy five hundred pounds "to be disposed of as She pleases by Will" and two slaves "to be disposed of as She pleases," and he committed fifty pounds to her brother's education as well.[36] This unique gift from man to intended wife may have been just what it took to overcome the objections of a hesitant young woman or her hesitant parents. The headstones that still mark their graves in the Old Blandford Cemetery reveal that William was a full forty years older than his bride.

In 1817, Lydia Thomas and John Stewart signed the contract that marked the first of several transitions in the character of marriage agreements. Lydia Thomas was not an heiress, nor, so far as can be determined, did she run a business. She was a free black, probably a widow, and the property she brought to the marriage—some furniture and a single slave—was of only modest market value.[37] In the decades that followed, most of the parties to marriage contracts would be more affluent than Thomas, yet Thomas introduced the coming trend: Neither great wealth nor a business was required to justify the creation of a separate estate at the time of marriage.

Through 1825, a third of the women who signed marriage agreements (6/18) were documentably in business before or at the time of marriage. The proportion fell to less than a tenth (6/78) in the years from 1826 to 1860. The female parties to marriage contracts in the antebellum period, in short, were less exceptional than their predecessors. They were also more likely to be marrying for the first time, or so it appears from the information available. The change came in the 1840s. From 1784 to 1840, the majority of the women who signed marriage contracts (20/32, with 9 additional cases unknown) were widows. This is no surprise, for a widow was more likely than a single woman to own property. More to the point, the widow was more likely to have children, and a marriage contract could do much to protect the child's interests from waste at the hands of an ill-disposed or unlucky stepfather. From 1841 to 1860, however, the majority of marriage contracts (23/41, with 13 additional cases unknown) were signed by women who had never married. As time went on, then, the female parties to marriage agreements less often had a fortune, a business, or a child to protect. For women of the privileged classes, commencing marriage with a contract was becoming less exceptional.

Marriage contracts did, in any case, become more frequent. From 1821 to 1860, one marriage in twenty-six (84/2,224) was covered by a contract, a substantial increase over the earlier ratio of one in sixty-two. There was also measurable improvement in the terms. Before the 1840s, only 14.3 percent (6/42) of the contracts empowered the woman to sell her property; from 1841 to 1860, that figure jumped to 62.3 percent (33/53). Authority to write a will had always been more readily reserved; even before the 1840s, two-thirds of the agreements included this power. From 1841 to 1860, the proportion grew to over 80 percent (43/53).

We can only guess whether the women themselves insisted on those liberal terms. There is no question, however, that women were increasingly assertive in matters of property and that the overall growth in the number of separate estates owed much to female initiative. A few women found in their dower rights a new means of establishing

separate estates for themselves. And by will and deed of
gift, women were increasingly active in establishing separate estates for one another.

Under the common law, the married woman's one
power was the power to refuse to relinquish her dower
rights in property her husband wished to convey. From
the 1830s on, some Petersburg women began to use it—to
trade their contingent rights of dower for active control
over a separate estate. Mary Boswell showed how it was
done. Mary's husband William was a merchant, and for
more than twenty years, he was one of Petersburg's big-
gest real estate owners. The crash came in 1842. William
mortgaged one lot after another in a desperate effort to
keep faith with his creditors, and time after time, Mary
signed away her dower rights. "How submissively and
cheerfully she bore this reverse of fortune," her obituary
later chirped. But Mary Boswell was no martyr. There
were two lots on High Street that Mary wanted for herself. In these, she refused to give up her dower, and in
exchange for the promise that she would relinquish her
rights in all of William's remaining lands, the two lots,
along with five slaves, were conveyed to a trustee for
Mary's separate use. The following year, William's mortgaged property went under the hammer. Mary's separate
property was preserved, and when she died a few years
later, she left all of it to her married daughter, likewise, as
a separate estate.[38]

From the mid 1830s until 1860, there were only twenty-
five recorded cases in which women parlayed dower rights
into separate estates.[39] But that was twenty-five cases more
than in the previous fifty years, a significant if small indicator of women's growing assertiveness. The more arresting measure was the frequency with which women
established separate estates for other women. Of the separate estates established by deed of gift from 1784 to 1840,
one-fifth were granted by women (11 / 52). In the twenty
years that followed, two-fifths (42 / 118) were granted by
women.[40] Wills were less often used to establish separate

estates, but here the agency of women was even more pronounced. Among the eighteen testators who left separate
estates from 1784 to 1840, five were women. After 1840,
women moved into the lead; fifteen of the twenty-six testators leaving separate estates were women. Altogether a
large third of the separate estates established by will and
deed of gift were established by women (88 / 234 = 37.6
percent).

This third was large indeed given women's place in the
structure of property holding. Although women as a group
were making gains, never did they add up to a third of
Petersburg's property owners. And they controlled
nowhere near a third of the wealth. Relative to the amount
of property they possessed, women were far more active
than men in establishing separate estates.

Their gifts expose the fraudulence of the adage that
women were their own worst enemies. From the letters
and diaries of nineteenth-century women, historians have
begun to recover evidence of an emotional universe in
which intimate relationships between women were central. Based on common work and shared experience, this
universe was characterized by strong bonds between
mothers and daughters and by friendships between women
that were long-lived and emotionally, sometimes sen-
sually, rich. The Petersburg women who granted separate
estates to other women add an economic dimension to this
portrait. Most often the grants were from mothers to their
daughters.[41] Women understood what it was to be legally
and financially vulnerable; more often than men, they tried
to see to it that their daughters were spared.

Yet this was not feminism. Or if it can be called feminism, it was feminism of the most inchoate and defensive
kind. The woman who granted her daughter a separate
estate was not rejecting male dominance for the sake of
equality or female autonomy. Equality and autonomy were
not ordinarily among the choices. Rather, the choice was
between the maintenance of the husband's dominance on
the one hand, and on the other, the guarantee of some economic security to a woman and her family, ends that were

both desired but often incompatible in the capricious economy of the nineteenth century. The provisions of estates established by women did not differ a great deal from those of estates set up by men. Women granted power to make a will somewhat more often than men did; provisions for writing a will were included by 20.7 percent of the women grantors (12 / 58) and 13.4 percent of the men (15 / 112). Power to sell the property was also granted a little more often by the women (18 / 58 = 31 percent) than by the men (25 / 112 = 22.3 percent). The great majority of grantors of both sexes, meanwhile, granted no powers at all. The principal and common target was security; the essential point was not to free the wife but to restrain the husband's creditors. The most that can be said for the women grantors is that they were somewhat less likely than were the men to equate security with utter passivity.

The rise of separate estates owed a great deal to female assertiveness and to sisterhood. The central, usually implicit demand was not, however, for equality, nor was it for autonomy. What was asked for was protection from gross exploitation. Whether this was enough to constitute feminism is largely a matter of definition. What is clearer is that in practice, protection exacted costs of its own. In its day-to-day application, equity could be full of complications.

First, there were complications with trustees. Trustees could be expensive. Although some waived their right to compensation, they were entitled to pocket 5 percent of whatever income the estate generated. Their appointment could also occasion considerable inconvenience; when a trustee died or resigned or moved away and no provision had been made for the selection of a replacement, then it was off to court for a decree naming the new trustee. And the more the trustee had to say about how the estate was managed, the more room there was for serious conflict.

Consider the case of Mary Ann Vizonneau and her trustee, John Bott. The episode began in 1813, when witnesses gathered at the deathbed of John Stewart to hear his final requests. No one knew quite what to expect. Stewart, a Scottish merchant, was quite well off, and his only heirs in Virginia were his illegitimate children Mary Ann and John, both of them born of a black woman. Mary Ann, moreover, had enraged her father several years before when she married André Thomas Vizonneau. But Stewart's last moments were moments of forgiveness, and he directed that Mary Ann be given "all the money he then had in the Bank and the house & Lot he then lived on," on the condition "that her husband (Andre Thomas Vizzoneau) might have no manner of Controul over, or right, to the same." By this time, Mary Ann herself was regretting the day she married André—she later called him a "confirmed maniac"—and it was probably her new economic independence that enabled her to make the final break. In 1818, a separation agreement made it official. Finding it "extremely disagreeable, uncomfortable & unpleasant for them to live together," Mary Ann and André promised to have nothing further to do with each other.[42]

That should have been the end of Mary Ann Vizonneau's problems, or so she undoubtedly thought as she struck out for New York City, leaving behind the scene of her disastrous marriage and leaving her separate estate in the hands of John Bott, a highly respected Petersburg doctor. Bott proved to be a poor investor. Assuming that the hard times of 1819 and 1820 would be of short duration and minor impact, Bott loaned the greater part of Vizonneau's trust fund to various Petersburg merchants. As the depression deepened, the merchants one by one defaulted. When Vizonneau heard the news, she hurried back to Virginia "much excited against Dr. Bott" and initiated legal proceedings to have him discharged from his trusteeship and to recover her wasted estate. Bott, it must be said, did the best he could. Perhaps a third of Vizonneau's funds were lost for good, but Bott made up the rest by selling his own farm and slaves "at a very great sacrifice" and by mortgaging his house in town. Vizonneau had nonetheless had enough of trustees; in acquiring her separate estate, she had simply traded one kind of contingency for another, and she was satisfied with neither. In 1824, she petitioned the legislature for permission to manage her estate independently. Of course, trustees were vulnerable as well. By 1825, John Bott was dead, his estate gutted, and his widow nearly impoverished. At length, Vizonneau composed herself enough to survey the wreckage, and before her return to New York, she deeded the house she had inherited from her father to Bott's widow Susannah.[43]

There were complications, too, in discerning exactly what assets were included in a given separate estate. Estates granted to wives by indebted husbands were particularly fertile ground for litigation as the courts tried to balance the welfare of the women against the rights of creditors. In 1860, for example, creditors sued Ella Dunn, asserting a claim to property her husband Thomas had set aside for her benefit several years earlier. The court ruled for Ella Dunn. The deed that originally established the separate estate, the court pointed out, specifically stated that the purpose of the trust was to provide support for Thomas Dunn's family. Had the property produced income beyond what was needed to maintain the Dunn family, the creditors might have had a case. As it was, there was no excess, and the creditors were thus out of luck.[44] The court's decree gave no further details, but it made one curious fact plain: A separate estate did not always contain a fixed amount of money or property, but could rather contain a variable amount that shifted with the changing needs of a family. It was left to the court to define what those needs might be.

Disputes over the contents of a separate estate could also stem from the absence of a clause permitting the conversion of assets from one form to another. Frances Bolling was born into Petersburg's richest family. She subsequently married John LeMessurier, French immigrant, importer of fine foods and wines, and as far as the Bolling family fortune was concerned, a veritable siphon. In 1814, Frances's mother wrote her will, and in order to prevent John from losing any further Bolling property, she made Frances's legacy a separate estate. The problem arose when

Frances used part of the income from her separate estate to buy household furnishings. The question: Did the furnishings become part of the separate estate, or were they outside the trust and therefore subject to the demands of her husband's ever eager creditors? John LeMessurier did not give his creditors a chance to test the issue in court; "fearing that the same might be considered as part of his property & be liable to seizure for the payment of his debts," he made a detailed inventory of the furnishings and conveyed them to a new set of trustees.[45] It took the establishment of a second trust to carry out the intentions of the first.

A single phrase could have spared LeMessurier the trouble. No second trust would have been necessary if the first had contained a few words stipulating that any property purchased with the separate estate's income likewise became part of the separate estate. In fact, such clauses did become more commonplace with experience and as more people chose to keep open the option of substituting new property for that originally placed in trust.[46] What the parties gained in flexibility, however, they sometimes lost in security. The woman who was empowered to alienate and invest her separate property might also be construed to have the power to lose it. Here were the materials for a third set of complications, complications regarding the woman's powers and obligations.

The justices of the circuit court seem to have believed that close judicial supervision was the best way to guarantee protection without sacrificing flexibility. Separate estates were occasionally created by order of the court; not one of the estates so created gave the woman general power to convey her property. Instead, if the woman wanted to alter the character of her holdings, she was to apply to the court for permission. Thus Catharine P. Smith made five trips to court in as many years, securing approval to invest in bonds, to buy a house, to furnish the house, to add a room to the house, to add a story to the new room, and to furnish the new rooms.[47] A sizable proportion of the litigation respecting separate estates consisted of cases like

Catharine Smith's, amicable suits requesting permission to buy, sell, or borrow, or to perform some other act not authorized by the deed that initially created the trust.[48] In each of these cases, there were costs—court costs, delays (the circuit court sat only twice a year), and the necessity of subjecting one's affairs to the scrutiny and possible disapproval of the judge.

In other cases, the women acted first and litigated later, and in these decidedly unamicable suits, equity showed its true capacity for subtlety, and consequently for unpredictability. Unhappily, most of the decrees tell us very little. The ruling in the case of *James, Rice, & James* v. *Mary A. McLemore,* however, does offer a glimpse of the intricacy of equitable reasoning. In 1847, when Mary Ann McLemore married for the third time, she entered into a marriage contract that covered her house and furniture, her one slave, all debts due her, and her "Goods, Wares and Merchandize"—the stock of a neighborhood grocery store, one guesses. The contract gave McLemore a good deal of discretion over her property. She reserved the power to use the property and its profits, to make a will, to rent out the house, to hire out the slave, and with her trustee's concurrence, to sell any of the property and reinvest the proceeds. In time, McLemore became indebted to the firm of James, Rice, & James—probably her wholesalers. McLemore either could not or would not pay her account, so in 1851 the firm sued, claiming that McLemore's separate estate was liable for payment of the debt.

The court thought otherwise. It was not that McLemore lacked the power to contract debts. Rather, the ruling hinged, as did so many decisions in equity, on the particular purpose the separate estate was intended to serve. The object of McLemore's separate estate was to provide for her "economical support," the court declared, and since McLemore's debt to James, Rice, & James defeated that object, it was not enforceable. Had McLemore's estate yielded an income above what was needed for her maintenance, James, Rice, & James would have had a claim to the excess. Instead, the firm had no choice but to absorb the loss and pay the costs of the suit as well.[49]

Protection, to repeat, could be complicated. While rulings of this sort got women like Mary Ann McLemore off the hook, their longer-range effect was to make debtor-creditor relations uncertain, confusing, and more productive than ever of litigation. As states one by one began to reform the statutory law of married women's property, the confusion assumed truly massive proportions.

We return to Mary Beard. Beginning in 1839 and continuing into the early twentieth century, state legislatures chipped away at the common-law disabilities of married women, in bits and pieces granting all married women ownership and control of their property and earnings. These married women's property acts, Beard contended, "merely transformed generally accepted equity principles into provisions of statutes." In this, Beard was absolutely right. She was well off the mark, however, in her treatment of the "positive riot" of interpretations handed down by the courts after the early married women's laws were enacted. Beard attributed the confusion to a misguided attempt to make the principle of equality the central principle in married women's property law. An opponent of the Equal Rights Amendment of her own time, Beard believed that the principle of equality was too vague and too simple to be of real utility in sorting out the complex issues that arose from the obligations of marriage and parenthood and from the several and sometimes conflicting interests of wives, husbands, children, extended kin, and creditors.[50]

Here Beard was half right. The social reality was (and always is) sufficiently complex to give rise to questions unanticipated by legislators. The key to this particular legal snarl, however, was the fact that equality was the last thing most legislators had in mind. The main engine behind the passage of the initial married women's property reforms was, as with separate estates, the desire to protect women's property from seizure when indebtedness was rampant and creditors impatient. (The only egalitarian impulse at work was the desire to extend to all women the protection that equity had offered to the privileged and the cautious.) Once all married women were given the right to own property, it was no easy task to decide what they should be allowed to do with it. The knowledge that some husbands were manipulative and malicious dictated that married women be given some powers over their property merely to hold house and home together. But if women were given full and equal powers, then the protective function of the law would be lost; the baby went out with the bathwater when women were permitted to assume the same obligations and risks as the men. The alternative was to grant women some powers while denying them others, aiming for a middle ground in which women would not be permitted to endanger their property. But this compromise only set the stage for an encore performance of the old equity drama. Now all married women operated in a legal twilight zone, and the results were widespread confusion and extensive litigation, this at a time when reformers were bent on simplifying the law. These special protective laws for women also inhibited the flow of capital. In time, most states gave up protection as a bad job and made married women subject to the same rules that governed everyone else.[51]

Equality would have made things much simpler, had equality in fact been the reigning principle from the beginning. But equality between the sexes was unthinkable to most people in the nineteenth century, as it had been for most of human history, and women thus continued to make do with the consequences of male self-interest. Not that men's interests were always clear-cut. Changing the law of married women's property required making choices among several desired but incompatible goals, that is, among male dominance, economic security for families, a uniform and streamlined body of law, and the free flow of commerce. The point stands nonetheless that change in the legal status of women came about as a choice among interests and not as a response to enlightened ideas about the proper relations between the sexes.

It may seem cranky to dwell on the less than admirable

motives behind improvements in the status of women. Happy results can, after all, emerge from questionable intentions, and this was the case with married women's property reforms. It was also the case with separate estates. Whatever the mix of love, prudence, sleaziness, and greed that caused separate estates to be established, women did gain by them. This is the clearest evidence Petersburg offers that women, at least middle- and upper-class women, were gaining power within marriage.

But motives did matter. Because financial security was the main motive, equity's full potential for freeing married women was only rarely realized; most separate estates left the woman well short of legal equality or independence. And this leads to questions about what women were able to do with whatever power they did gain. Surely economic independence is a key prerequisite to the achievement of genuine autonomy; no woman is free if she and her children can be starved, however subtly, into submission. At the same time, economic independence is no guarantee of freedom. What we simply do not know is whether Petersburg women were able to translate the economic power they gained through separate estates into decision-making power in other areas of life. We do not know whether marriages became more egalitarian; we do not know whether the women had more to say about children, sex, living arrangements, work, social life, or politics. It seems almost as likely that the acquisition of a separate estate could make for increased deference on the wife's part; in a time when men were licensed to govern and women told to obey, both sexes might feel pressure to try to restore the old, familiar imbalance of power.

In any case, the only sure way to escape the legal bondage of marriage was to stay away from marriage altogether. The next two chapters tell about some of the escapees.

4

Free Women of Color

In November 1853, Eliza Gallie, a free black woman of Petersburg, was arrested and charged with stealing cabbages from the patch of Alexander Stevens, a white man. She was tried in mayor's court and sentenced to thirty-nine lashes. There was nothing unusual in this; free black women were frequently accused of petty crimes, and for free blacks as for slaves, whipping was the punishment prescribed by law. What made the case a minor spectacle was that Eliza Gallie had resources, and she fought back. She filed an appeal immediately, and two weeks later she hired three of Petersburg's most eminent attorneys and one from Richmond as well. "If the Commonwealth, God bless her, has not met her match in Miss Liza," a local newspaper commented, "it won't be for lack of lawyers." The case came up in hustings court in March 1854. Gallie's lawyers argued first of all that her ancestors were of white and Indian blood and that she should therefore be tried as a white person. The court was unconvinced. On the trial's second day, her counsel argued that she was innocent of the theft. The court was again unconvinced. Gallie was pronounced guilty and sentenced to "twenty lashes on her bare back at the public whipping post. . . ." At first, she set another appeal in motion, but deciding that the case was hopeless, Eliza Gallie dismissed her lawyers and took her punishment.[1]

Gallie's case was in many ways an unusual one, and yet her story cuts straight to the central contradiction in our common image of the historic black woman. Eliza Gallie was, relatively speaking, a powerful woman, propertied, autonomous (divorced, actually), and assertive. But she was helpless in the end, the victim of the kind of deliberate humiliation that for most of us is past imagining. So it is with our perception of the history of black women as a group. On the one hand, we have been told that black women, in slavery and afterward, were formidable people, "matriarchs," in fact. And yet we know that all along, black women were dreadfully exploited. Rarely has so much power been attributed to so vulnerable a group.

The contradiction can be resolved, with sufficient attention to definition and evidence, and that is in large part the purpose of this chapter. But it needs to be understood from the beginning that the term "matriarch" would never have been applied to black women in the first place were it not for our culture's touchiness over reduced male authority within the family. It is a telling fact that matriarchy has most often been used as a relative term. That is, women are called matriarchs when the power they exercise relative to the men of their own group is in some respect greater than that defined as appropriate by the dominant culture. Given this standard, women need not be the equals of men, much less men's superiors, in order to qualify as matriarchs. The acquisition by women of just one commonly masculine prerogative will do, and hence it becomes possible to attribute matriarchal power to some of society's most disadvantaged people. The woman who had no vote, no money, and no protection under the law was nonetheless a "matriarch," so long as she also had no man present to compete with her for authority over her children.

Concern over the reduction of male authority has also been the touchstone of scholarship on black family life (very little has been written on the history of black women per

se). For all the disagreements among scholars on the character of the historic black family, it has been assumed on
almost all sides that female-headed families are, and were,
pathological. There were two key assertions, both related
to this issue, in the classic thesis advanced by E. Franklin
Frazier four decades ago and revived in 1965 in the Moynihan Report. First, as a result of slavery and continued
discrimination, an alarming proportion of black families
were "matriarchal," that is, the husband / father was either
absent or, Frazier added, present but of negligible influence. Second, the woman-dominant family was unstable
and disorganized, at once the symptom and cause of severe
social pathology among black people.[2] The Frazier-Moy-
nihan thesis came under heavy fire in the 1970s when
scholars began to check the matriarchy image for historical
accuracy. And yet the historians, too, reinforced the prevailing prejudice against female-headed households.
Working for the most part with census data from the second half of the nineteenth century, several historians found
that female-headed households were far outnumbered by
two-parent households. This, along with additional evidence of the statistical insignificance of the woman-headed
household, was offered in defense of the historic Afro-
American family: Black families were not generally
matriarchal / matrifocal / female-headed (the term varies);
therefore, they were not disorganized, unstable, or otherwise pathological after all.[3]

This is a dangerous line of defense, and its problems are
highlighted when we encounter evidence like that from
nineteenth-century Petersburg. From the early part of the
century through 1860, Petersburg was a town in which
well over half of the free black households were headed by
women. Shall we therefore label it a nest of social sickness?
It would make better sense to disentangle our evidence
from conventional, androcentric value judgments on what
is healthy and what is not.

For the time being, it would seem wise to set aside the
issue of the integrity of black family life (by what standard, after all, are we to judge it?) and to concentrate instead

on the impact of racial oppression on the status of women and on the distribution of power between the sexes. When we do this for Petersburg, we are confronted once again with the dual image of strength and exploitation. Women were prominent among free blacks; they outnumbered the men three to two, they headed more than half of the town's free black households, and they constituted almost half of the paid free black labor force. Yet this was all the product of wretched poverty and persistent discrimination. The "matriarch" and the victim, it turns out, were usually the same woman.

Still, the fact remains that among free blacks there was less inequality between the sexes than there was among whites; the possibility remains that some free black women valued their relative equality and did their best to maintain it. Among those free blacks who managed to accumulate property, a high proportion—40 to 50 percent—were women. And because they were more likely than their white counterparts to refrain from legal marriage, they were more likely to retain legal control over whatever property they did acquire. Free black women were in some respects Petersburg's most autonomous women. The tragedy was that the racism that made autonomy possible also made it contemptible.

For the free black people of Virginia, freedom was a fragile and changeable condition, its terms shifting with the anxiety levels of the men who ran the legislature and the local courts. In practice, periods of relatively benign neglect alternated with spells of close surveillance and sudden repression. In law, the story was one of progressive deterioration.[4]

In the new nation's first twenty years, white Virginians still took the rhetoric of the Revolution seriously. This is not to say that they extended their ideas about equality among men to blacks. The slave system was preserved intact, and the old colonial restrictions on free blacks (forbidding voting, service on juries, and testimony against whites in court) remained on the books. But the revolutionary generation did register its profound discomfort with slavery by making slaveholding a matter of individual conscience. The manumission law of 1782 empowered the owner to set free any slave under the age of forty-five by the stroke of a pen. For the first time, a substantial proportion of black Virginians would be free people.

In the towns, the change was dramatic. Petersburg's free black population more than tripled in the space of twenty years, its size swelled by a high rate of emancipation in the town itself and by the hundreds of newly freed migrants from the countryside who came in search of kin, work, and community. By 1810, there were more than a thousand free blacks in Petersburg, and they made up close to a third of the town's free population (31.2 percent). Free blacks and slaves together outnumbered the whites four to three.[5]

It was the very success of the manumission law that led to its demise. In 1805, Petersburg's common council begged the general assembly for some action to halt the growth of the free black population. The council feared an uprising, and with seeming good reason. Petersburg had welcomed its share of refugees from Saint-Domingue (Haiti), where dissatisfaction among free blacks had touched off protracted warfare; in 1803, the whites of Saint-Domingue were ousted altogether. When Petersburg's officials looked at their own burgeoning free black population, they imagined it happening all over again. "Already we hear of discontent among them—what is liberty say the well informed without the benefit of social intercourse—from such language among the free people of colour a train was laid, a mine sprung in St. Domingo that totally annihilated the whites. With such a population we are forever on the Watch. . . ."[6]

The legislature was quick to respond with two new statutes. One prohibited free blacks from carrying guns unless they obtained special permission from a court. The other was a cold-blooded new law of manumission. It was still legal to emancipate a slave, but the freed person was required to leave the state within a year, or else be sold back into slavery. For a time, the law was extremely effective. Five years passed before another slave was set free in Petersburg, and from 1810 to 1820, the town's free black community grew scarcely at all.[7]

In the meantime, white officialdom seems to have relaxed. In 1810 and 1824, Petersburg's common council passed ordinances reinforcing an old state law that required free blacks to carry certificates attesting to their free status, but the ordinances do not seem to have been enforced with any consistency. Instead, local whites placed their faith in voluntary measures as the movement to return free blacks to Africa gathered strength. In 1823, the *Republican* gleefully reported that "no less than ONE HUNDRED AND SIX persons, residents of this town," had signed up to help establish a colony in West Africa.[8] The state legislature, meanwhile, had made it easier for free blacks to remain in Virginia. In 1815, the general assembly revised the law of manumission, giving to the local courts power to grant newly emancipated blacks permission to reside permanently in the state. Emancipation rates began to rise again.

Then, in 1831, the axe fell once more, this time with terrible force. In August, a band of Southampton County slaves confirmed white Virginia's worst fears. Under the leadership of Nat Turner, slaves rose against their masters, and before they were stopped, they killed several dozen whites. The alarm bells rang all night in Petersburg as rumors flew that thousands of slaves were invading the town by the main highway from the south.[9] When the bells were quiet and the rumors quelled, Petersburg's whites joined in the statewide clamor for tighter controls on free blacks. The general assembly could hardly have been more obliging. In the session of 1831–32, teaching a black to read and write was made a criminal offense. Black preachers were silenced, and black congregations were denied the right of assembling without a white person present. Free blacks could no longer carry firearms under any circumstances. They could no longer buy slaves, unless the slaves were members of the purchaser's immediate family. Finally, free blacks were abruptly subjected to the criminal penalties prescribed for slaves. This meant that free blacks were denied jury trials except in capital cases. It also meant that most sentences would be carried out at the whipping post.

The legal cage constructed during the session of 1831–32 remained in place until 1865.[10] It was left to the local authorities to determine the intensity of enforcement. By 1860, there were more than three thousand free blacks in Petersburg, and the town government had neither the will nor the resources to maintain constant, watchful pressure. Sporadic humiliation was probably just as effective, however, and it took several forms. One was requiring blacks to produce their free papers on demand. Those who could not were jailed and then hired out until they had earned enough to pay the jailer the cost of their keep.[11] Another tactic was to whip free blacks who spoke "provoking" words to white people. In 1856, Esther Fells made the mistake of talking back to a white neighbor named Thomas Tucker, who had been disturbed by the noise coming from Fells's house. Tucker took it upon himself to give Fells "three cuts with a cowhide" and then had her taken to jail. The mayor ordered her fifteen lashes more "for being insolent to a white person."[12] The newspapers sometimes added insult to literal injury by using obnoxious metaphors to describe punishments; "they were both ordered medicine" and "nine drops of the essence of raw hide" were representative phrases from the *South-Side Democrat.*[13]

Local editors, indeed, wrote about free blacks with overt contempt, and nowhere was this more evident than in editorials on poverty. In the late 1850s, Petersburg's newspapers increasingly urged their readers to treat the white poor with generosity and understanding. Editorial comments on the free black poor were downright ugly:

. . . as they have not the face to apply openly for alms, they rely upon their ingenuity in rascality, and plan an attack upon the poultry, pork, or some other life preserver which the white man has put up for his own use; or, if perchance they are too lazy to steal, they will manage to get enough of "spirit brick" into their skulls to ensure them an introduction to Mayor Townes, who will send them to the poor-house, where they will remain until the opening of spring, when they again sally forth to bask in sunshine, and live another summer in idleness.[14]

Of course, the idea that blacks were inherently shiftless was a necessary link in the chain of arguments used to justify the maintenance of the slave system. The idea also justified the use of racially discriminatory means of squeezing the poor, specifically, the temporary enslavement of delinquent free black taxpayers. The order came in 1852: Free blacks who had not paid their taxes were to be taken into custody by the sergeant and hired out until they had worked off the amount due. In the past, the authorities had resorted to this measure only occasionally. Beginning in 1852, the order was sent down regularly.[15] Finally, a two-part ordinance of 1860 demonstrated the lengths to which the process of legal debasement could go. The first part of the ordinance made it unlawful for free blacks to ride in hacks (horse-drawn taxicabs) unless they had the permission of the mayor. The second required free blacks to step off the sidewalk to let white persons pass. Violators were to be whipped.[16]

It is not always clear just how much the actual condition of free black people was affected by the growing hostility of whites. With emancipation, however, the effects were plain. On the whole, emancipations became less frequent, especially for women; they were more often encumbered by conditions; and they were more frequently accomplished by free blacks themselves.

Before the legislature tied the hands of would-be emancipators in 1806, 173 slaves were manumitted in Petersburg. After the passage of the manumission law of 1806, emancipations came to a dead stop for five years. Thereafter, the slaves of Petersburg occasionally saw one of their number set free, but if there was renewed hope, there was also renewed disappointment. For some, manumission came only at the price of leaving Virginia for good. In the 1820s and 1830s, four of Petersburg's white slaveholders were moved in their last wills to free all of their slaves. But in three of the four cases, the slaves could claim their freedom only if they were willing to settle in Liberia.[17] Moreover, although the rate of emancipation did grow—some 400 slaves were freed in Petersburg from 1811 to 1860—it never approached the pace set before 1806.[18]

As the frequency of manumission declined, women were the disproportionate losers. Before 1806, women slaves had stood the better chance of emancipation; three-fifths of the adults freed by whites (49 / 82) were women.[19] Women lost this advantage after 1806; from 1811 to 1860, only two-fifths of the adults freed by whites were women. This was a serious reverse, and educated guesswork suggests at least two possible causes. One was the decline of antislavery ideology. It made sense to emancipate women in the revolutionary era, when antislavery feeling ran high. Under Virginia law, the child inherited the status of the mother. To free a man, therefore, was to free but one person. The emancipation of a woman in her childbearing years, however, struck a blow against the entire slave system, for that single act of emancipation might secure the freedom of generations. This incentive was, of course, eliminated in the antebellum period, when most southerners of the propertied classes developed a fixed commitment to the maintenance of chattel slavery.

Women may also have lost their edge in emancipation as a result of a change in sexual ethics. In the terse little deeds that set people free, emancipators did not usually reveal their motives, particularly when a sexual connection was involved. But there is reason to believe that as time went on, sexual intimacy with white men less often bought freedom for black women. At the end of the eighteenth century, Petersburg was still an urban frontier, a place in which white men outnumbered white women three to two, a commercial outpost manned by young merchants sent out from northern, English, and European trading houses.

Some French immigrants cohabited openly with black women; interracial couples were probably commonplace among other groups as well. The antebellum period broght changes. The sex ratio evened out among white people, and some men, at least, subscribed to a new code of sexual reticence and self-control. It is not clear whether this resulted in less sex between white men and slave women. It does seem probable that white men were less likely to acknowledge whatever intimacy had taken place, less likely to emancipate the women they had loved or exploited.

While whites backed away from emancipation, free blacks continued to buy relatives and friends whenever sellers were willing and savings sufficient. After 1806, a third of the slaves emancipated in Petersburg (133 / 410) were emancipated by free blacks.[20] This was a considerable increase (before 1806, blacks were responsible for one-sixth of Petersburg manumissions), and women accounted for a good part of it. All along, half of Petersburg's black emancipators were women. The difference between women and men, in the period before 1806, was that several of the men were able to liberate more than one slave; shoemaker Graham Bell managed to free a record ten slaves over a period of thirteen years.[21] As for the women emancipators, one each was the best they could do. After 1806, several women joined the ranks of the multiple emancipators, and no one, female or male, achieved more than Jane Minor. Jane Minor—or Gensey Snow, as she was called in slavery—had the skill of healing, and with this she had earned her own freedom. She was emancipated in 1825, after nursing several prominent citizens through an epidemic. It was her medical talent, too, that enabled her to become Petersburg's most active black emancipator. Altogether Jane Minor acquired and set free sixteen women and children.[22] Of all the slaves emancipated by free blacks after 1806, meanwhile, 45.1 percent (60/133) were freed by women.

Emancipation was itself a step up on the economic ladder; the woman at last owned her person and her labor. In Petersburg, she was not likely to own anything else, not in the beginning, anyhow. White emancipators expected their former slaves to fend for themselves. James Campbell made it explicit in 1802 when he freed forty-two-year-old Sally, "whom I have reason to believe is an honest woman, and one that will earn by her labour a proper support for herself."[23] A few emancipators may have granted their former slaves some kind of economic assistance, but in only one deed was something promised in writing. Women manumitted by will did not fare a great deal better. Of the more than seventy slaves directed freed by white testators, only twenty-three were given legacies, and two-thirds of these legatees were men.

The emancipators no doubt believed they were giving their former slaves an even chance. Given the circumstances under which many of the women were freed, however, making a living would be an uphill struggle. Roughly half of the women emancipated were emancipated along with their children, and while this spared the mothers from saving to buy their children (or from the frustration of being unable to save enough), it did mean extra mouths to be fed. Most of these women had one child or two, but three or four or five was not unusual. Most of the children were young, too young to be of much financial help.[24] The ages of the adults were important as well. Almost half of the women emancipated, and a full half of the men, were over forty.[25] These were people whose wages depended largely on muscle and endurance; their best earning years were already gone.

The most significant handicap for women, however, was the dearth of occupational options. Nothing made the women's occupational bind clearer than the apprenticeship orders issued by the court for free black children. Black boys, to be sure, had fewer choices than did white boys, but there were still a number of skilled trades open to them. Among the masters who took on free black boys as apprentices were carpenters, coopers, painters, brickmasons, blacksmiths, boatmen, bakers, and barbers. So limited were the girls' options that the clerk hardly ever wasted ink on specifying the trade. The few specific orders contained no surprises. In 1801, Lucy Cook was ordered bound "to learn the business of a Seamstress & Washer." On the same day, Polly Flood was "bound to Abby Cook, to learn to Sew & Wash &c untill of lawful age—being now about 9 years of age." Polly was bound to a second master "to learn Household business" five years later. The language had not changed by the end of the 1850s. In 1859, eleven-year-old Amelia A. E. Swan was ordered bound "to learn the art and trade of a Seamstress Washer Ironer & house-servant," while three orphaned sisters were apprenticed to a free black woman "to learn the business of washing and ironing, and sewing."[26]

A very few black women greeted freedom with special skills or resources that let them escape the pattern. Jane Minor was certainly one of these. Phebe Jackson was another. Emancipated in 1840 by Jane Minor, and perhaps trained by her, Jackson was well known to the people of Petersburg as a cupper and leecher. She saw her work as a business; she used an account book to keep track of visits and payments—a dollar for cupping, half again as much for leeching, and children bled for half price.[27] Among the medical women of Petersburg—cuppers and leechers, doctresses, nurses, and midwives—there were always several free black women. There were also a few free black women who ran small stores, grocery stores, taverns, and cookshops. In most instances, we do not know the exact character of these businesses; the reason we know they existed at all is that some of their owners were licensed, and others were arrested for lack of licenses. The one entrepreneur among black women to operate with real fanfare was Amelia Gallé. Gallé was the proprietor of a bathhouse, a business she had managed for years and then inherited in 1819 on the death of her lover. She believed in advertising. In the heat of August and the hard times of 1823, she placed her appeal in the local newspapers.

HEALTH
Purchased Cheap!

In consequence of *Small Change* being scarce, and wishing to contribute towards the health of the ladies and gentlemen, the

subscriber has the pleasure to inform her patrons and the public, that she has reduced the price of her baths to 25 CENTS
for a single one. She will make no comments on the necessity
of Bathing in warm weather:—suffice it to say, that with Mr.
Rambaut's FAMILY MEDICINES, and some Cold or Warm
BATHS, the health of her friends will keep at a proper degree
of the thermometer, without the aid of Calomel or any other
mineral Medicines.[28]

The great majority of gainfully employed free black
women, meanwhile, stuck with laundry, domestic service, sewing, or, from the 1820s on, stemming in the
tobacco factories. If the gentlemen of the grand jury had
been asked, they would probably have identified prostitution as a major enterprise of free black women. In 1804,
the grand jury registered a grievance against the invasion
of free black "strangers," many of whom "come only for
the purpose of Prostitution, to the ruin of the morals as
well as of the Health of the younger part of the community."[29] There is no telling how often free black women
resorted to prostitution—the scant surviving evidence on
prostitutes for the most part concerns whites—but the
grand jury was right about the invasion. Dismal as economic opportunities were in Petersburg, they were apparently worse in the countryside, particularly for women.

The migration of free blacks from the country to the
city may thus have been spearheaded by women; this in
turn may help account for the imbalance in the sex ratio.
Free black women outnumbered free black men everywhere in Virginia, but in the towns the imbalance was
extreme.[30] In Petersburg, there were never more than seventy free black men for every hundred free black women.
For the women, this was one more major economic dis-
advantage; relatively few free black women could count
on men to support them. When a woman got her free
papers, her struggle was hardly over.

The pattern was established early in the nineteenth century and held good at least until the Civil War: Free black
women assumed enormous burdens with pitifully slim

f headed Black or White households

resources; there developed among the free blacks of Petersburg a routine of female responsibility radically different from that prevailing among whites. Three sets of numbers outline the pattern. From census schedules, we learn that the majority of free black households were headed by women. The census schedules of 1860 tell us that a very high proportion of free black women were gainfully employed. And the tax books confirm what should have been readily guessed, that free black women were the poorest group in Petersburg.

The magnitude of responsibility shouldered by free black women begins to come into focus when we look at selected statistics on household composition. From 1810 (the first year for which census schedules are available for Petersburg) until 1860, over half of the town's free black households were headed by women—56.3 percent (138/245) in 1810 and 54 percent (472/874) in 1860. The proportion of white households headed by women, meanwhile, was 15.7 percent in 1810 and 15.2 percent in 1860. The focus becomes sharper when we consider where the children were. The earliest available statistics on children come from the census schedules for 1820 where, for the first time, free blacks were categorized by sex and age. There were relatively few children in the households headed by white women; in 1820, 17 percent of white households were headed by women, but only 13.3 percent of white children lived in them. But over half of the free black children lived in households headed by women. Women headed 58.1 percent of Petersburg's free black households in 1820, and they sheltered 57.3 percent of the town's free black children. Any attempt at finer analysis of household composition in 1820 amounts to a series of rough guesses. The best guess for free black households, however, is that the most comonplace household type was the female-headed family containing one woman and her children.[31]

The numbers for 1860 tell much the same story. A disproportionately small number of white children (10.7 percent) lived in households headed by women, while over half of Petersburg's free black children (55.2 percent) still lived in female-headed households. The greater detail provided by the 1860 census (the schedules gave the name, age, gender, and race of each person, though the relationships between persons were not stated) makes it possible to reconstruct household composition with somewhat more confidence; the household containing one woman and her children was still the most commonplace type among free blacks (191 / 874). Finally, the richer detail of the 1860 census makes it possible to discern where the mothers were. In 1860, there were about five hundred free black women in Petersburg who lived with their children. Only about two-fifths of them (188 / 492) lived with their husbands or in households that were headed by men. The remaining three-fifths lived in households of their own (269 / 492) or in households headed by other women (35 / 492).[32]

It would be fascinating to know exactly how they made ends meet. Of course, a great many free black women were gainfully employed. According to the census schedules for 1860—and this is undoubtedly an undercount—over half of free black females aged fourteen and above (678 / 1264 = 53.6 percent) were gainfully employed. (The comparable figure for whites was 9.5 percent.) Some free black women also sent their children to work, a choice that was probably made with relatively little soul searching, since their children did not have the alternative of going to school. A few hiring agreements from the tobacco factories still survive. The women made their marks and pledged the services of their sons; payments for the sons' labor were made directly to the mothers. In 1839, black women made at least a small gain when the court altered its policy regarding poor apprentices. The new system required masters to pay the mothers (or in rare cases, the fathers) for the services of children ordered bound by the court. James Andrew Jackson, for example, was twelve years old when the court apprenticed him to Charles Miller to learn the baker's trade. For his final year of service, Miller was to pay James Andrew thirty dollars. In the intervening years, Miller was to make payments—the amounts increasing with the experience of the apprentice—to James Andrew's mother, Judy Jackson.[33]

For all their economic difficulties, free black women did

not make many claims on the welfare system, such as it was. There were always a few free black women in the poorhouse, but their numbers were more or less commensurate with their proportion of the free population. From private white sources of assistance, they got even less. In February 1859, the Association for Improvement of the Condition of the Poor claimed to have given relief to 822 persons. Of these, 12 were black.[34]

The fact that free black women gained so little from charity is remarkable, for on the whole they were very poor. From extremely impoverished beginnings in the early part of the century, free black women had by 1860 made some progress. Even so, they remained by any measure the poorest of Petersburg's free people. There were fewer taxpayers among free black women than among any other group. In 1860, free black women made up only 6.1 percent of the town's owners of taxable property, while free black men were 7.9 percent, white women were 19 percent, and white men were 67 percent. With real estate alone, free black women were again the least blessed. In 1860, 8.9 percent of Petersburg's real estate owners were free black women, 10.5 percent were free black men, 19.8 percent were white women, and 60.8 percent were white men.[35] Of course, people who owned no real estate or other taxable property were not necessarily poor. Our best measure of rock-bottom poverty comes from the census taker's estimates of the value of all property owned by heads of households. According to the schedules of 1860, half of the free black women who headed households (51 percent) owned no property at all, not even five or ten dollars' worth. For free black men the comparable figure was 34.2 percent, for white women 12.1 percent, for white men 9.3 percent.

There is not much material here for romanticizing. In recent years, it has become commonplace to equate gainful employment for women with liberation. Even for the present this is far too simple. For the nineteenth century, it is utterly misleading, and it makes a mockery of women's real desperation. For free black women, the high rate of gainful employment, and the high incidence of female-headed households as well, were badges of oppression. Neither was chosen from a position of strength; both were the products of chronic economic deprivation and of a shortage of men. And yet there was autonomy of a kind; when black women of our own time say they have always been liberated, they have a point. The autonomy experienced by the free black women of Petersburg was relative freedom from day-by-day domination by black men. What we cannot see from this distance is whether the women themselves placed a positive value on their autonomy (or on particular aspects of it) and whether they took deliberate steps to maintain it. What we can see are two features of free black life that look positive through the lens of feminist hindsight. First, among those free blacks who did manage to acquire property, a high proportion were women. And second, for free black women it was not unusual to refrain from marriage, thereby retaining their legal autonomy.

With all the obstacles before them, the wonder was that free blacks as a group accomplished as much as they did. Except for limitations on the purchase of slaves, free blacks were never denied the right to acquire, use, and dispose of property. In this crucial area of status, there was considerable long-term progress. In 1810, 9.8 percent of Petersburg's real estate owners (23 / 235) were black. By 1860, free blacks were 19.4 percent of the town's real estate owners (207 / 1067), an especially notable increase considering that the proportion of blacks in the total free population had declined. It is impossible to say whether this measurable progress signified an overall improvement in the condition of free black people; how do we measure a gain in property holding against the loss of trial by jury or against the loss of the right to read?

What is clear and most to the point here is that women shared directly in the material gains. In 1810, women comprised just over a third of Petersburg's free black real estate owners (8 / 23). In 1860, women were 45.9 percent of

Petersburg's free black real estate owners (95 / 207), and the collective value of the land owned by women was greater than that owned by the men. These were stunning proportions. White women in 1810 were only 8.5 percent of Petersburg's white real estate owners (18 / 212). By 1860, white women had made marked advances, but they were still just 24.5 percent of white real estate owners (211 / 860).[36]

Black women, in other words, controlled a very large share of the small but growing amount of property controlled by the free black people of Petersburg. This was due in part to the high incidence of gainful employment among the women and to the fact that black men by and large did not earn very much. In 1860, three-fifths of Petersburg's gainfully employed free black men were either laborers or factory hands, and while there were a number of black men in the skilled trades, they were shut out by custom from high-income occupations, from the professions and from commerce on the grand scale.[37]

The high proportion of women among free black property owners was also a product of the tendency of black women to remain single. It is impossible to estimate how many of Petersburg's free black women shunned lawful matrimony, but the existing evidence suggests that the proportion was high, higher than among whites. The sex ratio, the law, poverty, and preference conspired to keep a great many free black women single, and to the extent that they remained single, they remained autonomous agents in the economic realm.

The sex ratio and the law together dictated the single life for one-third of Petersburg's free black women. Since blacks were not permitted to marry whites and slaves were not permitted to marry anyone, the pool of marriageable men was restricted to free blacks, and there were simply not enough of them to go around. A few black women did take up with whites, and more, apparently, were the partners of slaves. These matches yielded some interesting economic arrangements. When a free woman cohabited with a slave, here were the materials for a complete sex-role reversal, for the woman assumed all legal rights and responsibilities for the pair. In 1800, a slave named David White was jailed for going at large and trading as a free person. The fine for White's misdeeds fell on his mate, Polly Spruce, a free woman who had hired White for the year and who was therefore legally answerable for his behavior. Nearing her death several years later, Jane Cook found it necessary to make special provisions for her enslaved partner, Peter Matthews. Cook had purchased two small boats, "the Democrat and experiment," as Matthews's agent and with his money. These she bequeathed to Matthews, appointing a free black man to act as his agent and to stand guardian to her daughter, to whom she left her own property.[38] There were also a few women who owned their mates, and the women sometimes waited several years before setting their men free. In a bizarre case of 1832, a free woman emancipated her slave man in order to preserve her other property. Arthur Wyatt belonged to Martha Scott; she later testified that they "had been living for a considerable time as husband and wife – that during their coverture he had frequently fallen out with her, and several times threatened to burn her house." On one occasion, Wyatt actually set a fire, and Scott ultimately became so frightened of him that she had him locked up in the local jail. While he was confined, she executed a deed of emancipation, one that required him to leave the state immediately. Martha Scott's house burned to the ground shortly after Arthur Wyatt's release from jail.[39]

The women whose mates were white or enslaved had no choice but to remain technically single, but it is by no means certain that all of them would have married had they been given the chance. When free black women entered into partnerships with men who were likewise black and free, legal wedlock was not the inevitable result. Marrying did cost money, and for poor couples this could present a real obstacle. The clerk of the court charged for his services, and so, as a general rule, did white ministers (when a congregation stinted on the pastor's salary, the proceeds from performing weddings and funerals became

critical income). After the legislature abolished the black
clergy in the session of 1831–32, the problem of finding
ministers they could afford became acute among free
blacks, so much so that in 1839 scores of Petersburg whites
signed a petition proposing that black ministers be rein-
stated.[40]

Nonmarriage among free blacks, however, was evidently as much a matter of ethics as of expenses, for even
the propertied showed no consistent tendency to make their
conjugal ties legal ties. There were times when this led to
trouble. Thomas Walden was a good carpenter, and he
made a good living. In 1827, he managed to buy his slave
wife Nancy Munford and their two-year-old daughter. Five
years later he emancipated them, along with a second
daughter, but he never legalized his union with Nancy.
Then in 1845 Thomas was murdered. Nancy discovered
she was not entitled to a nickel. Thomas had left no will.
There having been no marriage, there were no legitimate
heirs, and Thomas's property was liable to escheat (to re-
vert, that is, to the state). Thomas's estate included a house,
three lots in town, and 150 acres in the country, and his
family was not about to let it be taken from them. In 1847,
"Nancy Munford alias Walden" and her daughters petitioned the legislature, their plea for justice accompanied by
white testimonials to the Walden family's respectability.
Thomas Walden, one of them warranted, had been a
"remarkable decent well behaved man and lived much better, than people of his grade generally (being a Carpenter
myself)." Another deposed that "upon the Marriage of
one of his [Walden's] daughters, the Ceremony was performed by the Rev^d Mr Levenworth, a highly respectable
minister of this town, and the Ceremony attended by several respectable White persons Male & female, this latter
statement is made merely to show, the very respectable
standing of Walden & his family." The legislature listened,
and the Walden women got their inheritance.[41]

Christian Scott averted this sort of difficulty in 1817, not
by marrying his mate, but by means of a deed of gift. Scott
was hardly well to do, but he did own some animals and a

goodly stock of household furniture. "Having for some time past lived with Charlotte Cook by whom I have a Son called Jesse Mitchell. . . ," Scott explained, "and being desirous from the friendship & Regard I bear to the said Charlotte Cook & affection to my said Son, to convey the property aforesaid to them," Scott deeded them the property, dividing it exactly as it would have been divided had Scott married Cook and then died intestate. James Vaughan, a barber, was far wealthier than Scott. He was also in deep trouble. In 1806, Vaughan was tried for the murder of "his supposed wife" Milly Johnston. After his conviction, a contrite Vaughan was permitted to write a will to direct the distribution of an estate that included cash and bonds worth over two thousand dollars, a town lot, three horses, and four slaves. Vaughan gave half of his estate to Sarah Vaughan, his daughter by Polly Hull. The other half went to John Vaughan, his son by Ann Stephens.[42] Whether James Vaughan's relationships with Johnston, Hull, and Stephens were simultaneous or sequential is both unclear and beside the point. The point is that he did not marry any of them.

So much the better for the women's control over their property and wages. Polly Hull, for example, bought a town lot a few months before James Vaughan wrote his will and was taxed on it for more than a decade thereafter.[43] There were other free black women in roughly similar circumstances. Charlotte Rollins was part of an uneasy triangle that included a free black named Captain Billy Ash and a slave named Julius. Ash was tried for "shooting and wounding" Julius in 1802, and Rollins's sister and brother-in-law were examined in the case. "On their being ask[ed] if Charlotte was wife of the prisoner, it was answered, that they both, the prisoner & Julius, resorted where she was." It is unclear what became of Billy Ash, but Charlotte Rollins never married him or anyone else. In 1810, she was listed as the head of a three-person family, and in 1817, she disposed of her household furniture and kitchen utensils by deed of gift, a probable substitute for the writing of a will.[44] Nelly White, unhappily,

Black marriage or cohabitation

108 | *The Free Women of Petersburg*

was unable to enjoy the property she had acquired in her baking business. In 1811, White was examined on suspicion of knifing a free man named Tom, and a witness described their relationship: "Tom & the Prisoner had lived in the same House, in different apartments – and been considered as man & wife but lived badly together after wrangling." White was convicted in district court and sent to the penitentiary. She left behind "some property & Estate," and the town sergeant was ordered to look after it while she served her sentence.[45]

A member of one of Petersburg's most prominent free black families, Molly Brander married once but opted for cohabitation the second time around. The first time, she married Nathan James. After his death in 1804, Molly began a new family, taking James Butler "as her husband tho not lawfully married" and adopting her orphaned niece. Because she did not marry Butler, Molly James retained her rights to the house and lot she had inherited from her first husband, and when she died intestate in 1812, her mother and brothers inherited the property in turn. Before her death, however, Molly James had told her family that she wanted the lot to pass to James Butler and her adoptive daughter. The family complied in 1815 with a deed of gift.[46]

Just how common it was for black women to acquire some kind of property and retain legal control over it by not marrying is a mystery, for evidence surfaces only sporadically in trial reports (hence the prevalence of violent crime in the preceding paragraphs) and in a very occasional deed. Moreover, these few documents give no clues as to whether the women deliberately decided against marriage for the sake of maintaining their legal rights. The legacy and continued presence of slavery no doubt provided cause enough. Slave marriages were necessarily based on mutual consent, and for a good many black couples, consent was sufficient in freedom as well. As late as 1860, the significance of legal marriage was still a debatable issue in the Gillfield Baptist Church. The church routinely disciplined its members for breaches of family and sexual ethics; next to fighting and disorderly conduct, the most common causes for expulsion from fellowship were adultery and being pregnant without a husband. In October 1859, another potential infraction was brought before the congregation: "Bro George Taylor ask a question [Does] the church allow her members man & Wife to stay in fellowship refusing to live With one a nother [?]" After deliberation, the church decided that it was wrong for husband and wife to live separately, and in short order, Maria L. Mabry was expelled for living apart from her husband. But this in turn raised the question of who was to be considered man and wife. In January 1860, a new decision was made. "It was moved & 2nd that the Past Action of the church be reconsidered of mutual concent being considered Man & Wife Carried – non considered Man & Wife But those joined together By Matrimony."[47]

Slavery may also have had a more direct influence on women's decisions against marriage. It may well have been that women so recently emancipated and women accustomed to providing for themselves did not give up their legal autonomy lightly. Unless the man owned property, legal marriage brought the woman no economic benefits. Moreover, free black women had unique incentives for staying single. For the woman who hoped to buy an enslaved relative, legal wedlock meant that her plan could be sabotaged at any time by her husband or by her husband's creditors. The common-law disabilities of married women added an ironic twist to chattel slavery's strange fusion of persons and property: Matrimony could pose a threat to the free black woman's family.

Once again, it is not clear what free black women themselves thought of their position of relative strength vis-à-vis black men. What is clear is that the relative equality between free black women and men was never granted any legitimacy by whites and was never used to call white gender arrangements into question. On the contrary, deviations from white standards of marital behavior were treated, if they were treated at all, as burlesque. The *South-Side Democrat,* for example, reported a domestic quarrel of 1856 between Mary Wright and William Smith, free blacks who, it was pointed out, lived together but were not married. The fight was over the question of "whether a lady or gentleman should preside at the head of the table." Such a question presumably would not have arisen among white ladies and gentlemen. In any case, William picked up an iron bar and struck Mary on the head with it; "had it hit her anywhere else," the reporter commented, "the blow might have killed her." The joke was completed when the mayor ordered William twenty lashes.[48]

This is not a pretty story by any telling, but if we take it seriously, we can learn more from it than the reporter from the *South-Side Democrat* did. And what we learn bears on whites as well as blacks. Mary Wright and William Smith were engaged in a real power struggle; while the evidence is too thin to permit firm judgment, it would stand to reason that among the free blacks of Petersburg, there was a relatively high degree of open antagonism between the sexes. Chapter 2 proposed that companionate marriage increased the incidence of overt conflict as wives assumed the right to opinions and as they gained new opportunities for encroachment on male territory. It is not clear whether "companionate" is an appropriate term for conjugal relations between free blacks, but the same reasoning applies: Free black women had relatively little cause to defer to their men, and the result may have been a substantial amount of conjugal conflict.

To say that there were battles between the sexes is not to risk giving aid and comfort to the old notion that there was something uniquely pathological about black family life. Pathology there undoubtedly was. Settling a dispute with an iron bar was a symptom of it; whatever William Smith's particular animus, poverty and the daily, personal assaults of racism on human character had to have done some damage. There was nothing inherently pathological about conflict between the sexes, however, no more than there was anything inherently pathological about female-headed households. Insofar as conflict grew out of leverage and assertiveness on the part of women, it was a sign of health; it was, in any case, better than routine, abject submission.

It should no longer be necessary to defend the historic black family by minimizing the existence of domestic conflict or by minimizing the importance of women. At the same time, it would be foolish to revive the old idea of a matriarchy; Mary Wright's assertiveness, after all, earned her a concussion. We are back once more to that unsettling pairing of autonomy with oppression, assertiveness with victimization. What needs emphasis here is that the experience of free black women represented in extreme and particularly visible form the experience of women as a group. First, much of the autonomy acquired by free black women was either a result of oppression or a form of punishment. Men were not present, or they were not free, or they did not make enough money; men let them down, and the women were left to do the best they could on their own. For women as a group, it was much the same story. Women were most likely to acquire separate estates when their husbands failed them. And as we shall see, they were most likely to enter the paid labor force out of an urgent need for money. Second, women ordinarily exercised power over small stakes. Free black women controlled close to half of the property controlled by free blacks, but free blacks controlled only a small fraction of the town's wealth. So it went, time and again, with women as a group. Women were most often appointed executors and guardians when estates were small. When they entered the paid labor force, as will become plain in Chapter 6, their earnings were generally paltry. In business, they were concentrated at the bottom of the scale, and when in the course of economic modernization new positions of authority were created, women were passed by. It was all enough to give autonomy a very bad name.

Nevertheless, some women did emerge with some genuine choices, and those choices should not be dismissed because they were few, or limited, or because their origins were suspect. We turn next to an exploration of what free women, black and white collectively, did with what they had. What we find are the outlines of a women's culture.

5

Women Alone: Property and Personalism

Much as we have learned recently about particular groups of American women, some stereotypes still stand between us and a clear vision of the past. One thinks of the stereotypical single woman in the nineteenth-century propertied family—dependent on the charity of her brother's household, useful after her fashion, and smelling of lavender and timidity. This is an image in urgent need of revision, because single women, and widows, too, are pivotal characters in the recovery of the female past.[1] For all the limitations on their lives, spinsters and widows did have the same legal options as men. As time went on, the single and widowed women of Petersburg became increasingly active in exercising these options. In the process, they set in place a series of windows on women's consciousness; when women were in a position to make decisions about money, about family, about slaves, and about their own capabilities, their choices were often different from those made by men. From this evidence, it looks very much as though women did indeed operate from a distinct female value system. And at its center, if it can be captured in a phrase, was a persistent personalism.

Mary Marshall Bolling was hardly the typical widow of

Petersburg, but no other woman in Petersburg illustrated better the great range of economic transactions open to the town's growing ranks of single and widowed women. Rarely did any one person demonstrate so well how a personalism characteristic of women could survive decades of transactions in the predominantly masculine world of business. Nothing is known of the first half of Mary Bolling's life except that she was born to wealth, that she married into an equally wealthy family in 1758, and that she raised five children to adulthood. Her husband died in about 1777, leaving Mary, who was then approaching forty, as head of Petersburg's most powerful household. According to the Marquis de Chastellux, she was more than equal to the task. Bolling, he beamed, "has but little resemblance to her country women; she is lively, active, and intelligent. . . ." She was not undone by the marquis's blue blood either, having received him "with much cordiality, without restraint or ceremony." By the time the marquis arrived in 1782, Bolling's courage in the face of the British enemy was already becoming legendary. When the British army stopped in Petersburg en route to Yorktown, the ranking officers quartered themselves at Bollingbrook, Mary Bolling's home. Bolling could have turned refugee, but instead stood her ground under house arrest to try to save her property from destruction. She did not talk the officers out of burning the tobacco stored in her several warehouses, nor could she prevent the confiscation of most of her horses, but she did persuade them to return her confiscated slaves, and the warehouse buildings themselves were spared.[2]

Thereafter, managing the Bolling estate was a more prosaic affair, and in the process Mary Bolling engaged in almost every conceivable kind of transaction. As was the case with many widows, Bolling's powers were restricted somewhat by the terms of her husband's will. She had a life estate in Bollingbrook itself, in all of Robert Bolling's town lots, in his five tobacco warehouses, and in half of his flour mill; and while these supplied a very healthy income, Mary could not convey them unless her son Robert, Jr., the reversionary heir, joined her. After dividing several plantations between his sons, however, Robert Bolling, Sr., had left the remainder of his colossal estate to Mary and her brother to distribute among the children as they saw fit. A good many of Mary Bolling's early conveyances carried the mark of her husband's will. She distributed some eighty slaves among her children; she gave her son Robert a free hand in developing a new residential section (reserving the ground rents for herself); and with Robert she conveyed several town lots. Later on she began making investments of her own. She bought several lots; she purchased slaves from the estate of her deceased son Thomas Tabb; and when branches of Virginia's two state banks were opened in Petersburg, she invested heavily in their stocks.

Conveyances and purchases, however, scarcely began the list of Mary Bolling's recorded activities. She was appointed her husband's executor, she served as a legal guardian, and she went bail for her son-in-law when he was named defendant in a civil suit. When debtors (probably her tenants) refused to pay what was due her, she took them to court. Like other proprietors, she paid taxes. Unlike most other proprietors, she managed to avoid paying taxes on slaves who, "on Account of their Age & infirmities," were no longer productive. Warehouse problems and her desire to see the streets of Petersburg paved prompted her to add her signature to petitions to the general assembly, while promoters of assorted public projects found in Mary Bolling a major contributor. In 1787, she donated a tract of land to the town for use as a site for "publick Buildings," and when the proprietors of Petersburg formed a fire company in 1791, Bolling, who had the most to lose, made the largest pledge. True, meanwhile, to local custom, she encouraged secular amusements with one hand and religious and charitable institutions with the other. Thomas Wade West's theatre company, the trustees of the Anglican church, and the officers of the Female Orphan Asylum were all beneficiaries of Mary Bolling's subscriptions.[3]

Just before she died in 1814, however, Mary Bolling

flouted local male custom when she issued the directions for the distribution of her estate among her heirs. Most of the men who left wills, regardless of their wealth, divided their assets equally among all their children, and when grandchildren were named, they too received equal shares. But Mary Bolling played favorites. This was an old source of contention within the Bolling clan. John Shore, the husband of Bolling's daughter Ann, had never been satisfied with the share his family had received when Bolling had distributed parts of her husband's estate by deed of gift, and when Shore wrote his own will in 1811, he made one last attempt to secure his family's due:

> I do request and enjoin it on my Executors, that they make personal application to Mrs Mary Bolling in behalf of my wife and children, for an equal division of the negroes and personal estate of my wifes father Mr Robert Bolling dec^d . . . and should Mrs Bolling still deny them that justice, so long withheld from them, I desire a suit to be instituted against her, with the least possible delay. . . .

Mary Bolling was not intimidated. Although she did leave a large portion of her estate to Ann Shore, she attached a menacing proviso to head off any litigation. "As to my daughters Ann Shore and Marianna Bolling, I repeat again that if they sue my estate for anything, they are to lose whatever is above devised and bequeathed to them. . . ."[4]

The remainder of Bolling's lengthy will sifted the chosen from among her numerous descendants. The legacy she granted Ann Shore, for example, was on Ann's death to be equally divided among Ann's children, but "with the exception of Thomas Shore, who is to have no part of either the land or the money." The will gave no hint of what Thomas Shore had done to offend his grandmother so deeply; neither did it explain why certain other grandchildren were singled out for special, favorable treatment. Two of Thomas Shore's siblings received sizable parcels of bank stock, while five did not. Another granddaughter, Rebecca LeMessurier, was given bank stock and a slave as well, but Rebecca's brother received no legacy of his own. And while Mary Bolling gave nothing to her son Robert (Robert had been amply provided for by his father), she did give three town lots to Robert's daughter Mary Banister and in addition gave bank stock to Banister's daughter. None of Robert's other children received anything.

This discrimination had no parallel in the wills left by fathers in the early national period. Among women, however, it was standard procedure. Whether we regard behavior like that of Mary Bolling as a positive assertion of the primacy of human feeling or as an ugly exercise in pettiness, the point remains that women made economic decisions according to their own standards of propriety and justice.

As time went on, moreover, a growing proportion of Petersburg's women were in a position to make those decisions. Among free black women, refraining from legal marriage was commonplace all along. Among white women, the proportion of widows and spinsters appears to have grown substantially over time. By 1860, more than a third of the white women living in Petersburg were either widowed or had never married at all.[5] Not all of these women were property owners, of course, but women as a group did by 1860 have more to work with than ever before. In 1790, only 7.3 percent of Petersburg's property taxpayers were women. By 1860, a full quarter of the town's taxpayers were women. A large minority of Petersburg's women were facing life as legally autonomous persons.

Autonomy did not come easily to nineteenth-century women, of course. For most white women of the propertied classes, taking charge of finances was an act fraught with ambivalence. Any judgments on the extent to which women did or did not seize their opportunities must be set against the fact that most women were neither trained nor rewarded for pursuing an independent course.

Eliza Ruffin made the point in a protest letter of 1828. Eliza had just turned twenty-one, and on that day her older brother Edmund, who had been serving as her legal guardian, divested himself of all responsibility for her affairs. Eliza was miffed at the suddenness of the transition, and she opened her letter to Edmund without so much as a "how are you." *"This legal independence—"* she began,

> what a mistaken notion is entertained of it! what an undesirable possession it is in my opinion, I am heartily tired of the pleasure already: but what is to be done? if 21 years have been realized, does it follow of course that they have brought along with them all the judgment and knowledge in the direction of such matters? am I any more competent to devise ways and means now, than formerly? . . . it really seems you expect me to metamorphose myself into a *man*, as it were by magic. . . .

In fact, when she discussed the details of particular transactions, Eliza seemed more than competent. "Mr Harrison has been to se[e] me," she wrote, "and the issue of our interview was, not the least change about his bond, I was perfectly satisfied with his statement of affairs and thought the security sufficient without any additional." The main sticking point, it seems, was that Edmund had initiated a lawsuit and then dumped it on Eliza, leaving her to play the aggressor. She would prefer taking a loss to continuing the suit, she claimed, "and a loser I had much rather be, than to meddle and render myself the subject of general talk and certain ridicule." The letter went on:

> You have brought me ridiculously and conspicuously into notice already by over anxiety to shake me off your hands and having done that, I am now left to go to the Bank personally, ask advice, hold consultations, all too because you wont receive the authority granted you. . . . Let me beg you to send no men to me; You ought to remember how disagreeable it must be for a female to be negotiating with every or any body— especially a *lady* of my *extreme refinement*.[6]

Eliza Ruffin, with characteristic Ruffin spunk, could express her qualms with tongue at least half in cheek. Mary Read Anderson, by contrast, was serious and harried, and problems with independence seemed built into her personality. Though she was well into her thirties, Anderson's financial moves kept her in a state of perpetual adolescence—now commanding, now defiant, but forever in need of rescue. When her husband died in 1813, Anderson knew that she had much to learn. Still stupefied with grief and fatigue, she qualified as executor of her husband's will and wrote to her brother Duncan Cameron to ask him to stand by as her adviser: ". . . I am a *novice* & feel myself *but illy* quallified to do any thing like business there is a kind of Stupidity which hangs about me that I have not yet been able to Shake off." When her brother did offer advice, however, Anderson ignored it. Cameron had tried to persuade his sister that her income as a widow would never be sufficient to maintain the household she had shared with her merchant husband and that her only course was to sell out and settle for a smaller place. But Anderson believed that her frugality would prevail, and she refused to move. Before the year was out, she was finding it necessary to dip into her sons' legacies to pay for their clothing (this was legal, but Anderson had hoped to avoid it): "I find I cannot with convenience cloathe them as I wished to do," she confessed to her brother; "I am already more in debt than I ever intended to be."[7]

Several years later, Anderson did give in and sell the Petersburg house, moving to North Carolina in 1817 to be near her sons, who had entered the university there. But the pattern was set in the first year of her widowhood and continued for more than twenty years: Expenses outran income; Duncan Cameron made up the difference; Anderson made excuses and promises of reform. "A woman is an helpless being," she wrote in 1819, "& that will [be], & I hope is appology sufficient for all the trouble I have been, or may be to you."[8]

It should be said in Anderson's behalf that her financial problems were not all of her own making. Women new to widowhood were regarded as easy marks and were often tested by sharp tradesmen and by slaves who saw the change of command as an opportunity to press their own interests. Mary Read Anderson encountered several tests in the early months of her widowhood. In an attempt to increase the long-term value of her slave boy Frederick, Anderson apprenticed him to a shoemaker named Hubbard. After some months in Hubbard's charge, Frederick became violently ill (Anderson thought this was Hubbard's fault for providing Frederick with such skimpy clothing), and it emerged that the boy had not been taught the first thing about shoemaking. None of Anderson's threats succeeded in getting Hubbard to live up to his obligations as a master craftsman, and she fell back on her brother once again, this time asking Cameron to arrange an apprenticeship that he himself could oversee. Two of Anderson's adult slaves, meanwhile, were sources of acute aggravation. Tom simply ran away. Peggy stole a bank note belonging to the estate of Anderson's husband, or so Anderson believed, and had gotten a white man to swear that the note had been acquired by legal means. Anderson resolved to sell Tom and Peggy at the first opportunity. As for Peggy's white accomplice, Anderson muttered, "it was well for the puppy I was not a man or I would have broken his head for his impertinence."[9]

As Mary Read Anderson clearly recognized, the lone woman suffered real disadvantages in the world of business. Anderson's particular response was to emphasize womanly weakness in order to justify her dependence on a male protector. Despite assertions that she desired self sufficiency—". . . you will readily see I wish that no one should be burdened with my expenses but myself," she wrote in 1819—Anderson's behavior kept her perpetually in her brother's debt and at its worst took on a quality of almost studied incompetence. Anderson destroyed all her bills and receipts when she moved away from Petersburg. When she returned for a visit, the bill collectors were standing in line. Anderson was certain she had paid all her bills before she had moved away, but as she had saved no records, she was obligated to pay everyone who presented a claim. Anderson did pay and wrote to her brother to ask for another loan.[10]

Insofar as she had choices, Mary Read Anderson chose dependency. Dependency takes two, however, and whenever Anderson played the lady in distress, Duncan Cameron suited up to play the white knight. Theirs was not an eccentric relationship. Legal autonomy was a frightening prospect, frightening in its sheer unfamiliarity and its loneliness. There were always opportunists willing to profit by a woman's inexperience; there were often well-intentioned men like Duncan Cameron who did just as much to reinforce a woman's diffidence. The wonder was that so many women overcame it.

People of both sexes had their doubts about the capacity of women to make independent financial decisions and transactions. Women, however, had fewer doubts than men did. In the wealthier classes, especially, women's ideas about their own abilities diverged sharply from those of their husbands. If in the early nineteenth century there was an attempt to make mere ornaments of upper-middle- and upper-class women, the attempt was made by men, and the women themselves resisted it.

The evidence comes from an analysis of appointments of executors and administrators. A great many of the widowed women of Petersburg began their independent economic careers as the executors or administrators of their deceased husbands' estates. The duties of an administrator were exactly the same as those assigned an executor. The administrator was obliged to dissolve partnerships, to collect and pay debts, to pursue litigation, to distribute the estate to the proper heirs, and to manage it in the meantime. The administrator was also compensated at the same rate as the executor; both were allowed to pocket 5 percent of the estate's income. The difference between an administrator and an executor lay in the appointment process. Executors were nominated by will, and the local court ordinarily endorsed the choice of the testator. When the will named no executor, when the named executor(s) refused to serve, or when no will was located, then the court appointed an administrator. The estate of a deeply indebted person might be committed to a creditor or to the town sergeant for distribution among creditors. Otherwise, the court was instructed by law to make the appointment "preferring first the husband or wife."[11]

The difference in how executors and administrators were selected may look like a minor procedural detail, but for us it is a critical difference. When the court made ready to appoint an administrator, it was ordinarily up to the widow to accept or refuse the task. In Petersburg, the women who made the choice based their decisions on considerations very different from those that moved men.

Recall from Chapter 2 that the nomination of wives as executors was closely related to wealth and that the richer the testator, the less likely he was to assign his wife any part in settling his estate. Men of means evidently believed that executorship stretched the wife's competence or undermined her status as a lady. This was most pronounced in the period before 1830, when not a single wealthy testator nominated his wife to serve as sole executor of his will. Men seem to have taken their wives' ages into account as well, apparently believing that women in their twenties were too inexperienced to assume the executor's responsibilities.

But none of this seemed to matter very much to the women, not to the women who made choices for or against administration. Unfortunately, it was only from 1808 to 1830 that the clerk made regular entries in the minute books specifying who refused administrations as well as who took them on; the figures are therefore small and cover a period of less than twenty-five years. They are, nonetheless, arresting. First, women did not feel that youthfulness should disqualify them. Widows in their twenties routinely accepted the administration of their husbands' estates. Second, widows of well-to-do men did not as a general rule shrink from administration, even though large estates usually brought more headaches than did small ones. Well over half of the widows in the upper income bracket (18 / 29) applied for and were granted appointments as administrators.[12] Each of these women assumed powers identical to those of a sole executor. Had their husbands left wills, chances were that none of them would have been given sole responsibility for settling the estate, and most of them would have been excluded altogether. While the relatively wealthy men of Petersburg in most cases thought the disposition of their estates beyond the abilities or inclinations of their wives, many of the wives themselves were willing to assume the authority.

Altogether, about three-fifths of the widows who were given the choice on administration decided to accept. Just why one would accept administration while another refused it is something of a mystery. The single most important factor may have been the condition of the estate; the case of Elizabeth Ann Somerville was an object lesson in why some women were well advised to leave the job to someone else. Somerville was only thirty when her husband John, a printer and bookseller, died in 1816. According to the commissioners who later reviewed her accounts of her administration, the experience had proved to be an unmixed disaster. Just a few days after she made official acceptance of the administration, Somerville left Petersburg for a time, perhaps to escape the fall sickly season. She appointed an attorney to act as her agent in her absence, and that was her first mistake. While she was away, some of the estate's household furnishings were sold on credit to various purchasers, but her agent managed to collect only a third of the payments due. Somerville had even less luck with the auctioneer she engaged to dispose of the unsold volumes remaining in her husband's bookstore. The auctioneer—or "vendue master," as the term was then—sold only the best of the books and then refused to turn over the proceeds. Somerville sued him, but as late as 1819 was still awaiting a judgment. That left the debts due John Somerville at the time of his death the one remaining source of income. Elizabeth Ann crisscrossed the town to secure their payment, but here again there was trouble. "The books of the Decedent contain a great number of accounts unsettled," the commissioners reported,

> but to most of them are Offsets and objections, and to get proof to substantiate them is impossible—Attempts have been

made but in vain. It is not probable that many more of the debts contained in those books can be collected. Everything relative to the estate was in the utmost confusion at the time of the death of John Somerville.

Elizabeth Ann was allotted an unusually large commission of 7.5 percent on the debts she did collect, an amount "barely equal, if equal, to the labour performed. . . ." It was well for her that she had some resources of her own. The estate was closed in its chaotic condition, and for thirty years more Elizabeth Ann Somerville would get along by taking in boarders and offering music lessons.[13]

For Elizabeth Ann Somerville, plagued by her own inexperience and by her husband's wretched bookkeeping, administration was more trouble than it was worth; the main thing to be said for her having accepted the administration was that she prevented someone else from doing a less conscientious job of it. It seems probable that anticipation of similar trials was sufficient to motivate other women to refuse the administration in the first place. There was nothing inherently satisfying, after all, in chasing debtors, in instigating litigation, or in any of the other chores that came with settling an estate. Unless the condition of the estate allowed the woman to turn a profit or to strengthen her position as an heir, incentives to accept administration were weak.

The state of the estate may have been the most important consideration in widows' decisions for or against administration, but there were plenty of other factors. Those women who were natives of far-off places and who had little but their marriages to tie them to Petersburg were only too glad to relinquish the right to administration so that they could leave town as soon as possible. Mary Parker, for example, relinquished her right in 1800, appointed an attorney to handle her other business, saw to the marking of her husband's grave, and was resettled in London by the end of 1801.[14] For the widow who stayed on, there was still much to consider. Her health, her age, the amount of time she had to spare, her previous experience with finances, her willingness to take on new ventures, the presence or absence of some trusted friend or relative willing to assume her right, and, possibly, literacy—any of these could make the difference.

Were enough known about each of the widows, these considerations might add up to some discernible pattern. As it is, their decisions appear to have been highly idiosyncratic; there seem to have been no conventions to guide the widows of Petersburg in their decisions for or against administration. Absence of convention likewise characterized the subsequent behavior of those widows who did accept, as they decided how much authority should be delegated. Although the administrator herself was legally responsible for the faithful performance of the trust, there was nothing to stop her from appointing others to do all or part of the work. Four days after Eliza Curtis filed as administrator in 1818, the notice she submitted to the *Republican* announced that she would act more or less as a figurehead:

> All persons having claims against the estate of Benj. Curtis, are desired to present them properly authenticated to Mr. Wm. Gilmour, who I have appointed my agent to settle the business of the estate; and all persons indebted to the said estate, are requested to make payment to him, as speedily as possible, that my administration may be closed without delay.

Mary Strange, to cite a contrary case, asked assistance from no one. Widow of the merchant who was one of Petersburg's wealthiest intestates, Strange mentioned no agent when she advertised the sale of her husband's personal estate, and the account she rendered of her administration showed she had tackled the most harrowing task of all, that of debt collection. It was the most lucrative task as well; in 1811, she paid herself more than $200, "the Administratrix's Commission 5 pr Cent . . . on $3143.84 received this year."[15]

While it is impossible to gauge with any accuracy just how active the appointed women were, scattered evidence suggests that the plurality of the women divided their responsibilities with friends, relatives, or attorneys. Elizabeth Murdock advertised a lot for rent shortly after her husband's death in 1815. "Apply to the subscriber," she directed, "on the premises." A year later, her brother submitted an ad for rental of the same "agreeable, healthy situation," signing the notice "For Elizabeth Murdock, EPPES SPAIN." Ann Harrison, meanwhile, hired a lawyer for an opinion on her husband's will and for some administrative services, but also allotted herself payments "for my Expences to Richmond to Collect Interest on Stock." And while Lucy Morris paid and collected numerous small debts, she found it necessary to send a lawyer after her husband's most stubborn debtors.[16]

Administration for women, then, was apparently a matter of personal preferences. While men nominated their executors more or less according to stereotype, women acted according to their own lights. In the process, they defied the masculine equation of wealth and youth with female passivity.[17] In time, their example may have had some influence on the men, for after 1830, some of the wealthier men who left wills began to nominate their wives as their sole executors, and more of the poorer men excluded their wives altogether. The implication is that for the first time, some of the men may have begun to ask their wives what they wanted to do. As for the women, the records unhappily do not permit any assessment of the nature or degree of change.

The pursuits of those who served as executors and administrators were closely regulated by law. These were positions of trust, and they did require managerial skill, but they did not generally license either women or men to do as they wished with the property for which they were responsible. The woman who was eligible to act as an executor or administrator was, however, equally eligible to operate on her own account—to buy and sell property and to extend credit and contract debts. While the majority of deals made by women (and by men) were not of the kind to be publicly recorded—real estate rentals, slave hires and purchases, and small loans only rarely surfaced in the record books—all sales and long-term leases of real property and a good many large loans were recorded. The recorded conveyances were highly conventionalized and uncommonly arid. Sort them out and add them up, however, and they do tell something of a story: In Petersburg, the women who had legal options tended to play it safe.

The most striking feature of the real estate bargains struck by Petersburg's women was the near absence of speculation. Jane C. Oliver was the exception who illuminated the rule; Oliver's splash in real estate development showed how much a woman could undertake. In the 1850s, southern cities were booming, and as Petersburg's newspapers took pains to point out, one of the side effects was a sudden shortage of housing. Jane C. Oliver, a well-to-do widow, was one of those who heard opportunity knocking. In 1854, 1855, and 1856, she purchased fourteen lots and set builders to work. This she did mainly on credit. She borrowed from all of Petersburg's new building and loan associations, she bought on time, and she promised to pay her workmen after their jobs were complete. It was a poor gamble. The new houses apparently did not sell quickly enough, and early in 1856, Oliver was sued from every direction. In March, she mortgaged everything she had to cover the judgments, and in subsequent months, she saw her lots, her plantation, and seven of her slaves sold to satisfy her creditors. Only her dower slaves—slaves in whom she had only a life estate—were spared.[18]

In fact, it may have been Jane Oliver's son who masterminded this whole dismal enterprise. Oliver had given her son a power of attorney—authorization, in other words, to transact business in her name—and many of her transactions were made under his signature.[19] Whatever the nature of her involvement, Jane Oliver's venture of 1854–56 was as close as any Petersburg woman came to speculation in high nineteenth-century style. For women as a group, the watchword was caution. They invested in land, but as the deeds show, they tended to hang on to it.

The eagerness of Petersburg's women to acquire and hold

real property was manifested in the fact that they did a great deal more buying than they did selling. From 1784 to 1860, women made only 209 real estate sales (in a third of these sales, the property had been acquired by inheritance). In the same period, women made 467 real estate purchases. [20] When we plot what the women then did with the property they purchased, the character of their financial conservatism becomes a little clearer. Women were cautious in part because their means were generally modest and their margin of error slim; the typical female real estate purchaser could afford only one property, a home for herself, one guesses, or, in some cases, a shop or rental property. Once she had made her purchase, chances were only one in three that she would ever sell. Most commonly, she kept the property intact for her heirs. When she did sell it was not always willingly. About a seventh of the women who sold out did so either because they could not make the payments, or because they had put up their real estate as collateral for other debts they could not pay. [21]

With credit, too, the women's approach tended to be conservative. The debts recorded in the deed books were secured debts. That is, the debtor conveyed the technical ownership of property to a trustee (the conveyance was thus called a deed of trust). If the debtor failed to pay the creditor on schedule, then the trustee was obliged to sell the property and pay the creditor whatever was due, returning any surplus to the debtor. From all appearances, the women of Petersburg did their best to avoid indebtedness altogether. Relatively few deeds of trust were executed by women; a woman was much more likely to purchase real estate at some time in her life than she was to enter into a deed of trust for any purpose. [22] The women who did borrow did so for a variety of causes. One of them needed bail money, another owed back rent, a third was in debt for slave hire, and a fourth was buying her slave husband on time. A few women secured loans to start new businesses or to keep foundering businesses from going under. Meanwhile, the majority of deeds did not say what the loans were for. Worth noting, however, is the fact that the largest identifiable group of loans—over 20 percent of the total—were obtained for the sake of buying real estate.

Women's roles as creditors are more difficult to read. The whole point of a deed of trust was to protect the interests of the creditor (the trustee, who did the dirty work if the debtor failed to pay on time, was often a near relative of the creditor). The behavior of the creditors who appear in the deeds of trust was therefore conservative by definition, and it should come as no surprise that there were more female creditors than debtors named in Petersburg's deeds of trust.[23] The creditors divided into two groups. First were those women who became creditors in the normal course of business. Elizabeth Taylor, for example, was a single woman who rented housing to tenants. One of her tenants, Joseph Council, had not been able to pay all the rent due for 1827, and as the new year opened, Council wrote out a deed of trust, leaving in the detail that lawyers tended to leave out.

> I being in loe health, and have a wife with but one hand, I leave you to judg that we must live some where as such I field a dispisition to secure Miss Taylor in the first step with what little property I now possess or what I might accumilate while I am on her Lot. Viz. One Sorrel Mare, Bridle and Saddle, Chart and whels, together with the household furniture of every sort or Kind.

One wonders whether Taylor held him to it. Other women became creditors in the course of hiring out their slaves, and women who ran businesses routinely extended credit to their customers. In 1855, for example, William F. Allen conveyed to a trustee his schooner *Cleopatra;* his purpose was to secure a debt due grocer Jane Perry "for provisions furnished him for said Schooner & hand hire paid for by her for him." Jane Perry did hold Allen to it. Thirty days passed with no repayment, and the *Cleopatra* was sold.[24]

The other principal class of female creditors was made

up of women with some capital who loaned money to others or who provided backing so that others could borrow from some third party. In a number of cases, the women were closely related to the borrowers. Most often these creditors were mothers, but there were also mothers-in-law, sisters, and aunts, and we are left to wonder which of the loans were acts of charity and which were investments for profit. John E. Riviere's confection and "segar" store had already failed at least once when his mother-in-law came through with a loan to allow him to begin again. John G. Orgain borrowed three hundred dollars from his mother to advance his gas pipe–fitting business. Thomas Shore, Mary Bolling's least-favored grandson, was more than three thousand dollars in debt to his mother.[25] It has long been observed by students of the American economy that women were an important source of reserve labor. If the deeds of Petersburg are any indication, women were also an important source of capital.

Meanwhile, the plainest fact about women creditors is that as time passed there were more of them. In the more than twenty-five years from 1784 to 1810, only one woman was named as a creditor in Petersburg's deeds of trust. By the 1840s and 1850s, an average of ninety women were named in each decade.

This leads to an essential point: Caution and passivity are not the same thing, and while Petersburg's women tended toward the conservative in their financial dealings, they appear to have become increasingly active in the acquisition and disposition of property. Table 5.1 shows the growth of women's participation in real estate and credit transactions. The significance of this growth would be clearer if we knew, for each period, what proportion of Petersburg's women had the legal capacity to make property transactions. We do know that after 1830 there was a marked increase in the numbers of women who were able to buy more than one parcel of real estate. Most of these women bought two properties, but a few bought as many as eight or ten or (enter Jane C. Oliver) fourteen. By 1860,

Table 5.1
WOMEN'S PARTICIPATION IN REAL ESTATE AND CREDIT
TRANSACTIONS, 1784–1860

	Real estate sales by women	Real estate purchases by women	Female debtors	Female creditors
1784–1800	7	18	3	0
1801–10	6	12	2	1
1811–20	20	28	10	13
1821–30	18	34	27	43
1831–40	30	70	28	44
1841–50	45	116	46	99
1851–60	83	189	61	81

28.7 percent of Petersburg's real estate owners were women. In 1820, the proportion had been 14 percent; in 1790, only 8.4 percent.[26]

The most dramatic upsurge in women's economic activity, meanwhile, was in the writing of wills. Here the numbers are startling. In the early going, women hardly ever left wills. From 1784 to 1800, only 7.1 percent (5 / 70) of the wills recorded in Petersburg had been written by women. In the first decade of the new century, women's wills appeared more frequently, and there was another spurt in the 1830s. By the 1840s, the activism of the women was nothing less than phenomenal. From 1841 to 1860, 44.4 percent of the wills recorded in Petersburg (99 / 223) were the work of women.

Once again, caution was not the same thing as passivity. With the writing of wills, women were, relatively speaking, more active than were men. The same was true of deeds of gift; all along, about 40 percent of Petersburg's deeds of gift (77 / 192) were executed by women.[27] Exploring why women were so active in the writing of wills and deeds of gift is in part a study of the peculiar legal constraints that bore on women. It is also, and more significantly, a study in values.

To understand why women wrote so many of the recorded deeds of gift, it helps to understand that a deed of gift could serve a variety of purposes. Some deeds of gift represented genuine acts of generosity, others were social security arrangements for the givers, and still others were substitutes for wills. And there were always the swindlers. In 1798, Moses Jeffreys made a deed of gift to his daughter-in-law Elizabeth, conveying to her his household furnishings and all his other movable property. Several years later, Jeffreys revealed his motive: " . . . a certain execution [was] issued against me for a debt, which I was not able to pay without entire ruin, and to avoid which I conveyed said property to my daughter-in-law; and without any consideration only as above." Jeffreys assumed that as soon as he got straight with his creditors, Elizabeth would reconvey the property to him. Bamboozled. Elizabeth not only refused, but by 1805 was remarried and to a man who, not surprisingly, supported her in her determination to maintain possession of the gift. Jeffreys vowed to fight their claim in court, but as he did not have a prayer at law, he probably derived his only satisfaction from taking out a newspaper ad to denounce the woman who "proved unworthy of my confidence. . . ."[28] It did not seem to trouble him that he might damage his own reputation in the process.

Jeffreys's moment of candor was unique in the annals of Petersburg. Fast moves were generally kept out of sight, and we can only guess at the frequency of attempted debt evasion through deeds of gift. Persons who merely wanted some security in their old age, meanwhile, had nothing to hide. About a tenth of the women who executed deeds of gift (8/77) and a smaller proportion of the men (3/115) were trading property for promises that they would be supported for the rest of their lives. Atty Ann Livesay exacted the most explicit commitment. In exchange for her two town lots, her son-in-law promised to "furnish her as long as she lives, with board and lodging, fuel, lights, washing, wearing apparel, medicines and medical attendance, and all other things and services which may be necessary & proper for the maintenance and comfort of an old lady in her position in society."[29] In a town that guaranteed its elderly nothing better than a berth in the poorhouse, a deed of gift, with strings, was one defense against a degraded old age.

A deed of gift could also serve as a substitute for a will. In several cases (7 / 77), the woman who bestowed the gift stipulated that the property was not to change hands until her death. For men, too, the deed of gift sometimes functioned as a will; in the spring of 1817, for example, Clotworthy Barber deeded all his household and kitchen goods to a relative to hold for his young son and daughter. Barber was dead before the summer was out.[30] While for men the incentive was the death of the body, women had civil death to contend with as well, and this was an important spur to the writing of deeds of gift. At least eight of the women who executed deeds of gift in Petersburg did so just prior to marrying. Nancy Curtis knew that her children stood in no immediate need of any gifts from her. Joanna was fifteen and Austin only eleven, neither of them about to establish households of their own. But she also knew that if she did not act quickly, she might never have the chance to give them anything. In December 1814, she deeded to each of her children a cow, a bed, and some other furniture, and to Joanna she gave her loom and spinning wheel as well. Two days later she married Jacob Brander and in one stroke lost her legal capacity to control property.[31]

Thus were women who were still in the prime of life prompted to make early settlements on their heirs. These legal constraints bore on women only, of course, and this helps account for the high proportion of women among the persons who executed deeds of gift. Legal constraints alone, however, cannot provide the whole explanation. The deeds of gift suggest, albeit faintly, real differences of attitude. They suggest that it was easier for women than it was for men to part with property, especially when economic security was pledged in return. They suggest that it was easier for women to anticipate and plan for death. But before this speculation proceeds further, it would be well to bring out the richer evidence of the wills.

In the 1840s and 1850s, nearly half of the wills recorded in Petersburg were written by women. This is an amazing proportion considering the obstacles: Most married women had no legal capacity to write wills; the women who had the legal capacity were less likely than were men to own property; the women who had the capacity and who did own property very often possessed only life estates (they could thus use the property but not will it). The conclusion is inescapable. Propertied women who had the legal capacity were more likely than were propertied men to dispose of their assets by will—actively, that is, and with deliberation.

Specific figures on intestacy (dying without a will) strengthen the case. During the period 1831 to 1860, nearly two-thirds of the propertied men who died in Petersburg (324 / 495 = 65.5 percent) died intestate. Among the women, the intestacy rate was substantially lower. Of those women who died with property and with the legal capacity to write a will, fewer than half (106 / 222 = 47.8 percent) died intestate.[32] It might be objected that gender was of no real significance here, that the operative factors were age and wealth; it stands to reason that those who die young and those who die relatively poor are less likely to leave wills than the old and wealthy. In fact, age and wealth did matter. But so did gender. As Table 5.2 shows, in every age category and in every category of wealth, women were more likely to leave wills than were men.

It seems odd on the face of it that women had the greater propensity to write wills, especially given their lesser experience with financial transactions. A plausible explanation, or set of explanations, lies in values—in attitudes toward death, wealth, family, and slavery.

To make a will was to acknowledge the inevitability of one's own death, and this may have been more difficult for men than for women. Daniel Anderson was well on in years when he suffered a stroke in 1806. The stroke left him half paralyzed, but Anderson would not write his will.

Table 5.2
INTESTACY, AGE, AND WEALTH, 1831–60

	Men dying intestate		Women dying intestate	
	#	%	#	%
Age 21–40	51 / 76	67.1	9 / 20	45.0
41–60	71 / 107	66.4	17 / 38	44.7
61 and older	27 / 56	48.2	16 / 49	32.7
Bond $2,000 or less	158 / 186	84.9	63 / 96	65.6
$2,100–$9,000	60 / 84	71.4	28 / 44	63.6
$10,000 or more	60 / 131	45.8	9 / 36	25.0

Anxious relatives tiptoed about him, at last deputing his best friend to impress on him the urgency of his case. Anderson, however, "did not wish to have any thing to say on the Subject.—His only answer . . . was – 'That he expected to get well in a short time, & then he would think of it.' " Continued prodding only caused him to dig in his heels. It was not until he had lived out three full years as an invalid that Anderson became resigned and produced a will.[33] It may have been that women, who looked at death with every pregnancy and who were more likely to be deeply religious, had less trouble making preparations for their dying.

To make a will was also to come to terms with one's financial standing. For men who had not done well—and in the nineteenth century it was easy to do badly—this was painful. There must have been many men who intended to make wills, but who died intestate nevertheless as they waited for the better day that never came. For women, on the other hand, wealth was a less important measure of one's worth as a human being; relative poverty was less likely to prove an obstacle to writing a will. Ann Peebles was an extreme case. Despite the fact that she owned next to nothing, Peebles did make a will. Her only legatees were the two women who were seeing her through her last illness. To her nurse, she left a dollar a day, and to her landlady, she left fifteen dollars "for her bed being so much damaged. . . ." That was all. Other women handed out their rather puny legacies with a good deal of relish. "I have nothing of consequence sufficient to make it necessary to write a will," Ann Birchett began, but she wrote one anyway, making very particular bequests to her nearest kin. To her son George, she gave her wedding ring and a fruit knife; to her daughter Jane, she gave one share of bank stock, a miniature portrait, and her white counterpane; and to her sister, she gave a cloak, a shawl, and some caps; and so it went.[34]

The care with which Ann Birchett selected particular items for particular persons suggests a third and probably the most important reason why women were more likely than were men to write wills. That is, women were more likely to be dissatisfied with what would be done with their property if they died intestate and left their estates to be distributed according to law. The central principle of Virginia probate law was equality. When a parent died intestate, the law saw to it that every child, male and female, received an equal share of the estate. This was perhaps laudable democracy, but most of the women had other ideas. While most of the men who left wills went along with the law, dividing their property equally among their children, women tended to play favorites. More precisely, of the 131 men who died in Petersburg leaving more than one child, 71 percent directed that all their children receive equal portions. Of the 43 women who left more than one child, only 16 (37.2 percent) called for an equal division. When there were both male and female children, the temptation to favoritism was greater, and here again the women more often filled their wills with discriminatory provisions. Among the men who left children of both sexes, 61.6 percent (53 / 86) still divided their property equally; those who favored one child over another usually favored sons. Among the women who left children of both sexes, only 26.7 percent (8 / 30) made equal divisions. The women, not surprisingly, ordinarily favored their daughters.[35]

Families are full of inequalities, inequalities of love and loyalty, inequalities of need. Women recognized this in the terms of their wills, and they were occasionally explicit about it. "I have not given any thing to my son Seth and daughter Susan purposely for reasons which they are apprized of"; "I do not wish for Henry Johnson'[s] child to have any posion of my estate being he is well enough off without my little estate"; "I hope my brother Robert and Sister Mary will not think that there is any want of affection on my part for them, I am only anxious to secure my little property to those of my family who need it most"; "I love all my children alike but my daughters I feel most attached to and think they ought to have what I own at my death, and therefore this disposition."[36]

While men for the most part distributed their property according to formula, women tended to pick and choose. There may have been an element of the power play in this; a propertied woman could keep her heirs on their good behavior for years, as long as she kept them guessing as to the terms of her last will. The women's wills were, in any case, highly personalized. They rewarded special qualities of loyalty and affection. They also funneled property into the hands of the heirs who needed it most, and here again the women's penchant for economic security was revealed. As the chapter on separate estates points out, women were more likely than were men to protect the legacies they gave their female heirs by making the legacies separate estates. (The desire to exempt bequests to married women from the control of husbands and husbands' creditors was in itself a major incentive for writing a will.) What is more, the women took the lead in a more novel procedure of establishing extra measures of economic security for sons. After 1820, there were ten wills that set up trusts for the benefit of adult sons. Eight of them were written by women.

Thus women had good reason to avoid intestacy: They wanted their property divided on the basis of personal merit and particular need, and they often wanted it conveyed on more protective terms than the ordinary course of probate law would permit. They also wanted, more often than did the men, special treatment for their slaves. "It is my first desire to make some comfortable provision for my servants as a just reward for their affection and fidelity."[37] So began the will that Dorothy Mitchell wrote in 1837, and as more women began to write wills, they left more evidence of a special relationship between southern white women and chattel slavery. It has been proposed by some observers that the white women of the South were covert abolitionists, or, at the least, that they lacked a full-scale commitment to the slave system.[38] The wills of Petersburg's white slaveholders, though their numbers are relatively small, give us a first opportunity to put this proposition to the test.

The results appear to be positive. First of all, more women than men used their wills to set slaves free. After 1840, twelve white women emancipated slaves by will; only eight white men did the same. (A much larger number of emancipations were performed by deed, and here, too, white women appear to have outdone the men in liberating slaves.)[39] Second, more women than men (again after 1840, eight women and five men) inserted clauses either to prevent their slaves from being moved or sold or to restrict the terms of sale. Lucy Frances Branch, a single woman of fifty, made herself very clear: "It is my express wish and desire to make such a disposition of my woman *Martha Graves* as to prevent her being removed farther from her mother and husband than she now lives." To that end, Branch stipulated that Graves was not to be moved or mortgaged, and that if a sale ever became unavoidable, Graves be permitted to choose her purchaser.[40]

Finally, women more often than men (twelve women, seven men) gave their slaves legacies, single cash payments in some cases, maintenance for life in others. For Mary Lithgow, the central clauses of her will, written more lovingly and in more detail than any of the provisions concerning her son and her grandchildren, were those written for the benefit of William Alexander, a seven-year-old boy whom she had recently freed. Lithgow directed that William be given fifty dollars a year until he turned twenty-one, that he receive five hundred dollars on his majority along with some furniture and traveling trunks, that he be put to a good trade, that he be educated in morals and religion, that he be allowed to stay in Virginia, and that, if this last request were impossible, he be placed with a gentleman of good standing in the North. Lithgow subsequently revised her will twice, and each revision brought a bonus for William Alexander. The first allotted the three hundred dollars Lithgow had stashed in her savings account to William's "plain education, so as to fit him for business." The second authorized him to buy members of his family, and at a fair price.[41]

So far as the wills let us judge, white women were kinder to their slaves than were men, and the women were more likely to set their slaves free. But was this a quiet form of abolitionism? Was it an implicit critique of the slave system?

The best answer seems to be that white women were in fact a subversive influence on chattel slavery, not so much because they opposed slavery as a system (the abstract merits of systems did not concern them much), but because they operated out of an essentially personal frame of reference. The women who wrote special provisions for their slaves into their wills worked from the same mentality that caused women as a group to divide property unevenly among their heirs: Women indulged particular attachments—they were alert to the special case, to the personal exception.

White women's thinking about slavery was almost always grounded in the particulars of day-to-day human interaction. Their letters and diaries, at least those that survive from Petersburg, said next to nothing about slavery as an institution. Instead, they spoke of individual slaves, as personalities and especially as workers. This is not to say they were above condescension and stereotyping. Kate Spaulding missed her family in Petersburg terribly, the more so as the rift between North and South widened. On Christmas Day 1860, she wrote from her new home in

New York, sending holiday greetings to "the dear darkies! If they *have* been the cause of so much fuss, they are dear to me as house-hold things!" Most often, however, women's comments on slaves were reports on the status of the household labor force—who performed which tasks and how well. Mary Cumming described her retinue to her Irish sister in 1811:

> And now to give a description of a large family in the kitchen. First there is old Nancy the cook, who is an excellent good one, Jennie the housemaid, who seems to be a very decent woman. She has four fine children, the eldest a girl about twelve years old, who is to be my little attendant, her name is Mary. Then there is Betty, Cora, and Joseph. They can all do something, Mary is a pretty good worker at her needle, she is now sitting beside me making a slip for herself. I think I shall make her very useful to me in some time. The man's name who attends at table is Palermo. This is an account of our family, the servants appear to be all regular and well behaved.

More than forty years later, Anna Campbell outlined the work of fourteen-year-old Lavinia and nine-year-old Solomon:

> . . . the former being a mulatto, is quite smart & really does a woman's work, helps me much with the children, occasionally sews a little. the latter runs errands blacks shoes cleans knives & forks, occasionally spills a bucket of water on the stairs, drops a tray full of dishes or a part of the dinner or breakfast as the case may be, but upon the whole is a good boy & rightly named, has only been caught stealing once. . . .

The mistresses were not always so well satisfied, of course. "We have engaged a woman for next year whose *appearance* is not very prepossessing," wrote Eliza K. Myers, "but I dare say she may suit us quite as well & I hope better than the last *incumbent*—or *incumbrance* whichever you please."[42] But the point is, while the mistresses' feelings ran the gamut from an almost comradely affection to extreme exasperation, they remained focused on individual slaves.

Consider by contrast the diary of Edmund Ruffin. Slaves must have been a constant presence in Ruffin's days, yanking off his boots, one imagines, stirring up his woodstove, serving his suppers. But Ruffin never talked about them. And this was not because he was writing an essentially public diary. Ruffin wrote pages on his aches and pains, on his flirtations with little children, on his leisure reading (which included a fair number of sentimental novels). He also wrote about the pamphlets he was composing to try to persuade his countrymen that western civilization owed its greatest achievements to chattel slavery.[43] Ruffin is remembered now as a major proslavery apologist. His refusal to acknowledge the living presence of particular slaves undoubtedly helped him to keep his theory clean.

Of all the Petersburg women who left some record, none gave any indication that she regarded slavery as a positive good. The closest any Petersburg woman came to an endorsement of slavery was a letter written by Ann T. Davis in 1859, after John Brown's raid had made it look as though the abolitionists were prepared to enflame the South in insurrection and war. Davis feared her sons would be marched off to fight; she prayed for the destruction of abolitionism, and, in a uniquely general statement, repeated the rather old-fashioned creed of the colonizationists:

> My trust is in God, who knows the great heart of the South, and who sees that they are doing all that they can do, for the comfort, and happiness of the slaves, providentially committed to their care. I, for one, would gladly hail the day, when every son and daughter of degraded Ham, were free and independent, in some country of their own, but until that can be peacefully effected, I believe that they had better remain in bondage under the care of good masters, than be free in the United States.[44]

This was faint praise. It may have been that women's propensity to look at life in personal terms prevented their becoming wholehearted defenders of the slave system; the auction block and the separation of families were too appallingly commonplace. At the same time, the personal approach—thinking about the immediate needs and talents and sins of particular slaves—must have helped white women get along day by day with an institution they believed to be evil in at least some respects. The alternative was not thinking. English immigrant Mary L. Simpson said it in 1821, after witnessing her first Christmas rush of slave hirings and auctions: "Now dont you often wonder how I can live contented and happy in such a quarter of the world? Why I assure you it is only when I leave out of the question or rather forget all these things." Then she added, "But a truce to *treason*."[45]

Mary L. Simpson made some sort of peace with slavery and in so doing became an accomplice to it. So did almost all white women of the slaveholding classes. But theirs was an unsteady complicity, for there was in women's willingness to make the personal exception a quality of sabotage. The will of Mary Lithgow was a case in point. Almost all of Lithgow's property was in her seven slaves, and she had her own family to consider. She had a son, and he had a wife, children, and chronic financial problems. So six of Lithgow's slaves were to remain in bondage. Three of them she had placed in trust, the income to be applied to the support of her son's family. Three of them she ordered sold, though not to slavetraders. The seventh was the boy William Alexander, to whom she granted freedom, property, and education. Mary Lithgow was no abolitionist. On the other hand, it was widely believed that free black people undermined the slave system by their very existence. Mary Lithgow could hardly have been unaware of this.

It is worth pausing to appreciate the importance of the deeds and wills for the recovery of values. It seems logical enough that a set of distinctive values should have grown out of women's distinctive experiences, out of their experience with nurture, with personal service, and with the maintenance of life day by day. But it is difficult to describe those values with any precision, and it is equally difficult to discern when and how much they informed women's behavior in activities other than marriage and mothering. We know, for example, that in Petersburg and elsewhere, women took the lead in religion and organized charity; this story will be taken up in Chapter 7. But it is hard to say how much this activity was an expression of female values, and how much it merely reflected the fact that women were allowed to do church and charity work while they were not allowed to enter formal politics, the professions, big business, or the military. There were not many occasions in the nineteenth century when women exercised something approximating free choice. There were even fewer occasions when women's choices were systematically recorded and rendered comparable to the choices made by men.

This is what makes the deeds and wills so special, and here, in one list, are the documentable components of a women's value system. Women, more than men, noticed and responded to the needs and merits of particular persons. This showed in their tendency to reward favorite slaves and to distribute their property unevenly among their heirs. It also showed in their ability to make independent judgments about their own fitness to administer estates. Women were particularly sensitive to the interests of other women and to their precarious economic position; this was demonstrated in favoritism toward female heirs and in the establishment of separate estates. As their real estate and credit transactions suggest, women wanted financial security for themselves as well as for others. Beyond that they were not as ego-invested as were men in the control of wealth. Our list grows a bit longer if we add the more ambiguous evidence derived from women's vanguard action in providing relief to the poor and in promoting religion. Women as a group were more invested than were men in Christian communities and the life of the spirit. And in their efforts to give assistance to the poor, both personalism and regard for other women surfaced again;

the poor were mainly women and children, most of whom cannot have "deserved" their poverty.

The people who wrote the antebellum period's popular literature have been trying to tell us all along that women were different from men, better than men in some respects. Perhaps it is time we took their message more seriously. The Petersburg evidence does help explain why the nineteenth century's theory of gender differences was so long-lived and so powerful: The cult of true womanhood owed its pervasiveness to the fact that it was in some fundamental way plausible. That portion of the cult that addressed spheres of activity always generated a certain amount of controversy and was always subject to additions and corrections, for in the real world the limits of acceptable female activity were in constant flux. But the portion of the cult that dealt with character was obdurately uncontroversial. By the end of the century, even woman suffragists fell into line, insisting along with everyone else that human kindness, moral virtue, and religious devotion were the distinguishing traits of the female character.[46]

And so they were. If Petersburg is any indication, the cult of true womanhood carried the day in part because some of its claims conformed closely to observed female behavior. This is not to say that the women of Petersburg were true women down the line. In the literature of true womanhood, the focus was on relationships between women and their men, and women were told that they owed their husbands, even cruel husbands, uncomplaining obedience. Real-life women of Petersburg, however, were deeply engaged in the lives of other females, as well as males, and as they demonstrated in the granting of separate estates, they were quite willing to undercut male authority when the welfare of a beloved kinswoman was at stake. Otherwise, purveyors of the cult of true womanhood would have found in the behavior of Petersburg's women a lot to like. Women *were* first in piety and benevolence, including, it appears, benevolence toward slaves—a dimension of true womanhood peculiar to the South—just as the popular literature claimed.

If we take gender differences as seriously as the nine-teenth century did, the implications for the way we look at history are enormous. Most existing scholarship implicitly takes men as the measure. That is, events and ideas are evaluated on the basis of how much they helped women achieve what men already had. This is obviously an essential line of inquiry. But it needs to be balanced with the recognition that women had standards of their own. One of the cult of true womanhood's many messages—and this is the one worth saving in our own time—is that there were two standards, two scales of achievement, two sets of values. In the antebellum period, of course, it could not be admitted that the values of women might be subversive; writers brightly insisted that the respective roles of men and women were harmonious and complementary. Whether we are dealing with harmony or subversion, the issue needs to be explored for as many times and as many places as the sources permit.[47] The Petersburg evidence suggests that it is possible to reconstruct female values in considerable detail. This is precisely what we need to take us beyond compensatory women's history, beyond the weary and ultimately impoverishing process of testing how women measured up on a masculine scale. The past, as a result, is going to look different—richer, more complex, probably more embattled.

For the future, emphasis on gender differences has great promise and great strategic risks. The risks derive from the difficulty we have in thinking in genuinely egalitarian terms; "different" is readily translated into "inferior," and thus is discrimination justified. The promise lies farther off. If we find that all along women have managed to create and sustain countercultures, then the chances increase that as women come to power, a more humane social order will indeed come with them. This is a hopeful vision, but not necessarily a utopian one; we may be talking about the realm of the small improvement.

That returns us to Petersburg and to the concrete terms that Petersburg's women found most congenial. The immediate significance of the women's value system was that some slaves were freed, some orphans were fed, and some daughters were protected from economic exploitation. That was not so very little.

6

Women Working

Willy Whitlow—"Miss Willy," as everyone called her—
was a familiar sight in the town, darting from house to
house, full of gossip, swinging her sewing bag before her
with unfailing exuberance. She was the dressmaker—poor,
overworked, plain, without family. She had her fleeting
moments of self-pity, a little pang of jealousy now and
again when she stitched a party dress for a young beauty
like Virginia Pendleton, but she always emerged as chip-
per as ever. Virginia, for her part, did not know what to
make of Miss Willy, could not fathom the source of her
vitality, her uncanny happiness. In time, Virginia herself
reached middle age, and it was then that she began to
understand (as well as she understood anything, for she
had not been raised to reason): " 'I used to pity Miss Willy
because she was obliged to work,' she thought with surprise, 'but now I almost envy her. I wonder if it is work
that keeps her so young and brisk? She's never had anything in her life, and yet she is so much happier than some
people who have had everything.' " Virginia's insight did
not change anything. Miss Willy, now elderly, went on as
before, cheerfully saving up for her tombstone. Virginia
slid further into despairing nothingness, deserted by a hus-

band who had long ago lost interest in her, paralyzed by the knowledge that her grown children no longer needed her. She had "outlived her usefulness."

Miss Willy and Virginia were women of the fictionalized Petersburg that was the setting for Ellen Glasgow's 1913 novel *Virginia*.[1] With the rebirth of feminism, Miss Willy is having her day (as is Ellen Glasgow). Contempt for the work of housewives has become more pronounced than ever as salaried work has become an increasingly powerful symbol of women's emancipation. That makes it all the more difficult for us to grasp the seriousness with which the nineteenth century took women's unpaid labor in the home. *Virginia* could not have been written a century or even a half century earlier. In the middle of the nineteenth century, the story would have to have taken a different turn. Virginia would have glowed with the gratitude of lovingly raised children, and if her husband insisted on leaving her, she would have scored a moral victory and rested in the assurance of some heavenly reward. Miss Willy, meanwhile, would have been the object of pity, or perhaps comedy. In the antebellum period, the angels, or at any rate the didactic writers, were on the side of domesticity.

Understanding the nineteenth century's obsession with domesticity is no easy task, but a look at the character of the work available to women helps explain why women themselves might have put more stock in housework and child care and less in gainful employment. Housework could be frustrating and exhausting, but because it was still productive and not yet divorced from money, it was not as difficult as it has since become for women to believe that their work was important. Besides, gainful employment hardly presented an appealing alternative. Women's occupational options were few. The pay was paltry. Women were not generally allowed to work in the same jobs as men; white women generally did not work in the same jobs as free black women. Feminists in our own time try to combat the trivialization of housewifery, insisting that housework and child care are critically important forms of work, and they point out that for most women, participation in the paid labor force is a less than liberating phenomenon. Our society still resists these truths. In the nineteenth century, they were easier to believe.

Still, it is by no means a settled conclusion that women themselves "chose" domesticity over gainful employment or that women sought paid work only when driven to it by the threat of destitution. Petersburg's free black women entered the paid labor force in large enough numbers to suggest that many of them subscribed to some sort of positive paid-work ethic. Among white women, meanwhile, there was a small group of successful businesswomen who stayed on the job even though they had children and were married to responsible providers. When paid work proved sufficiently rewarding, women sought it out and stayed with it.

The first point about women's work in the home is simple, and it has been made before, but it will probably have to be made again and again: Housewives in the nineteenth century performed immense quantities of essential labor. This was as true in the slave South as it was in the North. As Anne Firor Scott has made plain, leisure was not the lot of the typical southern lady; the slave system in fact ensured that most plantation mistresses would work and work hard.[2] The evidence from Petersburg suggests that for city women, too, hard work was the normal experience.

The second point about women's work in the home is that it was still overtly productive. Well into the nineteenth century, even in the towns, women still produced the most basic of goods; they grew and processed food, and they made clothing. This brings us to the question of how productive labor affected the status of women; we are back to the thesis of decline. When scholars first constructed an interpretation of long-term change in the status of American women, productivity was a major theme. Because the economy of colonial America was a domestic economy—most essential goods were produced at home—

women were engaged in the mainstream of economic production. The pivotal assumption here was that participation in productive labor conferred on women relatively high status. After the colonial period, therefore, women had nowhere to go but down. In the nineteenth century, production began to move out of the home, women were increasingly left with mere service functions, and the alleged result was a severe loss of status.[3]

Challengers of the thesis of decline have already pointed out that there was no necessary connection between productive labor and high status; slaves, to name the most obvious example, hardly achieved prestige or power as a result of their roles as productive workers.[4] The Petersburg evidence, meanwhile, suggests that the debate over production and status needs to be refined in at least three ways. First, the removal of production from the home has to be understood as a gradual process; whatever the effect of the loss of productive labor on women's status, it did not happen all at once.[5] Second, class distinctions were important. The women who benefited most from the continuation of production in the home were the women of the elite, women who had substantial amounts of slave help. (Because the analysis that follows is taken largely from letters and diaries, it concentrates on elite women to an unfortunate degree.) For women who had little or no slave help, the benefits of productive labor were probably outweighed by the burdens. Third, we need to be very explicit about what kinds of benefits productive labor entailed. Petersburg provides no evidence that women's productive work in the home gained them either respect or power. What it could gain them was a certain measure of self-respect. Petersburg's women seem to have believed that their work mattered, and that goes some way toward explaining why so few of them questioned their role.

Mary L. Simpson said it well in 1821: Housekeeping in Petersburg, she wrote, was "a sort of half farming life." Advertisements for some of the town's most desirable residences underscored the point. When Mary Read Anderson decided to sell her Petersburg "establishment" in 1817, she advertised not only the house itself, but a cowbarn, dairy, wine vault, icehouse, smokehouse, greenhouse, garden, and orchard as well. And E. C. Baxter said it again in 1858. Baxter wanted to get away from Petersburg for a time, "but the chickins and the milk and butter [and] the old man I dont no witch is the worst to leave."[6] Virginians who could afford the space, in other words, brought the plantation to town. There was thus a certain barnyard ambiance to city living, and this was something the people of Petersburg took for granted. The mooing and clucking, the smells of manure and straw, seemed such natural qualities of the urban atmosphere that the women who wrote letters never described them. But they did write about the work. As long as life in the city remained a "half farming life," women remained engaged in the production of food, and for some this was a source of considerable satisfaction.

Petersburg women wrote with special fondness and verve about their gardens. Mary Cumming fixed her ambition almost as soon as she stepped off the boat from Ireland in 1811. "I mean to turn gardener," she announced, and when spring came she filled her letters home with reports on the status of her young vegetables. "Do you know I have become a great gardener of late? I have got a variety of seeds sown long since, and a great many are coming up. My peas will be ready for rodding in a day or two, my cabbages are doing very well, and this week I intend getting my melons and cucumbers sown in a large square." In the beginning, Mary Cumming walked a half mile each way to her garden plot, and she did most of the work herself. This changed after her first harvest, however; her baby daughter died, her health failed her, and she sometimes went for months too weak and too depressed even to write home. She did return to her garden, though, expanded her acreage, hired a gardener, and turned entrepreneur: ". . . I hope to make a great deal of money by the produce of our garden, for we cannot use one quarter of the vegetables and fruit which we raise, so that we send a quantity to market every morning. I generally receive from three shillings to four-and-six a day, which is my money.

When Mrs. Bell lived here she once told me she made forty dollars by her asparagus alone."[7]

Mrs. Bell's asparagus was a telling commodity. No doctrine of proper spheres prevented women—even upper-middle-class women—from turning their domestic pursuits into profit-making pursuits in the local market. As Mary Cumming told it, "Almost everyone who has a garden raises vegetables for market and some make very large sums of money." And no code of gentility prevented the same women from engaging in physical labor. Mistresses did at times put slaves to work in their gardens, but the mistresses themselves planted and picked and weeded, too. In May 1857, Lizzie Partin assessed the state of her garden: "Nothing extra," she called it, "but very good considering the force to attend to it"—herself, that is, and one woman slave. Mildred W. Campbell's enthusiastic gardening had earned her some strained muscles (she was seventy years old and had been cutting down trees), so she hired a man to spend half a day spading up ground. But she still thought that she and her elderly woman slave Charlotte together could do all the planting. In physical exertion, it seems, was much of the pleasure. More than any other household task, gardening brought women some peace.[8]

Life on the urban farm included livestock, too—dairy cows mainly, and poultry. Alas for the chickens, poultry did not inspire much devotion or commentary from Petersburg's letter-writing women. Anne Dade Bolling did, in 1840, instruct her son to look after her "poor birds," but the main evidence for there having been numerous chickens in the backyards of Petersburg comes from newspapers of 1859, which reported a wave of henhouse raids in all parts of town.[9] Cows, on the other hand, came in for considerable discussion. "There is scarcely a family in the place that does not keep a Cow," Mary Simpson reported in 1821. Mary Cumming kept at least one cow. So did Mary Read Anderson, and when she prepared to move to North Carolina in 1817, she let her needs be known: "Has any good body looked out a Cow or two for me," she asked, "it is half my living & I will be lost without a dairy." Eliza K. Myers had grown up with a cow on the place, but had managed to avoid learning how to take care of one. In 1836, however, mistress of her own household and mother of a young child, she arranged to buy a cow from the neighbors and wrote to her own mother for some "cow *larning* . . . I should be glad of a few hints from you, my dear Mrs. Mordecai, for you know your children always say you make better butter than any body else."[10] Through the 1850s, newspapers routinely carried advertisements of cows strayed, cows taken up, and cows for sale ("raised in the city").[11]

Just as urban women maintained a role in the production of food, they retained a major role in the production of clothing. This role did change over time. From the time of the Revolution to roughly 1820, town women as well as plantation women knew what it was to start from scratch. Spinning wheels and cards for cotton and wool appeared in estate inventories with sufficient frequency to suggest that processing the raw materials was common-place if never universal in urban households.[12] For a time, spinning took on new prestige, as domestic manufacturing became a weapon in the war for economic independence from Great Britain. At the local Fourth of July celebration of 1809, the obligatory toast to the ladies—this was ordi-narily proposed after a long series of toasts to the heroes of the Revolution, to the presidents, and to assorted republican principles—was not to the women's smiles, or even to their patriotism, but was instead to their work. "The fair daughters of Columbia—" the orator called out with whatever clarity he could summon (this was the sev-enteenth toast), "may their manufactures (if possible) exceed their beauty."[13]

In Petersburg, the production of yarn and cloth in households apparently fell off quickly after about 1820, when factory-produced textiles, some of them manufac-tured locally, became widely available. But there was still much to be done in order to transform bolts of cloth into usable goods, and here the efforts of women at home were critical. Sewing and mending were still done entirely by hand; sewing machines were not mass-marketed until the late 1850s, and the first evidence that anyone in Petersburg owned one comes from 1861.[14] That being the case, the women's inventories of work completed and work waiting to be done were all the more impressive. "I made four pairs of sheets and hemmed four pocket hkfs this last week, and have in prospectus six shirts to make for Sam and some night gowns for myself besides bolster cases, collars, and various odd jobs which will afford me a great deal of amusement for some time to come." "I have finished all Mr Ligons Shirts, and made me up a sett of night gowns underfrocks *pillow*-cases and am now making Shimmies. I had *Marie* to help me. . . . I made Jimmie four new Shirts and Mr Ligon 8, so they wont want any more shortly." "Worked hard & finished another shirt it being the tenth. have three more to make still."[15] When a woman referred to "my work," she meant her sewing.

There was plenty of other work, of course, but the women hardly ever wrote about it. It was productive labor, the growing of food and the making of clothing, that gave them the purest sense of accomplishment. What needs emphasis here is that this was very much a matter of class. The women who derived the greatest benefit from the continued productivity of the household were the women of the elite, women who could count on the labor of three or four healthy adult slaves. For the majority of housewives, women who had no slave help or very little, the satisfaction derived from productive tasks was offset, even cancelled, by the tremendous energy and time they exacted; too often all tasks melted into a blur of drudgery.

Statistics on slaveholding help us appreciate the ordinary housewife's dilemma, and they suggest that her dilemma—and the slave's burden—were growing worse. To begin, in a large proportion of households headed by white people there were no slaves at all. In 1810, 47 percent of white households (243 / 517) kept no slaves. By 1860, the proportion of white households keeping no slaves rose to well over half, 55.8 percent (1,062 / 1,905). Some of these families may have hired help from time to time (if money was available, it would go first for a washerwoman), but otherwise the wives were on their own. Secondly, among families who did keep slaves, there was a decline in the number of slaves working in each household. In 1810, half of the households keeping slaves (136 / 274) contained more than two slaves over the age of twelve. By 1860, only 36.7 percent (309 / 843) of slaveholding households contained more than two slaves over the age of twelve. The plurality of slaveholders in 1860 (41.5 percent) kept only one slave; 21.8 percent (184 / 843) kept two.[16]

If Anna Campbell's experience is any indication, one or two were simply not enough. Campbell's diary is our best record of the housewife's frustration and fatigue, and her story is the more poignant in that her marriage began as a life of leisure. It was to relieve her boredom, in fact, that her husband suggested that she chronicle an average day. "I am induced to write it out here on the spot," she began. Anna Campbell rose at seven "after due consideration & grave deliberation," washed, opened the windows, took in the April air, and said prayers. Then it was time for breakfast with her husband Charles (as they were boarders in her mother-in-law's home, Anna had nothing to do with the planning or preparation of meals), and afterward she sat with him while he read the paper. He went off to his schoolroom; she went up to their bedroom. Aunt Charlotte, a slave, had made a fresh fire. Anna herself dusted, tidied up, and made the bed—"sometimes for a change, I turn the bedstead around, (ie) put the head where the foot was & 'vice versa.' " That much accomplished, Anna sat down to read for half an hour, "to think over matters & things," and to wait for Charles, who sometimes popped in for a mid-morning hello: "By the way there has been a falling off of late in these ten o clock visits which I regret exceedingly, as any change, however slight, tends to mar the monotony of the even tenor of these days." Anna then dressed and went downstairs. After a while, she went back upstairs, took up some mending, read the paper perhaps, or wrote a letter. At noon, Charles popped in again to

announce he was going to the post office. Anna speculated
on getting mail. From one o'clock until three, Anna would
read, sew, or sleep. School was out at three, and shortly
after, the family sat down to dinner. Then it was time for
an after-dinner stroll. Anna and Charles walked down-
town together, stopping to chat with friends they met along
the way. At twilight, they returned home and sat together
until they were called to tea. "After this Charles *lounges*
upon the lounge & reads & I read, drum a little on the
Piano or sew until bed time or prayer time rather, after
that say good night . . . & ascend to our dormitory."[17]

This was leisure all right, a life that consisted mostly of
desultory reading and sewing and of waiting for Charles.
The point, however, is that it lasted only a few months.
Anna Campbell's life changed as soon as she gave birth to
her first child, and by the time she took up her diary again
(some three years after she described her typical day), the
pace of her days had changed utterly. To her cousin, she
wrote that she was merely busy. "I have been very constantly occupied during the time preserving fruit & vegetables for winter use, sewing, repairing old & making new
garments. . . ." To her diary, she confided that she was
almost desperately harried. Anna and Charles had set up
housekeeping for themselves four months earlier, "& so
far I cannot say much for it. . . . The school is flourishing
29 scholars. I assist every day. this, with taking care of my
children, house keeping & trying to keep things in something like order . . . stockings darned & a thousand things
too trifling to mention seems to fill up every moment but
I have not the satisfaction of feeling that any thing is well
done. why is this? . . . I am continually oppressed by a
feeling of *inability* to do what I ought to & a consciousness
of a great lack of system, so that the day is hurried through
& the close finds me tired in body & mind with no feeling
of satisfaction & the heart sickening prospect of days &
days still to come, fac similes of the one just gone—Why
is it," she asked again, ". . . all is confusion *all is wrong.*"
Not much had changed when Anna Campbell read over
her diary several years later. "More than three years ago I

wrote these bitter things against myself, & here again I am ready to repeat them with additional of the same nature." This time, however, her words conveyed less struggle. "I have no nurse now, & no one but Charlotte & Mary to do the work. the former is old & but poor dependance. things are badly done & the children take all my time & attention so that the housekeeping is not after a good or pleasant fashion."[18] Frustration, apparently, had become routine.

Ann T. Davis would have understood. Davis's children were nearly grown, and she had the help of several slaves. But as was often the case, she was burdened with the care of children not her own. Married to a minister and professor in one of the new female colleges of the 1850s, Davis's duties as a housewife had expanded to accommodate her husband's work. Not only was she in charge of student boarders, but she was also obliged to offer hospitality to a stream of ministerial visitors. "I am heartily tired of the bustle, and confusions, and constant, and heavy responsibility, of a school," she wrote her son in 1860. Although the demands on her were enough to wear out a much younger woman, Ann Davis regarded her unhappiness as a personal failing. "I know that while I ought to be the light and happiness of my home," she wrote in her diary, "from every surrounding circumstance, from every holy motive of gratitude, to God, and to the best of husbands, and loving, and dear children, yet to my shame be it written I am the cause of most of their trials. Disturbing them with my murmurs and complaints." She ended her lament, as women usually did, with a prayer for Christian resignation. "Help me I pray thee O God, to be a more faithful and happy christian mother, and wife. I am trying to be a christian, but am often faint. Strengthen then me."[19]

Anna Campbell and Ann T. Davis despaired, blamed themselves, and prayed for greater faith and strength. We are led to wonder how far they spoke for generations of housewives. It may have been that their dissatisfaction was mainly a result of their personal circumstances. Housework, after all, was largely personal service, and feelings about the work were very much entangled with feelings about the persons for whom the work was done. For Anna Campbell, whose marriage had become strained and at times riddled with conflict, the feeling that nothing was ever done properly must have been reinforced by the fact that no amount of domestic efficiency could win her any real appreciation from her husband. Ann T. Davis, meanwhile, carried special burdens as the wife of a minister. Still, there is cause to believe that the despair articulated by Campbell and Davis would have evoked ready and profound recognition from countless women.[20] Whatever their diverse personal circumstances, the majority of housewives faced the same set of problematic facts. First, maintaining a household in the antebellum period required an enormous amount of labor. Second, standards of housekeeping and child care were going up. Third, in most households there were not enough hands to meet those standards. For the overworked majority, the eventual removal of production from the home was probably an improvement if not quite a case of good riddance. Housewives sacrificed some of their most enjoyable work, but this was still progress in the battle against dumb exhaustion.

The continuation of production within the home was an unmixed blessing only for women of the elite, mistresses of at least three or four full-time house servants. In Petersburg, these women did not adopt an ethic of genteel inactivity; if there was any notion afoot that an idle wife conferred social prestige on her husband, the women themselves did not subscribe to it. The 1850s, in fact, brought opportunities to parade their achievements before the general public, and women of the elite took advantage of this. Each October, thousands of people crowded into Petersburg, jammed the hotels and houses of friends, and endured the dust in order to take in the sights and events of the agricultural fair. For the women, the main gathering place was the Department of Household and Domestic Manufactures. Here it was that women submitted and judged entries of food, needlework, crafts, and art. Among the exhibitors were dozens of women from Petersburg, and many of them belonged to the town's most prestigious families.[21]

Elite women did not generally withdraw from work. Instead, they used their resources to expand the productivity of their households—it took capital to obtain the space for a garden, after all—and they used the slave system to reserve for themselves the tasks that gave them the most satisfaction—productive tasks, child care, and work for church and charity. To the slaves was left the worst of the drudgery. No Petersburg person has left us a detailed account of how work was divided, but from scattered evidence it is clear that slaves relieved wealthy mistresses from most of the grubby, sooty, routine, and never-done aspects of housework.

Like any privileged group, the mistresses were only half aware of what they had until they lost it. For many, the Civil War was an education. Petersburg went under siege in June 1864, and by July, Margaret S. Beckwith and her family were driven out by the shelling. The Beckwiths' cook had been killed, but the other slaves stayed on, scrounged for food, and helped make do in the hardscrabble conditions of the failing Confederacy. When peace came, however, the Beckwith slaves set off to claim their freedom, and for the first time, the white Beckwith women were confronted with cooking and laundry. "We find the cooking easy enough, as there is very little to do," Margaret wrote in her journal, "but the washing is the rub. . . ." This, they discovered, was steamy, backbreaking work, and after two weeks of struggle, they contrived to send the wash out. But this did not end their problems. "Same old tune of washing, ironing & cooking may be heard here daily – Last week, our third week's experience of being maids of all work – was the worst of all." Margaret and her sisters spent days doing the ironing and then hung the clothes out to air. Along came a rainstorm. The clothes were drenched, a week's work ruined.[22]

Thus was Margaret Beckwith rudely awakened to the full range of women's work. In elite households, laundry, routine cooking, cleaning, and scrubbing fell entirely to the slaves. There were also a number of tasks that slaves shared with their mistresses—sewing, gardening, serving guests, and looking after children. The result was that mistresses had some choices about the work they themselves would do. As we have seen, most of them sewed, and some of them took up gardening or dairying with a will. Sometimes they chose the kitchen. Ellen Mordecai baked a cake to sell for the benefit of the Female Orphan Asylum. Mary Cumming boasted about her poppy-seed cake and sent to her sister for a receipe for currant wine. Eliza K. Myers praised her own first attempt at preserving fruit— *"it looks beautifully"*—and sent away for a recipe for eggplant, "for your way I know is à la Francaise – and Sam says no cooking ought to be à la any thing else."[23]

Above all, women of the elite were free to invest in their children. The nineteenth century, as historians have recently portrayed it, was the century of the child. Families became child-centered, emotional bonds between parents and children intensified, and the responsibility for giving children a proper start in life was transferred from fathers to mothers.[24] Petersburg women gave every indication that they took this assignment seriously; their letters breathe passionate attachment to their children.[25]

Mary Cumming was sitting up in bed less than twenty-four hours after her daughter's birth, writing to her sister about the happy event. "It would be impossible, my beloved Margaret, to describe the rapture I felt on the birth of my darling little daughter. . . ." In the weeks that followed, Cumming's letters home brimmed with delighted commentary on her daughter's winning qualities. Imagine her grief, then, when the child became ill and died at only four months. It was over a month before Cumming could bring herself to write about it:

> Oh, dearest Margaret! it almost breaks my heart when I think that my lovely baby is gone for ever. Oh, that you had seen her, you would not wonder at my sorrow. She was one of the most beautiful infants I ever beheld, and so good, she was too

good to stay in this troublesome world. I believe she knew me, for when I would go to take her out of her little crib-bed, the darling would look up at me and laugh, she was beginning to take notice of everything, but she is an angel in heaven, and in that happy place I trust in God I shall meet my little Mary.

It will be long before I can get the better of her loss, for I am so lonely without my sweet pet, but I will try all I can to be resigned to the will of Providence.[26]

It was a tragically commonplace refrain. While we cannot calculate what a newborn's chances were—birth and death registers simply were not kept—the available evidence suggests that in the early nineteenth century, infant mortality rates were terrifyingly high. Mary Cumming, after the death of her first child, became pregnant again. This second child was stillborn, and Cumming herself died the next year. Mary Read Anderson raised two sons to adulthood. Three other sons she buried, one at one year, one at seven months, and one at nine days. Jean Syme's first pregnancy ended in miscarriage; she raised only one child to adulthood. Several of Mary L. Simpson's children did survive to adulthood. Her first daughter, however, was stillborn, and so were three others, two of them within eighteen months of each other. Her son George lived only fifteen months. Her son Freddy died at the age of three.

The precariousness of infant life did nothing to diminish the devotion of the mothers. As Mary Read Anderson explained in 1801, the knowledge that her child might die only intensified her dedication. "I acknowledge My dear Brother my weakness in allowing my own happiness to be too much dependent on the health of my darling Son, but in spite of all my own arguments to overcome it I cannot. . . . Oh My Duncan I have lost two!—that ought alone to teach me the vanity of placing too fondly my affections on any one object, yet alas it rather serves to weaken where it ought to strengthen me most." Anderson nursed her sons through all their illnesses ("I have a great aversion to Doctors for children . . .") and as the years passed, she never relaxed her style of vigilant maternity.[27] When her sons were nearly grown, they went off to school at the University of North Carolina. Anderson, by this time a widow, moved to Carolina to be near them.

Petersburg mothers remained closely involved with their children long after the children were grown. Fanny Bernard expressed it to her son by means of invidious comparison: "With out the society of my beloved children what would this life be; to me, perfectly void of pleasure, the feelings of my children are more congenial to mine than those of your Father's although he is truly affectionate & kind to me, but then he has so little to say that interests me." Anne Dade Bolling, who had traveled to Culpeper to see her daughter through childbirth, chided her son for his failure to send news from Petersburg. "I catch a few moments to enquire what has become of you and yours, how so engaged as not to have written me a line *no* not a solitary word have I heard from any of you. . . . In the midst of anxious cares here I have not forgotten others Dear to me, You know me too well, not to think that your silence would cause me much anxiety and uneasiness." Bolling was still willing to make sacrifices, though. "I left home rather unexpectedly and hurried, it was a great undertaking for me, but it seames that a mother cannot forget her child, Indeed I feel as if I was willing to spend and be spent for them if sickness or peril required it, although perhaps," and here came the hook, "they may not take into consideration my age and infirmities or feel a proper interest for my comfort and peace, however," and here she fell back on aphorism, "it is a sweet consolation to know that we have not lived for ourselves alone."[28]

Spend and be spent—would that there were some accounting, hour by hour, of how much time women like Anne Dade Bolling actually spent with their children. We do not know how many elite women translated their profound devotion to their children into round-the-clock, intensive mothering. We do not know how many delivered major responsibility for child care into the hands of slaves and other servants. The point for the moment is that elite women had some choice.

To say that elite women had some choices and that choices made their working lives easier is not to say that they were uniformly satisfied with the roles available to them. For Anne Dade Bolling, widow of Petersburg's wealthiest man, to write about motherhood was to use the language of ambivalence. "Your sister has another daughter born on the twenty sixth of May," she wrote ten days after the birth, "she is doing pretty well, but the best is bad enough, yet we should be thankful for all that is directed by the Almighty." And in announcing her willingness to sacrifice for her children, Bolling managed to string together a "but" and an "although" and a "however" in a single run-on sentence. Self-sacrifice did not come without a struggle.[29]

For that very reason, one suspects, antebellum women were barraged with literature assuring them that their work was essential to the nation's well-being. Much the same thing occurred in the middle decades of the twentieth century, of course; American women of the late 1940s and the 1950s were greeted on every hand by the feminine mystique, by the insistence that the only work that mattered for women was marriage, housework, and child care. The question, or one of the many questions, is why nineteenth-century women were more likely to believe it, why the notion that woman's main work was in the home came under so little fire from women themselves.

While this is a very complex question, part of the answer must lie in the changing character of the work itself. In the antebellum period, work in the home was for most women physically and emotionally taxing, and there is no persuasive evidence that it conferred on them any actual power or prestige. Yet for all the difficulties, and despite the paucity of rewards, it was still possible for a woman to believe that her work was important. This was what was so badly eroded by the mid-twentieth century. In the antebellum period, as we have seen, household labor still included productive labor. By the 1950s it did not. In the antebellum period, there was at least implicit recognition that household tasks were varied, specialized, and took

some skill. This was the message of advertisements posted
by slaveholders who wished to sell or hire out female
domestics:

> For Private Sale, a Family of Young Negroes; . . . The man is
> a good shoe-maker, and the woman an excellent washer, ironer
> and spinner, and a tolerable plain cook.

> For hire on accommodating terms, two very likely Negro
> Girls,—One is a good cook, washer and ironer, and is also
> accustomed to wait in the House—the other is a good seam-
> stress, and a very capable house servant.[30]

By the 1950s, this, too, had changed. "Labor-saving"
devices, and the advertisements designed to sell them, portrayed housework as push-button work that any fool could
do.

Finally, housework in the nineteenth century was not
yet divorced from money. This was partly because household tasks could still be converted to cash. For many families, the income from a boarder, from livestock or a
garden, or from sewing made a critical difference. The
monetary association was reinforced by the slave system.
Champions of today's housewife find it useful to inform
husbands of how much it would cost to hire workers to
perform all the chores their wives perform gratis. Such
consciousness raising was hardly necessary in a society in
which the cost of hiring domestic labor was an item of
daily conversation. Work in the home, like work on the
outside, had a clear market value. This, too, was lost in
the first half of the twentieth century, when the proportion
of families employing domestic servants declined precipi-
tously.[31]

It was not until the middle of the twentieth century, in
other words, that women's work in the home was thoroughly trivialized. In the antebellum period, housewives
could still believe their work counted for something. This
is not to say that they actively chose the home, and it is
not to say that domesticity was a font of personal happi-

ness. It is to say that there was nothing in women's experience that caused them to question the assignment of housework and child care to women alone. It is also to say that there was nothing in their experience that made them think they had a right to any other kind of life. Discontent, therefore, was largely contained within the domestic sphere. Women who felt the need for a change tried to change themselves, or they tried to change their domestic arrangements. Anna Campbell moved back in with her mother-in-law, and she substituted a young hired nurse for one who was old and slow. She also encouraged lengthy visits from a close friend, Elizabeth Wilson, who helped fill Anna's need for emotional support as well as for household help. Ann T. Davis, meanwhile, repeatedly urged her husband to take a position as pastor in a quiet parish, where her energy would be more equal to her tasks.[32] The belief that their work mattered was positive incentive for redoubling their efforts to make domesticity work for them.

The other incentive, of course, was the shortage of attractive alternatives. If women focused their energies on their households, it was partly because the gainful employment situation was so bleak.

The men who edited Petersburg's newspapers were well aware of the dismal prospects that faced the woman who needed paying work. "WHAT can she do?" asked the *American Constellation* in 1834. "There are but very few avenues of business in which women are privileged to walk. The wages paid for female labor is very trifling; and when she has others besides herself to provide for, it seems almost impossible that a woman can succeed."[33] The editors knew all about the discouraging facts that historians have been rediscovering ever since: Occupational choices were few, earnings were pitiful, and economic independence was very difficult to achieve.

It may be instructive to notice what the editors chose to make of these facts. The *Constellation* article of 1834 went on to document the economic heroics of a North Carolina widow who, at the age of sixty, walked to Tennessee with her grandchildren. First, she knitted purses as she walked, selling them to meet her expenses along the way. Once arrived in Tennessee, she rented a garden plot and sold gourds for drinking cups. Then she acquired a cow and marketed the milk. Finally, "by her frugality and industry, she was enabled at her death, to leave each of her grandchildren a snug farm." The moral for womankind: "Her strength and courage will rise in proportion to the difficulties which surround her, and kept in intense exercise, her love seems, like the fire which the prophet invoked from heaven, after the water had been poured upon the sacrifice, to annihilate every obstacle in her path."

Love, in other words, conquers all. This may have been the most pernicious assessment of women's economic problems ever set forth in a Petersburg publication. Editors in the 1850s showed a somewhat keener sensitivity to discriminatory reality, and in editorials surprisingly unconcerned that woman might venture too far beyond her sphere, they gave hearty endorsement to the entry of women into new lines of work. "It has long been a source of just complaint that the circle of female occupations was too contracted," said the *South-Side Democrat* in 1855. This editorial went on to advocate the hiring of female store clerks. Another came out for women physicians. "For ourselves we see the most manifest propriety in it, and the wonder is that a silly prejudice has for so long a period kept the sex out of this profession to the serious and irreparable detriment of humanity, particularly their own sex." A third editorial argued that typesetting ought to be opened to women. "The circle of female employment," the *Democrat* said again, "should be enlarged."[34]

Be it recorded that the editor of the *South-Side Democrat* did not hire women to set type in his own printshop. Nor did he take pains to inquire about who profited from the system that kept women's options limited and their wages low. Rather, the *South-Side Democrat* attributed discrimination in the paid labor force to mere "silly prejudice." The implication was that the problems of the working woman would be solved as soon as the world learned to get by on a little less silliness. In the meantime, there remained the individual solution. The primary message of an editorial of 1858 was that the success ethic was as good for women as it was for men, that persistent, hard work was bound to be rewarded. The story was headlined "An Encouraging Instance of Womanly Ambition," and it plotted the rise of a young woman whose career had begun in one of Petersburg's cotton mills. A millhand by day, she studied at night until at length she quit the mill and opened a school. The school was a flop because the children in the mill district were either enrolled in the free school or were millhands themselves. Our unnamed heroine then went out into the country to teach. After two years of roundly successful teaching, she struck out for Arkansas where she concluded her "noble struggle for womanly independence" by marrying a rich planter. "She was still a school-teacher, but as her charms, and her ambition were of no ordinary nature, she made quick work of the conquest, and now enjoys all the happiness which youth and love, an immense plantation on the Red river, and plenty of money can bestow."[35]

It comes as no surprise that success for women was defined as marrying well. What is worth special notice is the author's easy assurance that such success awaited any woman who had the requisite virtues. "Honest industry ever carries with it its own reward, health and happiness—besides holding in perspective a sure guarantee of future eminence in social position." America, the land of the self-made man, was also the land of the self-made woman. Even by the standards of nineteenth-century journalism (objectivity was not a high priority), this was preposterous. It is also understandable. To look squarely at the economic plight of women was to confront the fundamental unfairness of the American economic system, and this the editor was manifestly unwilling to do. Instead, he glanced at the harsh reality and then rebounded into platitudes on virtue and reward.

Getting beyond glances and platitudes is no easy task for us either, though for us the main problem is with evidence. The problem is not that the evidence is limited in quantity. The problem is that very little of the existing evidence can be profitably subjected to systematic analysis. The federal census did not report women's occupations until 1860. While a map of women's places in the occupational structure can thus be drawn for 1860, there are flaws due to underreporting, and there is nothing to tell us how the situation in 1860 may have differed from the situation in previous decades. Existing business and factory papers are almost completely devoid of personnel records.[36] Petersburg did not get its first city directory until 1858, and here the only women listed with occupations were the proprietors of businesses. Long-term changes in the character of gainful employment for women simply cannot be charted with precision.

We make do, then, with large quantities of evidence that resists system. Clues on gainfully employed women turn up almost everywhere. In the newspapers, there was advertising—over the years, hundreds of businesswomen took out ads in Petersburg's papers—and there were occasional references to employment in local news columns as well. We know that Lucretia Updike was a laundress, for example, because the *South-Side Democrat* in 1855 reported her arrest on a charge of having stolen a watch from the pocket of a vest she had been hired to wash. Relatively large numbers of retailers and innkeepers were entered on the tax lists or in the minute books when they obtained licenses, and some who ducked the license law appeared in the minute books when the grand jury caught up with them. Executors, administrators, and guardians also identified scores of gainfully employed women, as the most careful accounts of expenditures included the name of the woman employed, the service she rendered, and the amount she was paid: "Jane Douglas for Washing blankets after the death of deceased pd ____.75," read an entry of 1825, followed by "To Cash pd Jinsey Snow, Nursing deceased 6.00."[37] As time went on, new high-yield sources appeared. Beginning in 1845, local agents working for R. G. Dun & Company made periodic evaluations of the creditworthiness of Petersburg entrepreneurs, women as well as men. And beginning in 1853, a new concern for the collection of vital statistics resulted in the keeping of a death register in which occupations of the decedents were recorded.

For the entire period, meanwhile, sporadic information on gainfully employed women crops up in every kind of source, in the odd deed, will, letter, diary entry, legislative petition, and court report. For example, newspaper advertising is the richest source for identifying women who took in boarders. But many keepers of boardinghouses never did advertise, and these quiet proprietors must be sought out in a variety of alternative sources. Eliza Drummond appeared frequently in the local records as a property owner, and when the war came she went to work immediately as an organizer of soldiers' relief efforts. Her activity as a boardinghouse keeper would not have been known at all, however, were it not for the diary of a New Jersey minister's wife, who stayed at Mrs. Drummond's in 1850 and who recorded the names and religious denominations of her fellow boarders. The occupations of Mary Bowman and Mary Bartlett came to light when they went to court to testify against boarders accused of theft. Elizabeth Pope kept at least one boarder; we know this by virtue of the fact that the said boarder ran up a bill of more than three hundred dollars and then mortgaged all the shoes in his shoestore to cover the debt.[38]

A thorough search of local records thus yields more information on gainfully employed women than there was any reason to expect. Altogether for the period 1784 to 1860, specific occupations can be identified for more than 1,700 Petersburg women. Of course, there were untold numbers of employed women whose occupations cannot be determined, and some occupations are far less visible than others. We know the names of 172 teachers; we know the names of only 6 prostitutes. One hardly knows whether to be impressed with the evidence that does exist or to mourn what can never be recovered.

Either way, tentativeness is the appropriate tone for

generalizations on the long-term changes in gainful employment for women. Industrialization and a more general expansion of scale in manufacturing, it is certain, created hundreds of new factory jobs for both white and black women. What is uncertain is whether women of the working classes were better or worse off as a result. As for the more traditional lines of women's work, what we call progress or loss changes with the frame of reference. If we compare the situation of women entrepreneurs in the 1850s with the situation of women entrepreneurs several decades earlier, there appears to have been little change. If we compare the opportunities available to women with those opening up to men, the story is one of relative loss, for as professionalization and economic modernization created new positions of authority, women were shunted aside.

The best known case of displacement is midwifery. For centuries, as many historians have pointed out, delivering babies had been the exclusive work of women. Then, in the late eighteenth century, male physicians began to compete with midwives for a share of the childbirth market.[39] Just how quickly the doctors triumphed is still a matter of speculation, but it is generally agreed that midwives no longer served well-to-do women after midcentury.

Petersburg's women at first resisted the doctors' claims to superior wisdom and skill. In 1808, one physician did announce "that in future he will attend more constantly to the different Branches of his Profession, and particularly to the OBSTETRICK ART, to which, his close and lengthy application, added to his success, entitle him to the first consideration." It seems unlikely that the doctor found many customers, however. Dr. James T. Hubard kept an account of all his visits from 1798 to 1800, and there was not a single obstetrical case on the list. And no one thought to call a doctor when Mary Cumming gave birth to her first child in 1812. Mary was attended instead by Elizabeth Swail, who was, in William Cumming's words, "a great favourite among the ladies here."[40]

After Elizabeth Swail died in 1813, the mantle fell to

Sarah Weatherly, "an old matron," as William Simpson described her in 1823, "(a sort of Mrs Middleton by profession) in very great repute here among the ladies & always in request on these occasions whenever disengaged." During Sarah Weatherly's term as Petersburg's most trusted midwife, however, physicians seem to have taken a long step toward dominance in the lying-in room. In the 1820s, Mary L. Simpson gave birth to four children, and Sarah Weatherly was called each time.[41] A male physician was also called each time. For women who could afford it, having a physician on hand during labor was apparently becoming routine procedure.

It is not clear when well-to-do women stopped sending for the midwife altogether. It is clear that money was important, both as an incentive for doctors and as a guarantee that midwifery would live on among the poor. From the beginning, doctors commanded shockingly high fees for their services to pregnant women. In 1800, six Petersburg physicians met to set standard fees for their various services. For an ordinary visit in town, the charge was six shillings. The charge for a call in the middle of the night went up to one pound, ten shillings. The fee for delivering a child, "with or without Instruments," was eleven pounds, five shillings. The only service that even began to approach the price for childbirth was treatment for syphilis, and that was three pounds. For the female midwife who delivered a child, meanwhile, the standard fee was twelve shillings. This radical gap between the earnings of doctors and the earnings of midwives persisted. In the 1850s, Dr. John L. Peebles kept a careful account of his patients and their payments. For the great majority of calls, Peebles charged one dollar or sometimes two. In obstetrical cases, he charged from twenty to twenty-five dollars. The standard fee for a midwife delivery in the same years was three dollars.[42]

For the time being, doctors were willing to leave attendance on slaves and the relatively poor to midwives, and as a result, the number of women who practiced midwifery probably did not decline substantially before 1860. The social profile of midwives seems not to have changed either. Midwifery was taken up by both black women and

white, and there was considerable range in what its practitioners were able to achieve economically. In the 1850s,
as before, about one midwife in three or four made enough
to buy real estate.[43] Midwifery remained an occupation in
which a few skilled women—but only a few—could make
a decent living.

The next rung down on the medical ladder was nursing
and leeching. Nursing, according to the classical medical
history of Virginia, was usually left to "slovenly old
women without skill, kindness or good morals." How
much of this is truth and how much libel is not certain. It
is true that most of the women who were paid for nursing
in Petersburg were obscure. Cuppers and leechers, nurses
who specialized in drawing blood, did advertise on rare
occasions. Virginia Manly, for instance, let the Petersburg
public know "that she has secured a large supply of
AMERICAN LEECHES, which are so requisite in leeching children." But on the whole, leechers and women who
performed more general nursing services are nearly invisible, and they are nearly invisible because they were poor.
Of all the women known to have been paid for nursing in
Petersburg, only Jane Minor acquired any substantial
property. Emancipated in 1825 for her healing gift, Minor
was in demand in sickrooms all over town, and with her
considerable earnings, she helped to free sixteen slaves. Her
achievement is the more spectacular considering the usual
poverty of women in her calling; Petersburg's nurses were
generally unable to acquire taxable property.[44]

Still below the nurses in the medical hierarchy, or outside the hierarchy altogether, were folk healers. The *Press*
in 1860 reported the practice of "an Obeah woman" in the
eastern part of town. She was a "little, cunning, old, white
woman," and according to the *Press,* the following was
her method: When she heard of illness in a free black
household, she would go to the house secretly in the night
and plant some special pellets there. The next day she
would return, announcing that the house was filled by an
evil spirit, which she could chase away, if she could find
some mysterious pellets. For this she charged three dollars, and she was reported doing very well. As the *Press*

saw it, this was one more example of "genius diverted to base purposes."[45] For us, it hints at the existence of an important medical underworld in which women may well have been the main practitioners.

It was only at the top, in any case, that no women were to be found. Male doctors elevated childbirth among the well-to-do to an expensive and prestigious aspect of regular medical practice and then succeeded in reserving it for themselves. Moreover, the physicians who organized to upgrade their profession, and to exclude those they believed to be quacks, formed an all-male club. In 1852, eighteen Petersburg doctors petitioned the legislature to establish a board of medical examiners. There were no women among the petitioners.[46]

A parallel process took place in the business of education. In the early part of the nineteenth century, opportunities for women teachers mushroomed as Petersburgers joined the national campaign for improved female education. "Parents in Virginia," wrote William S. Simpson in 1820, "are bent upon having 'accomplished' daughters & are by no means sparing of their money to attain this end."[47] As time passed, women continued to do most of the teaching of children and young women. As supervisors, however, women lost ground to men. In the new schools of the 1850s, men were the principals, the presidents, and the professors.

With the opening of the new century, a number of people in Petersburg wanted something done to make the education of girls more formal and more thorough. By 1808, their concern was urgent, and nothing could have made this clearer than the advertisement posted by the mayor:

A SCHOOL MISTRESS
WANTED

To a lady who will establish a SCHOOL in THIS TOWN, and confine herself to the education of twenty-five GIRLS,

ONE THOUSAND DOLLARS

will be given, per annum.

To prevent useless applications, it is deemed proper to state, that she must be well recommended as to *character, attention,* and *mildness of disposition,* and must also possess *every accomplishment* essential to complete the education of the young ladies who may be placed under her care.

It is not known whether this fabulous offer found a taker. By 1820, however, the age of formal schooling for young ladies was well underway. Jane Taylor, a longtime resident of Petersburg and a woman known for her learning and wit, opened a school for young women in 1817. Mary L. Simpson, just married and just arrived from London, opened her school in 1820 and had to turn students away.[48] For the entire period 1784 to 1820, there were twenty identifiable women teachers in Petersburg. Sixteen of them first appeared between 1816 and 1820.

The demand was not only for more schools, but for more versatile and learned instructors as well. Before about 1815, the standard curriculum for girls was reading, writing, sometimes arithmetic, and needlework. Needlework, as we have seen, was no joke; women of every class sewed for themselves and their families, and depending on the circumstances, needlework was an important form of personal expression or source of income. Teachers offering the short curriculum still found students after 1815, but the fact that students were older and parents more ambitious cleared the way for highly fortified courses. Mrs. Barbour's academy opened in 1817, promising instruction in "orthography, reading, writing, grammar, composition: belle-lettres, geography, natural history, history of nations, chronology, natural philosophy and chemistry," and Mary Simpson's Seminary for Young Ladies offered "arithmetic and geography, with the use of the globes, history, natural and experimental philosophy, drawing, &c." along with language skills. The new schools may not all have delivered as much as they promised, but the best of them were rigorous. "Mrs. Taylor," the local rector reported in 1824, "makes her pupils read the Grecian, Roman, and English historians at large, not in the abridged form."[49]

In the new style of female education, the cultivation of character was important, too. Students were expected to absorb the personal virtues of their teachers, and to that end, most of the women who ran academies sacrificed their privacy and took in several students as boarders. Mary Simpson's family was typically swelled by the presence of at least six "Parlour-Boarders," and Jane Taylor, when she first opened her school in 1817, explained the rationale: "Although I shall not refuse day scholars, my first wish is to receive boarders: I shall feel equally accountable to both, but the power of making proper impressions on the minds of my boarders will be much greater. They will always be with me; I can understand the peculiar cast of their minds, and at proper times, fix on them principles calculated to render them useful and rational companions."[50]

Student boarders were sources of extra income, of course, and that underscores an essential point about teaching in Virginia in the first half of the nineteenth century: Teaching was a business. Until the 1850s, there was only one free school in Petersburg. That was the Anderson Seminary, founded for poor children by a private endowment in 1821 and kept alive thereafter by small supplements of tax money. The great majority of Petersburg's young scholars attended private schools. Teachers were therefore entrepreneurs, competing for students on the open market, and they were understandably preoccupied with the number of students they managed to sign on. Some of them did consistently well. William Simpson, who assisted his wife in her Seminary for Young Ladies, sent the good news to his sister in 1826: "Our school continues very full, too full indeed but there is no resisting it." There was more good news in 1828. "The school still ranks A1 in these parts – ergo – we have as many pupils as we wish." Mary Ann Peabody, a newcomer from New England, found the going rougher. "I am engaged in teaching a part of every day," she wrote in 1843, "and have a fine set of scholars, but schools are so numerous here, that our number is small."[51] Teachers fought for patronage, bought or rented classroom space, charged what they thought the market would bear, kept accounts, dunned debtors, and took out ads in the papers.

This was significant for women. As long as teaching remained a small business, women remained in charge. In some of the larger schools, it is true, women teachers did work for others. But they generally worked for other women. What happened in the 1850s was the establishment of new educational institutions that were run by men. First, Petersburg developed something like a public school system for the sons and daughters of the poor. New free schools were established on the west side of town in 1851 and on the east side in 1855. That made three free schools altogether, and all three employed female teachers. All three were run, however, by male superintendents.[52] Meanwhile, the old-style academies for young ladies were faced with a new set of competitors—schools founded by men who emphasized intellectual toughness. The Petersburg Female College, chartered in 1854, promised "the cultivation of habits of concentrated attention, and accurate, clear, vigorous and self-relying thought," as well as instruction in the traditional accomplishments. A broadside for A. J. Leavenworth's seminary claimed *"mental discipline"* as the main object. "Hence it is our aim, not only to give a clear and thorough comprehension of the lessons taught; but to do this, by exciting the powers of the pupil herself, and teaching *her* to THINK—to reason, investigate, compare, methodize, and judge."[53] The persons who set out to accomplish these things were mainly men, and they were ambitious. In the 1850s, three different groups asked for and were granted acts of incorporation by the legislature. Power in each of the schools thus incorporated—the Petersburg Female College, Leavenworth's Female Seminary, and the Davidson Female College—was vested in a board of trustees. All of the trustees were men. The presidents or principals were men. Men were also in charge of instruction. In the Petersburg Female College, for example, there were four male faculty members. The four female faculty members were all termed "assistants," except for Miss Lacey, who was given the less prestigious title of "Teacher" of drawing, painting, and needlework.[54]

As education expanded in scale, then, women were excluded from the new positions of authority. Much the same process was at work in the growth of business, and here the culprit was the corporation. It was true that women were always concentrated in a fairly narrow range of enterprises. Women's main businesses were millinery, dressmaking (or mantuamaking, as it was then called), retailing groceries, keeping inns and boardinghouses, and prostitution. It was also true, however, that at the beginning of the nineteenth century there was no business from which women were automatically excluded. Among the dozen persons who manufactured tobacco in the early years of licensing, there were three women. (Elizabeth Cook's operation suffered a setback in 1804, however, when she was caught red-handed with fifteen kegs of processed tobacco and no license. The tobacco and her equipment were confiscated and sold, and the proceeds went to the town.) Mary Fleming was the dominant partner in T. Dunn & Company, a trans-Atlantic trading firm. Mary Bolling and Eliza Spencer were both proprietors of tobacco warehouses.[55] As long as the individual proprietorship and the partnership were the only forms of business organization, the exceptional woman could be found in every sort of enterprise.

That changed with the rise of the corporation. The great age of the corporation did not arrive until after the Civil War, but in the antebellum period, a fair number of expensive, large-scale Petersburg enterprises were granted corporate status by the state legislature. There were internal improvement companies, corporations designed to build canals, turnpikes, plank roads, and, above all, railroads. There were banks and insurance companies. There were several cotton mills. And there were other diverse enterprises—a lumber company, a gas light company, and a locomotive factory. All of the incorporators were men.

All of the officers were men. Women were free to buy stock, of course, but there is no evidence that stockholding, even in the early days of the corporation, brought women any active role in making company policy.

So women were left out of the new economic order, at least as managers and directors, and had no choice but to concentrate on the businesses that had been open to them all along. How they fared from one decade to the next is difficult to say. Our only measure of women's participation in retailing comes from lists of licenses, lists that were kept sporadically between 1805 and 1819 and more consistently (though for different purposes) in the 1840s and 1850s. The lists of the earlier period gave the names of those merchants who paid a twenty-dollar fee for licenses to sell goods imported from abroad. Only one woman appeared on the first of these lists, and for the period 1805 to 1809, the proportion of licensees who were women was a tiny 2.6 percent (8 / 307). The proportion did grow to a less tiny 5 percent (24 / 485) for the period 1817 to 1819.[56] The proportions of women among licensees of the 1840s and 1850s were somewhat higher, but these licenses were issued for the sale of liquor, an enterprise more likely to include women than was the selling of imports. From 1844 to 1850, 8.2 percent (58 / 712) of liquor licenses went to women. From 1851 to 1857, the figure was 6.1 percent (46 / 749).[57]

At no time did women own even a tenth of Petersburg's legitimate businesses. Illegitimate businesses were another matter. In the 1780s and 1790s, the town clerk was reasonably conscientious about recording the names of persons who obtained tavern licenses ("ordinary licenses," they were called at the time) and the names of those hauled in for operating without licenses. Among those licensed, just under one-fifth (11 / 54) were women. Among those presented for failure to obtain licenses about 30 percent (13 / 44) were women, and it was a woman, Ann Forbes, who held the town record for liquor sale violations. Forbes ran afoul of the grand jury four times, for "Selling Spiritous

Liquors without License," "for retailing Liquors on Sunday, to Negroes, without License," and "for dealing unlawfully with Slaves."[58] The more disreputable the business, it seems, the more women were to be found in it.

Or to put it more generally, in those businesses in which women and men competed, the women's enterprises tended to be smaller in scale and more marginal in prestige. The provision of meals and lodging is a good example. Countless Petersburg women took in boarders, their enterprises ranging from the smalltime and informal—taking pay from a nephew who bedded down in the corner—to the supervision of a large house with a large staff of slaves. Until roughly 1820, women also retained a reasonable share of the tavern and innkeeping business. Beginning in the 1820s, however, the taverns were gradually replaced by hotels ("Hot-tle, Hot-tle, what the devil is a Hottle," an unenlightened local was heard to ask).[59] The new hotels had some pretensions to elegance and grandeur. All of them were operated by men.

There were parallels in the grocery business, where men monopolized wholesaling and women were concentrated in the lowliest ranks of neighborhood retailing. The women who ran groceries and cookshops were a scrappy lot. Nelly Butler, convicted in 1857 of selling liquor without a license, threatened one of the witnesses against her: "She would make him swallow his teeth if she were a *man,*" she said. Indeed she would have. A year earlier Butler had foiled an attempted robbery in her store by catching the thief in a rat trap. Another would-be thief met his match in the Market Square when he tried to walk away from a cookshop without paying for his food. The two free black women who ran the place tackled him and "levied" on his boots for their payment. Maria Downing could tackle, too. When she observed two men taking beer mugs from her store, she followed them out, "tumbled both in the gutter and recovered her property." She prosecuted the two as well.[60] Other women storekeepers asserted themselves in more decorous ways. Margaret Kenny, Catherine McFall, and their daughters, along with Ann Moran and Catharine Bissett, were all Irish and all grocers, and all of them applied to the court to become naturalized citizens of the United States. This was highly unusual and was probably meant to give the women unobstructed rights to inherit and bequeath property.[61] The same women, meanwhile, were central figures in the community that built Petersburg's first Catholic church. Margaret Kenny, Catherine Bissett, and Ann Moran served, with men, on the church's building-fund committee.[62] In no other white church did women serve on committees with men.

For all their assertiveness, however, Petersburg's women grocers remained little fish in a fairly large pond. In all the years that agents for R. G. Dun & Company monitored Petersburg businesses, only three women grocers— Moran, Kenny, and McFall—did enough business to earn them credit ratings. Most women grocers ran little neighborhood stores that doubled as gathering places and grog shops. They did not usually advertise, and they apparently had no role at all as wholesalers. In the business directories of 1859 and 1860, about 5 percent of the persons listed as retail grocers were women. In wholesaling, where the bigger money was, no women were listed.[63]

The only businesses in which women were well represented at the top of the scale were those businesses in which there were no men. Prostitution was apparently one of these. Because polite people did not talk about it, and because the authorities did not prosecute those who participated in it, we are left with only occasional hints as to prostitution's existence and character. We know that women of both races were involved; while the grand jury in 1804 registered a grievance against free black women who moved to Petersburg "only for the purpose of Prostitution," the few women who were actually arrested on charges of "keeping a Bawdy House & House of bad fame" were white.[64] Beyond that, about all we know is that some prostitutes lived in groups from early in the century. For this information, we are indebted to the testimony of several Petersburg men who in 1813 submitted affidavits supporting the petition of Alexander Crossland for a divorce from his wife Catherine. All of them testified that Catherine had been a common prostitute in Petersburg for several years. John Loughridge deposed that she had been "living with women of infamous character," and Martin Eanes also added that she had been "living with lewd & profligate Women." Eanes was in a good position to judge, having "frequently and repeatedly had carnal knowledge of the body of the said Catherine within the last five years." A bit more evidence surfaced in 1856 when a fire destroyed a house owned by two free black women. The *South-Side Democrat* reported merely that the house had been "inhabited by some needle women. . . ." For the *Express,* however, the fire was the occasion for some fun: "Many we are told, of both sexes were seen jumping out of windows, dressed very *light,* and taking refuge where they could. Several young gentlemen from down town were observed taking the back track for their legitimate lodgings, some only partially apparrelled, and others, less fortunate, the victims of sacrifice, in breeches, vests, broadcloth coats, and gold watches."[65]

Millinery and mantuamaking (or dressmaking), were the other major businesses monopolized by women and were easily their most visible and most lucrative enterprises. Every fall and every spring, Petersburg's milliners advertised the opening of the new season's stock of goods; every fall and every spring, they offered the same phrases and the same promises of reasonable prices and the latest fashions from more fashionable places. They also offered to restore worn bonnets: "Bleaching and ironing old Bonnets, done with dispatch." They advertised for apprentices and assistants and like Ann Kerr, who had "brought on from N. York persons competent to execute good and fashionable work," announced the hiring of new employees when the employees brought with them some fashionable lustre. By the late 1850s, there were fifteen or sixteen going millinery and mantua concerns in Petersburg, many of them employing several skilled craftswomen.[66]

More than any other enterprise, millinery made for success stories. Mary Phepoe first appeared in the papers advertising her stock of *"elegant dress,* and *undress Bonnets"* in 1808. A few months later she made her first appearance in the official records when she hauled her husband into court for a breach of the peace. That was the first and last heard from Richard Phepoe, who either died without a trace (and thus without property) or deserted his wife and daughter before 1810 when the census taker named Mary the head of the family. The millinery business was good to Mary Phepoe. By 1819, she had saved enough to pay twenty-five hundred dollars outright for a house and lot, and that same year she acquired her first slave. The next year she acquired a second slave, sufficient property altogether to place her in the top third of Petersburg's taxpayers.[67] Phepoe moved to Richmond in the late 1820s, leaving the field clearer for A. D. Williams. Williams was single when she began her millinery career in Petersburg in 1819. She married the next year and may have quit her business for a time. Her new husband was a drunk, however (she bounced him in 1835 and acquired a separate estate in the meantime), and Williams was soon back in her shop working to support herself and her three small children. She succeeded marvelously well. In the 1840s, R. G. Dun & Company reported her worth from ten thousand to fifteen thousand dollars. "Remarkable business woman," the agent mused.[68]

While A. D. Williams was probably Petersburg's most impressive self-made woman, the Dun ledgers suggest that a number of women were able to succeed in the millinery business. Adeline V. Sleppy: "Know her well, very good. . . ." Isabella Lyon: "Stands very well." Sarah J. Toole: "Doing very well, generally meets her notes before maturity." Mrs. Kayton: "Getting on well, good for contracts making money." Caroline Kennedy: "A worthy woman who educated 3 children by her own industry. . . ." Mary Robbins: "Has become rich & retired from business."[69]

The majority of Petersburg's gainfully employed women did not run shops or schools or brothels. They worked in factories, or did laundry, or sewed for whoever could pay them. In this labor force, with a few exceptions, women were sharply divided by race. Among seamstresses, there were both blacks and whites.[70] Almost all of Petersburg's washerwomen were black, however, and the factory labor force until the late 1850s was cleanly divided: The tobacco factories hired free black women; the cotton factories hired white women.

The era of the factory began in Petersburg in the 1820s, and from the beginning, women and girls were mainstays of the industrial labor force. Petersburg's first cotton mill opened in 1827. By 1850, six of them were reported operating in Petersburg or on its outskirts, employing altogether more than seven hundred female hands. Tobacco manufacture was even bigger business. It took relatively little capital to launch a tobacco factory—tobacco manufacture did not require much in the way of expensive machinery—and by 1835, at least six factories were in operation. By 1860, there were twenty tobacco factories in Petersburg, and they employed more than twenty-five hundred hands.[71]

The tobacco factories ran mainly on the labor of slaves, but they were also a major employer of free black women. In 1860, the census taker listed 299 free black females as stemmers; this was the largest single occupation listed for free black women. Most of Petersburg's factories produced plug and twist tobacco. The stemmers, most of whom were women (about a tenth of the stemmers listed in 1860 were young men ranging in age from twelve to twenty), performed the first steps. The tobacco was dampened, and the leaf was then stripped from its center rib. The best leaves were set aside to be used in wrapping the plug or twist, and the remaining leaves were tied in bunches (these were called "hands") to dry. Subsequent steps were apparently performed mainly by men (altogether, male workers outnumbered female workers by about two to one). While the tasks were divided by sex, everyone joined in making music to lighten the work. A northern visitor described the scene in 1850: "In passing a long, narrow, low building, which we were told was a 'tobacco factory' our attention was attracted by singing within. On going around to the door, we saw in one end of the building about 60 colored persons men, women & children busily engaged at their work and all uniting heartily in singing a lively tune. The music was truly delightful. We listened a long time and it ceased not. They seemed to be singing a hymn, though the only words I could distinguish were 'I'll take my staff & travel on.' "[72]

For young white women, meanwhile, the sound of the factory was racket and clatter. Work in the cotton mills cannot have been easy, but unfortunately there were few local witnesses to tell us about it. One editorial in 1856 was dedicated to "the little girls who are now toiling away their precious lives in our cotton mills. Early each morning," the editor effused, "long ere light streaks the eastern skies, the bells ring them from their warm beds and humble homes; the day passes with them amidst the unwholesome fumes of cotton and oil, and with but brief intermissions, few and far between, their tiny hands are kept toiling until a late evening hour." The factory brought not only hard labor, but moral corruption as well:

> It is just, too, at an age to commence the development of the intellect, when their young minds are susceptible of receiving and retaining moral impressions; but the unrelenting hand of poverty points them to the loathsome factory—there they must delve; there be crushed all their childish aspirations, bright hopes and beautiful fantasies. Though there are some whom the benificent influence of Sabbath schools has visited, there are many whose young minds are strangers to a teacher's voice and the benign lessons of the Bible. It is here and in this situation that they form associations which pervert their natural dispositions, and they grow up without the fair and spotless name which should always crown the life of that gentle, radiant being—woman.[73]

The essay went on to no particular purpose. There was no moral, and no remedies were proposed. Yet it was significant that one voice suggested that the factory labor system left something to be desired. It was one thing to condemn the industrial labor system of the North; the southern press called it "wage slavery" in an attempt to demonstrate the relative benevolence of the southern slave system. It was quite another thing to face up to the plight of free factory workers at home. Most of Petersburg's editors kept factory workers out of sight and presumably out of mind.

The only time a Petersburg editor gave any sustained attention to factory workers was in 1858, when the *Express* carried on a campaign to turn free blacks out of their jobs in the tobacco factories and to replace them with white women. This was one more move in the broader assault on the rights of free blacks in the 1850s. It was also, or so it appears, a response to high rates of unemployment among whites. The depression of 1857 set back both cotton and tobacco production—there were massive layoffs in both industries—but cotton was hit harder and took longer to recover; the Merchants' Mills shut down for almost a year, and one reporter estimated that a thousand millhands in all were thrown out of work. It was in that context that the *Express* took up the cause of white labor in the tobacco factories. Local factory owners who had tried the experiment, the *Express* claimed, had found that white women "are more industrious than the blacks, learn the particular duties for which they are employed, with far more rapidity, and being more moral, more temperate, and in all other respects so vastly superior to the blacks, they are more reliable and of course far more preferable."[74]

The owners were not persuaded for very long. By 1859, the *Express* was admitting that "many" factories had gone back to hiring free blacks after having given white labor a trial. It may have been that the provision of separate entrances and work rooms for the whites cost more than the manufacturers were willing to pay (in the two factories described by the *Express,* black and white workers were rigidly segregated).[75] In any case, the census schedules for 1860 listed only about two dozen white female tobacco stemmers. Petersburg's factory women remained divided by race, as they had been from the beginning.

Racial divisions did not stop there, of course. Black women were far more likely than were white women to enter the paid labor force. According to the census of 1860, over half of all free black females aged fourteen and above were gainfully employed (678 / 1264 = 53.6 percent). Among white females of fourteen and above, the census indicated that only 9.5 percent (298 / 3146) were gainfully employed.[76] When we ask why women worked for pay, the Petersburg evidence largely confirms the findings of other historians. Women in Petersburg sought paying work because they needed the money; the women most likely to be found in the paid labor force were widows; young, single women from poor families; and women, often black, who had children to support.

To leave it at that, however, is to reinforce the myth that women ordinarily chose the home and to imply that no self-respecting nineteenth-century woman would enter the labor market as long as she had a husband to support her. Two points need making here. The first concerns numbers: There were a great many more married, middle-class women who contributed directly to family earnings than the census reveals. The second point concerns attitudes toward work and family. The most successful businesswomen in Petersburg were the milliners, and they did not abandon their businesses when they married and had children. Instead, they kept right on stitching and selling, and their families found ways to adapt to this. The implication is that women were willing to place a high priority on their careers, as soon as their careers proved sufficiently rewarding.

In the meantime, most Petersburg women seem to have entered the paid labor force out of stark necessity. A few of them made this explicit. Mildred W. Campbell, a widow getting on in years, wrote to her daughter-in-law as September drew near: "I find I must go to school keeping again in order to keep house Taxes and everything else so high. My shop not rented and not likely to be at a good price. So I can see no other way but to go to work again."[77] On rare occasions, they made their need public. E. H. Page hoped that her "extreme unfortunate situation" would induce customers to patronize her "genteel" boarding-house. Virginia R. and Jane D. Lownes made their motives plain when they reopened their infant school in 1831: "The object of the continuation of this Institution, is the support of the Orphan Family of the late Mrs. A. W. Lownes." Elizabeth Ann Tenain, Petersburg's most spirited adver-tiser, opened a secondhand-clothing store and with her "POVERTY PANACEA" tried to help everyone make a virtue of necessity in the hard times of 1838. "The neces-sities of her family requires that she should turn her hand to any thing by which she can make an honest penny. Adversity hath taught her, that *Pride without Money* is worse than *Pudding without Sauce*. She has therefore discarded those feelings which more halcyon days enabled her to cherish."[78]

Most of Petersburg's needy women did not advertise their misfortune, but dozens of hard luck stories can be reconstructed from assorted records. On a spring after-noon in 1817, Daniel Organ was going about his usual business as a hardware clerk. A shot was heard, and Organ fell to the floor, the victim of a stray bullet accidentally discharged by a drayman unloading muskets from a cart on the street outside. Organ's widow Pamela proved resourceful in the emergency. By his will, Daniel had left her and their infant son all his property, "should there be any in [my] hands at my decease," but the inventory of his estate amounted to only "1 cutting box" and "1 time piece" worth but ten dollars total. Within three months of her husband's untimely death, Pamela Organ was tendering "her services as a SCHOOL MISTRESS for Young Ladies," offering instruction in "Reading, Writing, Gram-mar and Orthography, with Plain and Fancy Needle-Work" and for an additional fee, "Geography, History, Drawing and Painting. . . ."[79] Sally Nash, who entered the ranks of the gainfully employed the following year, had probably seen it coming for some time. Like Daniel Organ, Paul Nash had left all his estate to his children and his "dear & truly faithful" wife, and like Organ, Nash had nothing to leave them when the time came. Nash's mercantile plans never seemed to work out, and from 1815 to 1817, Sally Nash stood by and watched her husband's holdings go on the block to satisfy his creditors. First to go was their house, then the best of their household furnishings, "A large variety of Elegant Prints . . . 1 pair large Elegant Looking Glasses; Best plated Tea and Coffee Urns; China and Cut Glass Pitchers; Dining and Card Tables; Mahogany Chairs &c.," then eight house slaves, and then what was left of the furniture. When Paul Nash died in 1817, his creditors were still hovering, waiting to get what they could from the remaining estate. His widow left the messy distribution to the town sergeant and for her part announced her readiness to take in "a few genteel boarders."[80] The tales of economic woe could be multiplied almost indefinitely.

Statistics, rough as they are, tell much the same story. The census schedules for 1860 are the best source we have on factory hands, seamstresses, and washerwomen. Among seamstresses and washerwomen, a high proportion headed their own households (two-thirds of the blacks and over half of the whites). A high proportion were supporting children (half of the blacks and over a third of the whites). Those who did not head households of their own for the most part appear to have been single women or widows who boarded in the homes of others.[81] The factory labor force looked somewhat different, and there were more pronounced differences between whites and blacks. White female factory hands were mainly young (fourteen to twenty-four) and single; almost half of them lived with their parents, either with widowed mothers or in two-parent households in which the father was a laborer or a millhand himself. Another 30 percent of the white female factory hands were apparently self-supporting boarders. Only a seventh of white women factory hands headed households of their own. Free black factory hands were a more diverse group. About 40 percent headed households; about a third were supporting children; 17 percent appear to have been self-supporting boarders; and a tenth were unmarried daughters helping to support mothers, or in a few cases, both parents.[82]

What black women workers and white women workers had in common was economic need. The main difference between them, at least according to the census schedules, was that for free blacks, marriage was less likely to stand in the way of gainful employment. Among free black laundresses and seamstresses, 16.1 percent (20 / 124) appear to have been married. For whites, the comparable number was 1.1 percent (1 / 92). The same gap was visible among factory workers; 20.5 percent (60 / 293) of black female factory workers appear to have been married, while for whites the figure was 7.8 percent (21 / 269).

Petersburg is not the first community to yield up this sort of data. Other historians have observed that married black women were more likely to be gainfully employed than were married white women, and three possible explanations present themselves. One is economic. Assuming that unemployment and underemployment were more widespread problems for black men than for white men, it would stand to reason that more black wives would feel compelled to seek paying work. A second explanation is cultural. It has been argued that all other things being equal, including the ability or inability of men to earn a living, black wives were still more likely to be gainfully employed. This, it has been proposed, was a continuation of the slave experience, in which marriage and childbearing never exempted women from working for their owners. (The slave tradition of communal child care may have been equally important.)[83] Both explanations seem plausible for Petersburg. A third explanation, however, would suggest that we have less explaining to do than we thought. That is, the incidence of gainful employment among white women may have been much higher than the census reveals.

For some of women's most important occupations, Petersburg's 1860 census schedules are woefully deficient. The census listed only three women—one "doctress," one leecher, and one midwife—in medical occupations. A search of all the other available records reveals the names of twelve medical women, all of whom were practicing in 1860. The census listed only nine women as teachers. Other sources show that there were at least forty women teaching in Petersburg in 1860. The census listed nine women keepers of boardinghouses. The business section of the city directory for the same year listed eighteen female boardinghouse keepers, and in the personal section of the same directory, ninety women were named as having taken in boarders. It is not clear whether the census taker was not asking or whether the people were not telling, but the result was serious undercounting of gainfully employed women, especially married women, especially those in genteel occupations.

Alternative sources suggest that married women were far more active than the census admits; eighteenth-century patterns of female enterprise survived well into the nineteenth century. For one thing, it was not unusual for a woman to take major responsibility in running her husband's business. In most lines of work, one learned the business by helping out, day by day; formal training and formal credentials were not required. Moreover, the separation of home space from business space was not yet complete. This kept husbands closer to home and wives and children closer to the business, as Samuel Mordecai noticed in 1842. Mordecai was having some trouble with his business partner, "and I believe his wife dont like me, because I dont encourage all the Children white & Black to stay in the Counting room." The fact that his partner's wife "makes a nursery and Servants hall of the Store and Counting room" was a nuisance for Mordecai, but for some families the proximity of business and home meant that the wife could make direct contributions to the family income.[84]

The enterprises most likely to engage the wife as a full-time manager were tavern and hotel keeping, and advertisers sometimes acknowledged the fact. Richard Bate in 1805 announced that his club at the New Market racetrack would stay open "under the management of Mr. and Mrs. Bonner, whose ability and desire to give satisfaction is generally known and acknowledged." In 1818, Drury Burge announced that he was giving up the tavern business due to his wife's sickness. "The ill health of my wife," he explained, "and my own occupation being such that the necessary attention cannot be devoted to this establishment, I offer it for sale." Even in the 1850s, when the day of the hotel had long since arrived, the wife's role was still essential. "My wife will see that the ladies who patronize the hotel shall have every wish gratified," the Bollingbrook's proprietor promised in 1855. Overseeing the poorhouse was a two-person job as well. In 1856, the *South-Side Democrat* gave "Mr. Wilson and his lady" the credit for a neatly managed institution.[85] Any man who made it his business to provide lodging and meals was well advised to marry a managerial woman.

Wives also helped with, and sometimes ran, businesses less closely identified with domesticity. Mary Ann Currie Haines knew enough about her husband's newspaper business to settle bills for him while he was away. "I wish you to send for Mr. Drummond and have a settlement of his Cash Account," Hiram Haines wrote in 1836; "the Theatre Bill with the old balance due, cannot be less than $30.— perhaps more." Ann Donegan minded her husband's shoestore and had the bad luck to be in charge on an April day in 1822 when a customer made off with five odd boots. A few months later, William Hawthorn's wife was in her husband's store and caught a robber with his hand literally in the till. She snatched the money back and later testified for the prosecution. Charlotte Miller, from May to September, managed the ice cream saloon associated with her husband's confectionary business. N. D. Johnson's wife helped him with his business as a hatter. Thomas W. Bell had a reputation for intemperance, but his wife "has about reformed him," and they stayed solvent by virtue of the fact that she managed his jewelry business.[86]

Such women, if they were widowed, could carry on the business without missing a beat. In Petersburg, there were several women who owned "masculine" businesses, and almost all of them were widows who took over from their husbands. Judith Cary, a free black, apparently engaged in the river traffic. "My Will and desire is," her husband had written in his will, "That my said wife, shall keep and run my Water Craft called the Shark, as long as the said Vessell is Capable of running." Mary Thayer went into partnership with her son after her husband was mysteriously murdered in 1826. As "Mrs. Thayer & Son" they ran a blacksmith shop. Mary Lee and Ann L. Pace continued their husbands' butcher businesses. Martha Couch and Jane Steward continued in the saddle and harness business.[87] In a time when on-the-job training was the only way to learn a business, marriage provided a few women with access to unusual occupations.

One last list of entrepreneurial women is in order. This is the list of married women who carried on businesses of their own while their husbands engaged in some separate line of work. Rebecca Brodnax Hicks, the wife of a country doctor, edited a literary magazine called the *Kaleidoscope*. Mrs. George J. Smith opened a large boardinghouse next door to Leavenworth's Female Seminary, reserving one room for her husband's medical office.[88] Mary L. Simpson ran her school for three decades; her husband assisted her at times, acted as an agent for local merchants, and eventually settled into selling insurance. Susannah Beasley, Susan Musser, Mary Ann Pollard, Emily Holland, Isabella Potter, Mrs. Morriss, and Mrs. Solomon were all milliners. They were married, respectively, to an innkeeper, a railroad conductor, a saddler, a carpenter, a straw goods dealer, a furniture maker, and a furniture dealer. Mary and William M'Cay occupied the same tenement and advertised back to back (she was a milliner, he a watchmaker), as did Jane and William Ingram, at least until 1855 when William's "United States Bazaar" burned to the ground and he was tried on suspicion of arson.[89]

These women were not extraordinary. An analysis of the marital status of teachers, store or tavern keepers, boardinghouse keepers, and proprietors of millinery and mantua shops shows a substantial portion of married women in each group. Teaching was the occupation that drew the most single women. Well over half of the teachers whose marital status can be determined had never married. Still, a quarter of Petersburg's female teachers were married, as were more than a third of the store and tavern keepers, more than two-fifths of the boardinghouse keepers, and half of the milliners and mantuamakers.[90]

For some of these women, of course, gainful employment was an emergency measure; husbands fell ill or drank to incapacity or made poor investments. But there is evidence that other married women engaged in trade because they liked the work, they enjoyed the benefits of two incomes, they were doing well, and they saw no reason to stop. This was especially true of the milliners. Caroline Kennedy may have assisted her tailor husband during her first marriage. As soon as her first husband died in 1826, she announced her intention to carry on the millinery and mantuamaking business, and when she married again in 1836, she protected her business with a marriage contract. Kennedy continued her business through her second marriage, and before she died in 1852, she taught her daughters to do the same. In the 1850s, Sarah Jane Toole and Adeline V. Sleppy ran two of Petersburg's most important millinery and mantua shops (Toole began as a milliner and added mantuamaking later; Sleppy did just the reverse). Both were daughters of Caroline Kennedy, both made a respectable living, and both were married and mothers.[91] Mary Ann Pollard's millinery career in Petersburg spanned more than three decades. Pollard first advertised the opening of her shop in 1821, two years after she married saddler John Pollard. John Pollard did experience some financial disappointments—he had a way of losing money by backing friends—but these only prevented him from becoming rich. His own business was sound as could be, and he retired in 1855, very comfortably off. Mary Ann, meanwhile, had at least one child and remained in business year in and year out; "old Sister Pollard," as one of her customers called her, finally retired in 1857, two years after the retirement of her husband.[92]

We are left speculating on how Petersburg's gainfully employed women coped with jobs and young children all at once. We do know that they could not always manage both. Jean Syme gave one example: ". . . the Mantuamaker I allways employ, has at this time two Children lying dangerously ill with the Meazels, & could not take any work." Anna Campbell provided another: "I must tell you how my plan of teaching has turned out. —I rose early after quite a good night with the baby, & bathed & dressed her & myself in time for breakfast – & so thought to begin finely." Then came trouble: ". . . poor Aunt Fathey's head became *so bad* she had to give up [and] go to bed. I sent Calley for her Doctor . . . & also told him he might dismiss the boys who had come, to say that they need come no more this week. You see I could'nt help myself. no one to take the baby." The women who did manage to keep going satisfactorily on both fronts seem to have had extraordinary support services. Mary L. Simpson was married to a man who could drop his own work and take over her school whenever he was needed; he was especially helpful after Mary was laid low by difficult pregnancies. The Simpsons, moreover, kept at least four slaves.[93]

Mary L. Simpson's situation was exceptional, of course; very few enterprising women made enough to support a full retinue of domestic servants. But the women who did make enough—milliners, mainly, and a small number of other proprietors—are an illuminating minority. More than any other group, they beam light on the relations between domesticity and gainful employment for white women of the nineteenth century. They show us that women did seek careers, highly visible careers, and that they stayed with their careers, despite marriage and motherhood, *when it paid*. But there was not very much room at the top, and for most white women it made more sense to stay home, picking up what earnings they could by taking in a boarder, sewing, or selling milk or garden produce. This was not a rejection of regular employment outside the home per se. It was a rejection of employment on the terms the nineteenth century offered. Most housewives were overworked as it was. Where was energy to do additional work to come from? The paid work available to most women did not generate enough income to allow them to hire labor to replace themselves at home. In fact, attempts to earn money sometimes ended in total disappointment. Mildred Campbell in 1858 remarked on a friend who had just quit the boarding business: "Done with keeping boarders, nothing made by it."[94]

So most white women stayed home, making the best of a nearly inescapable situation, probably trying to be grateful that they were no worse off than they were. They did not have to look far for examples of how bad things could be. Of the 822 persons sufficiently desperate to receive assistance from the Association for Improvement of the Condition of the Poor in 1859, 728 were women and children.[95] Limited opportunity in gainful employment meant that poverty was primarily a women's problem. Poverty also became a women's project. In Petersburg, women took the lead in organized efforts to bring relief to the poor. The next chapter tells their story.

7

Women Together: Organizations

When Eliza Spencer died in 1800, Petersburg lost one of its most notable women of affairs. The town lost a curiously representative character as well, for in her last will, Spencer captured a critical shift in the public roles of Petersburg's women. Parts of her will crackled with the crusty independence of the prosperous eighteenth-century widow. In a bold hand, Spencer directed that any ambiguities be settled by her executors and not by litigation: "Let no lawyer nor Doctor," she insisted, "have a shilling of what I leave." But in providing for the education of the poorest of her nieces and nephews, Spencer struck the altruistic keynote for the women of the century to come:

> My heart clings and cleaves to the poor while young. O help the young, push them forward, pray do, a shilling to the young is far better than a pound to the old. How many is [in] want all their lives for want of a friend to assist them while young. O my friends when I am gone remem[ber] the young, push them forward with what little I leave and I hope God Almighty will Help both you and them with his choisest blessings both hear and hear after.[1]

A few years later, the white women of Spencer's class made her plea the basis for collective action in the public sphere. The landmark was the official incorporation of the Female Orphan Asylum in 1813; then and thereafter women made it their particular business to organize on behalf of charity and the church. This was something new. Earlier, on the few occasions when Petersburg women attempted to exert some public influence, they did so as individual proprietors. Women could not vote or hold office, but they did have the right to petition the Virginia legislature, and beginning in the 1780s, taxpaying widows joined men in the exercise of that right. Eliza Spencer herself signed several petitions, one (granted) to make a single corporation of the town's three settlements, another (not granted) to dissolve that corporation, and a third to build a new tobacco warehouse (granted, and the warehouse was built on Spencer's land).[2]

In the new century, women taxpayers continued to sign the occasional petitions in which they had some immediate interest. But the more prominent form of public activity by far was organization, initially for the benefit of the female poor and subsequently for the spread of the gospel. Such organizations were mushrooming all over the country, of course, and historians have rightly identified them as essential to the changing status and developing consciousness of nineteenth-century women. To what ends they were essential, however, is the subject of some controversy, a controversy that is part of the larger argument over the value of women's separate "sphere." Most scholars would agree that the growth of organized benevolence brought women a number of short-term benefits—an area for activity outside the home, a heightened sense of personal usefulness, a deeper appreciation of the needs and abilities of other women, and a chance to develop leadership and organizing skills and to participate in democratic decision making. The debate centers on what all of this had to do with the origins of organized feminism and the growth of feminist consciousness. It has been contended on the one hand that the women's rights movement was a direct outgrowth of organized benevolence. It can also be argued that organized benevolence inhibited the development of feminism, first by perpetuating the image of woman as possessed of a special mission (as opposed to equal capacities) and second by encouraging women to engage in projects that gave them the semblance but not the substance of power. The compromise position is that benevolent activity helped women to become conscious of themselves as a group, a necessary precondition for feminist protest, though not in itself a sufficient cause.[3]

Different as these conclusions are from one another, their defenders in fact share considerable ground. First, most of them work within what might be called a feminist-whig framework. That is, the progress of feminism is the featured story, and the importance of organized benevolence is reckoned primarily according to the magnitude of its impact, for good or for ill, on feminist thinking and organization. This may in time prove to be an extremely fruitful approach, but it may also limit our capacity to see organizations whole, particularly for the period before 1860 when only a minute fraction of American women were conscious feminists. Students of women's benevolent societies also share a tendency to focus solely on women, without providing comparable information on the men. This is an understandable choice given the youth of our enterprise and the enormous number of women's organizations that remain to be studied. Yet it leaves us with no very clear idea of how much gender really mattered in the proliferation of voluntary associations that characterized the first half of the nineteenth century.

Local records can help, and in several ways. Petersburg's records, first of all, make it abundantly clear that there were indeed women's organizations in the antebellum South, a fact that has generally escaped the notice of historians of southern culture.[4] Second, it takes immersion in local detail to arrive at sufficiently refined answers to the questions of why organizations were created and how they served their members. The local approach, moreover, makes a manageable task of keeping tabs on the organizational lives of men, and this introduces all kinds of new analytic possibilities, clarifying some issues while complicating others. One fairly simple question, the question of whether voluntary associations provided more opportunities for women than for men, begets a fairly simple answer: Men had it better, especially in the white lower classes. Comparison of the organizational lives of women and men also makes it possible to clarify the boundaries of a distinct women's culture. The concept of a women's culture may well be the most important concept introduced by historians of women to date, but it remains rather fuzzily defined. We need to know to what degree the organizational lives of men and women were in fact separate from each other; we need to know, even more urgently, whether women's collective behavior in fact differed from that of men. The evidence from Petersburg suggests that there was indeed an identifiable women's culture and that its public manifestations were special contributions in the realms of religion and social welfare.

However, and here come the complications, while comparison of male and female organizations highlights the separation of the sexes, it also reveals the development of new forms of togetherness. In the 1850s, for example, after decades in which poor relief had been left to the women, men adopted the cause as their own. There were convergences in organizational structure as well; after several decades in which single-sex societies were the rule, the 1850s witnessed the rise of mixed associations in which the women usually assumed auxiliary roles. The 1840s and 1850s also brought new forms of ritual submission, as women were increasingly identified by their husbands' names (Mary Smith became Mrs. John Smith) and as females were decisively denied the privilege of public speech.

However these developments may be interpreted, they make one point clear: "Woman's sphere" was never a fixed space. True enough, the nineteenth century's basic ideology of male and female spheres was already ossified by 1820; women were endlessly told that they belonged in the home while their men braved the crueler worlds of commerce, politics, and war. But this left a considerable quantity of social space unaccounted for. Rigid as nineteenth-century Americans were in defining sex roles, with voluntary associations they left themselves room for invention, maneuver, and experimentation. The results were intriguing.

The women who organized the asylum in Petersburg behaved as though the need for an orphanage for girls was self-evident. If in the beginning they found it necessary to plead their case before the townspeople, none of their propaganda was preserved. The fragments that have survived reveal a no-nonsense approach to institution building that might have won an approving smile from Eliza Spencer. The scheme was evidently hatched in the winter of 1811–12. By March 1812, the women had collected enough subscriptions and contributions to open a school, if not to operate a full-fledged caretaking institution, and the leaders called a meeting "for the purpose of making the necessary arrangements for immediately putting the SCHOOL into operation—." Within the week the subscribers met, unanimously passed "such laws as were deemed necessary for the government of the Society and the School," and elected officers and directors. No sooner were the directors elected than they hired a matron to supervise the school. It was in a subdued, we-told-you-so style that the women then appealed for further support from the people of Petersburg:

> There is now no doubt but the institution will be carried into effect, and it is hoped that those who have not yet contributed, under an impression that the plan could not succeed, will now, that the prospect of success is so flattering, come forward, and by their patronage, aid and assist in more fully accomplishing the designs and wishes, not only of the Society, but also of the whole community.[5]

The subscribers were confident that they had launched a laudable project; the point was to persuade potential donors that they were quite capable of following through on their good intentions.

Contributors had every reason to hold out for some promise of success, for Petersburg's one previous experiment in quasi-public education had been a disappointment. The Petersburg Academy was chartered in 1794. Nearly two decades later, the academy had yet to be built.[6] The women of the orphan asylum probably had the phantom academy in mind when they petitioned the general assembly for legal incorporation late in 1812: ". . . the fate of other Institutions of a similar description," they explained, "has taught your petitioners that such compacts however ardently entered into, in the moment of enthusiasm, will decline, and finally perish as that enthusiasm abates, unless protected by an Act of Incorporation which will enable the Society to bind and punish refractory members."[7] A steady income was essential. With an eye to relatively long-term commitments, the society had already determined that membership was to be for a five-year period; but without incorporation, there was no sure means of seeing to it that members fulfilled their pledges. When inspiration gave way to routine, the association might need power to take its delinquent subscribers to court.

Control over their own membership was evidently the petitioners' first concern, but they wanted other powers as well, powers to control both their financial assets and the girls in their care. In concise paragraphs that were markedly free of the deference that informed most petitions of the time, the subscribers asked for power to hold and convey property and for the right to participate in litigation. (Standing in court was necessary not only for suing recalcitrant subscribers, but was also an essential condition for engaging in property transactions.) And they wanted a free hand with the children themselves. They requested power to manage any inheritance an orphan might bring with her; the society, in other words, intended to act as a corporate legal guardian, looking after the girl's estate until she was old enough to manage it herself. A legal guardian, however, controlled only the child's property and not her person. To meet all contingencies, the petitioners asked "that they may be vested with the authority of controuling in every respect, the Orphan Female Children, whom they may take under their protection, until they shall respectively attain their lawfull ages."

The women did not get everything they asked for. They were indeed duly incorporated by the general assembly in January 1813, but the statute made no reference to control of the orphans. The legislators probably decided that the existing law of apprenticeship would suffice. Just two years earlier the legislature had empowered the local authorities to apprentice destitute children to institutions; under the law of apprenticeship, the asylum managers exercised day-to-day authority over the child until she turned eighteen, but the local court retained power to revoke the apprenticeship if the child was mistreated. On all other counts, the "Act for incorporating the female association for providing a female orphan asylum in the town of Petersburg" gave the petitioners what they wanted.[8] The powers to make laws, elect officers, deal in property, and appear in court were the standard provisions of acts of incorporation, but for women they took on special significance. Here the wives among them assumed rights that they were ordinarily denied by law. In concert with one another, the petitioners opened a large loophole in the common-law doctrine of civil death for married women.

Within a year of the association's incorporation, the orphanage was in full operation. In 1814, the society rented a house on High Street, and that summer the court ordered that "such Orphans as may be under their care" be bound out from time to time as the directors stipulated. The asylum itself was intended to harbor and instruct only the younger girls, while those old enough to be apprenticed were placed with selected families or with women in the skilled needle trades. No other evidence on the early program of the asylum exists, but the court's order made one thing clear: The elected officials had transferred their lawful responsibility for one group of Petersburg's poor—"the most helpless and interesting of the community," in the women's words—to the organized women.[9] It was a small slice of public authority, but it was public authority nonetheless.

The question remains: Why the asylum? A pioneering

article painted early women's charity as the offspring of the churches, one of many Christian outreach efforts inspired by revival-style religion.[10] But this will not do for Petersburg. The town retained its reputation for godlessness until a revival finally took hold in 1821–22; certainly none of Petersburg's struggling little congregations showed any signs of missionary or benevolent zeal before 1812. For Petersburg, it makes more sense to begin where the founders did, by looking at the condition of the poor.

Poverty was becoming more widespread in the early nineteenth century, and the most vulnerable poor people of all were orphaned girls. In some other time, this might not have evoked an organized response. At this time, however, wealthier women had both the leisure and the need to organize. The leisure, of course, came from their positions of privilege in the same economy that made throwaways of the orphaned daughters of the poor. The need seems to have sprung from education. The founders had some education, enough to create ambitions that neither domestic nor social routines could satisfy. To them, learning was precious. Poor girls, meanwhile, had no access at all to formal schooling, and that must have made their plight seem all the more desolate.

Petersburg's women spelled out their explanation of the need for an asylum in the preamble to their 1812 petition to the legislature: ". . . your petitioners," they wrote,

> deeply impressed with the forlorn and helpless Situation of poor Orphan female Children, in the town of Petersburg, left entirely destitute of the means wherewith to support, and educate themselves; and aware of the many incalculable benefits to be derived to them, from moral and usefull education, in whatever situations in life they may in future be placed— and deprecating the many evils, almost too sure to come upon them, if left to struggle through this life, without good precept and example, have associated themselves together, with the view and wish to snatch from ignorance and ruin, as many of that class of children, as the funds to be raised from their association will admit. . . .

The petitioners had cause for concern. Ignorance, sexual abuse, destitution, prostitution—these were the standard elements of female debasement. None of these was new, but a close search of the local records suggests that all of them may have been growing more serious.

In the eighteenth century, as in this century, poverty was primarily a woman's problem, and all the signs for Petersburg indicate that the problem was getting worse. While there is no direct, numerical evidence for the period after 1797, when the town clerk ceased reporting allocations to impoverished individuals, the numbers for the 1790s suggest increasing economic distress among women. From 1789 to 1793, the substantial majority of the town's adult poor were women (18 / 28), even though females were but 37 percent of the town's free white population. Between 1794 and 1797, the proportion of the poor who were female grew to 80 percent (35 / 44). There is no reason to believe the trend was reversed as time went on. From 1790 to 1810, Petersburg's total population doubled, but the number of persons who owned taxable property increased by only 11 percent. Of course, not everyone who paid no tax could be classified as poor, but the fastest growing segment of the population was clearly the lower class.[11] The most spectacular growth rate was that of the free blacks, who more than tripled their numbers during the two decades. All in all, Petersburg's population was becoming younger, more female, blacker, and, even among the white men, poorer.

It seems probable that the relief supplied by the local officials was not keeping pace with the need. For the orphaned daughters of the poor, the court was instructed to provide both maintenance and a skill through apprenticeship, but the apprenticeship system was apparently on the decline. For one thing, some children were very likely neglected altogether as the town grew and the poor consequently decreased in visibility. While the number of female children had probably increased some two and a half times since 1790, the number of orphaned girls bound out by the court was not much greater in the first decade of the nineteenth century than it had been in the last decade of the eighteenth.[12] It may also have been the case that some of the girls who were apprenticed were regarded as cheap labor, emerging from their indenture at eighteen with few skills and without prospects; the overseers of the poor, in any case, do not appear to have exercised ongoing supervision of the treatment of apprentices. Finally, for half orphans the system was discriminatory. Poor boys whose fathers had died were customarily taken from their mothers and bound to skilled craftsmen. Girls in a like situation were usually kept with their mothers and took their chances with what they could learn at home. While there was perhaps much to be said for keeping families together, the daughters stood to inherit their mothers' dependent status.

They also stood to inherit their mothers' ignorance, this in a time when the education of young women was assuming new importance. As Linda K. Kerber has shown, stock in female education was going up. Educational reformers argued that a republic could not survive unless its citizens were virtuous and that its citizens would not be virtuous unless they were properly instructed from an early age. Mothers, therefore, played a pivotal role, and they could not play it well unless they themselves were well educated; some went so far as to claim that the fate of the nation hinged on the education of its mothers.[13] While educational theorists debated what sort of schooling would best accomplish the desired object, Petersburg provided no public schooling of any kind. This was a hardship for poor children of both sexes, but for the girls the deprivation was greater; girls were less likely than their brothers to achieve a degree of literacy through apprenticeship.

The founders of the asylum no doubt saw all this as the fast path to prostitution, a particularly worrisome development given the fact that the public authorities made next to no effort to regulate sexual behavior. The grand jury rode roughshod on unlicensed purveyors of liquor and made periodic forays against gamblers. The single case "relative to keeping a Bawdy House & House of bad fame," however, was dismissed. The criminal docket, meanwhile, had been free of rape accusations since Andrew Edwards had been found not guilty of beating and raping Fanny Gibson back in 1791. That same year two men had been summoned on charges of fathering bastard children; one further case—dismissed—in 1807 was the only paternity suit in recent memory.[14] A girl without family evidently could not look to the judicial system for protection or redress. The asylum could offer her physical shelter in the short run and moral instruction and a trade for the longer haul, all preventive measures in a town where no punitive ones were in sight.

Orphaned girls, in short, were sexually endangered, intellectually disadvantaged, and economically vulnerable—more so than orphaned boys. In our own time, the word "asylum" calls up images of psychosis and gloom. In the early nineteenth century, it meant only a place of safety. This is what the founders of Petersburg's Female Orphan Asylum meant to provide.

What was in it for the founders themselves? Obviously, in organizing and sustaining the asylum, they made a place for themselves beyond their homes, engaging in work of community-wide significance. The magnitude of this departure should not be missed. While founding an orphanage for girls may seem unremarkable to us, it is important to remember that any such organizing on the part of women was unprecedented; before the asylum, organized, public life was entirely in the hands of men: the legislature, the court, the vestry, the militia. The founding of the asylum was an act of assertiveness that needs to be accounted for.

The best guess is that education made the difference; the founding of the asylum marked the coming of age of Petersburg's first generation of educated women.[15] How they acquired their learning is not quite clear. It was probably acquired at home, from their brothers' tutors and from indulgent parents, and continued afterward by reading and conversation. Their achievement was most evident in their letters; they wrote with verve, with humor sometimes, and with command of the language. Education may also have propelled them toward a wider sphere of usefulness. The domestic routine, much as the women were committed to it, made little use of their schooling. The social routine, much as they may have enjoyed it, was unsuited to their seriousness of purpose. Founding the asylum was a partial solution.

In the forefront were women of formidable personality and considerable learning. Jane Taylor was one of them. Taylor makes her appearance in local histories partly by virtue of blood; Chief Justice John Marshall was her brother, and her husband, George Keith Taylor, was Petersburg's leading attorney and one of Virginia's outstanding legislators. But she was an outstanding character in her own right, "a lady of genius and information," a visiting minister wrote of her in 1828. In asylum-founding days, she had a reputation for being downright intimidating. "Often before I had the pleasure of knowing this lady I had heard of her," Mary Cumming wrote. "I was told she was extremely lively, witty, and sensible, keen in her remarks, and will have her laugh no matter at whose expense." Cumming happily found the reality less frightening than the reputation: ". . . I thought I should feel rather afraid of her, but my opinion changed the first time she came to see me, I found her lively, cheerful, and agreeable. . . ." Within three years of the founding of the asylum, George Keith Taylor was dead, and despite the fact that she had a handsome income and three young daughters, Jane Taylor would embark on a long and distinguished, at times controversial, teaching career.[16]

Then there was Mildred Walker Campbell. As with Taylor, Campbell's teaching career began only after death claimed her husband; in the 1840s, she was the one female instructor in the Petersburg Classical Institute, a prestigious academy for boys. In 1812, she and her husband, an ordained minister turned bookseller, were the town trendsetters in literary taste. "Mr. Campbell," an elderly citizen reminisced in 1868, "was not more esteemed for learning and scholarship than was his accomplished lady." The author went on to recall an incident of some fifty years before when two attorneys got into a wrangle over a point of grammar: ". . . Mrs. C. was selected as umpire, being, as was agreed on all hands, to be better qualified than any other person in the place to decide." So impressive was Mildred Campbell's intelligence that her friend Edmund Ruffin found it necessary to exempt her from her gender: "Her mind is masculine," Ruffin wrote, "& of superior order."[17]

It may have been the broadening effect of education that led the asylum's founders to concern themselves with events taking place outside their homes; they did, in any case, feel free to express political opinions. To an immigrant like Mary Cumming, women's interest in politics was remarkable. "Men, women, and children are all politicians in this country, politics is the general topic of conversation among the gentlemen and even of the ladies of this place. Some of the females of my acquaintance," she added, "are most violent democrats."[18]

In 1812, meanwhile, Campbell, Taylor, Cumming, and their friends were deeply enmeshed in conventionally feminine tasks, or so it appears from the surviving evidence on the asylum's founders. Forty-six women signed the incorporation petition of 1812. For forty-one of them, some information on family and income is available, and the profile that emerges bears a striking resemblance to the classic profile of the American volunteer; the founders of the asylum were for the most part young, educated mothers of the upper middle class. Conspicuously absent from the petition were the signatures of Petersburg's female entrepreneurs. The one exception was Elizabeth Goodwyn, whose husband had died just a few months before, leaving her his inn and the administration of his estate.[19] There was only one other widow among the subscribers. The great majority (32) were married, and almost all of the married women were rearing young children. Of the seven single women, six were young and would soon marry. None of the unmarried women headed households of their own. Most lived with their parents, and the one permanent spinster kept house for her brother.[20]

Financially, most of the subscribers were comfortable. The men who headed their households were mostly merchants who engaged in the unspecialized commerce of the day, and there were several professionals as well. While their relative wealth is difficult to determine with any precision, thirty of these men appeared on the 1810 tax list, nine of them in the top tenth of Petersburg taxpayers and twenty-five in the top third. All but one were slaveholders, and all but four kept one or more adult female slaves to do household chores.[21] A few of the men were struggling financially, but like bookseller John Wilson Campbell, their relative poverty was offset by the prestige they won as members of the local intellectual elite.

If we may draw from the numbers and from imagination a portrait of the typical subscriber, her story reads something like this: She was in her early thirties and the mother of three young children; she had lost another child in its infancy; she was a white, native Virginian, raised and educated on a plantation in the country; marriage had brought her to the city some ten years before;[22] marriage had also brought her relative financial comfort and leisure, at least to the extent that her slaves could look after household and children when she was away; whatever marriage had meant in the beginning—the new experience of town life, of running a household, of sexuality, of childbirth—the excitement and trauma had since worn into something more like routine; in short, she was in a position to be getting restless.

Still, it would not be fair to see in the founding of the asylum a simple flight from domesticity. Education may well have been responsible for the women fixing their visions beyond the confines of their own households, but it was probably motherhood—the passionate concern for the shape of the world their children would grow up in— that moved them to action. Education and maternity together, one suspects, were powerful fuel for volunteer activity, and probably remained so well into this century. Moreover, in any probe of the relations between the domestic world that women inhabited and the public roles they created, one should guard against seeing in the nineteenth century problems that became acute only in the twentieth. It has become customary to portray the upper-middle-class housewife as a person beset by feelings of boredom, uselessness, and isolation. Whatever the justice of this description for the present, it only half applies, at most, to the early nineteenth century. Boredom there may have been, and there was undoubtedly a desire to feel useful beyond one's own household. Isolation, however, is a relatively recent addition. In early Petersburg, as in much of the rest of the country, women of the upper middle class were engaged in a dense network of relationships with other women.

The network was based on kinship, neighborhood, and common experience, and from it grew the asylum. The list of subscribers is a genealogist's delight, for at least half the subscribers were related to some other subscriber. There were three sets of mothers and daughters, four of aunts and nieces, and five of sisters, as well as more distant connections. But the network went beyond kin groups and expanded to take in newcomers, as Mary Cumming discovered when she arrived a young bride from the north of Ireland in 1811. "I have had a great many visitors since I wrote last," she told her sister, "indeed, the ladies are remarkably kind and attentive to me, I never met with more pleasing people. I have got several little presents sent me by them, knowing I was a young beginner."[23] The women who formed Cumming's welcoming committee—Clara Colquhoun, Mary Haxall, Sarah Freeland, Mary Read Anderson, Ann Robinson, Mary Moore—all knew one another, and all of them soon became promoters of the orphan asylum.

Polite calls, however, did not constitute the essence of the women's community. The stronger bonds were those that grew from mutual support in times of childbirth, sickness, and mourning. Again Mary Cumming is the witness. In the fall of 1812, both Mary and her husband William were helpless with fever, a disease that had already taken the life of their infant daughter. "I do not know what

I should have done during my illness if it had not been for Mrs. Freeland," Mary wrote. "I never experienced so much kindness and attention from any stranger as I have done from her at the time poor William and I were so much distressed that we could do nothing. She came here, ordered everything to be done that was necessary, and indeed appeared more like a kind relation than an acquaintance." Sarah Freeland and her fifteen-year-old daughter Agnes were soon Mary Cumming's intimate friends, and they were on hand again when her second daughter was stillborn. "As usual, my good and kind friend, Mrs. Freeland, has paid me the greatest attention of late. She was with me when I was confined, and for a week after she stayed day and night, nursed me as if I was her own daughter, my dear Agnes was my housekeeper. Never, never shall I forget what I owe to that family."[24]

The asylum was an affirmation of women's role as friend in need; the founding of the orphanage was not so much a rejection of woman's sphere as it was an attempt to give institutional form and public importance to its most positive features.[25] Women valued and protected other women. Organization in turn reinforced the women's network. Given who her friends were, it was no surprise that Mary Cumming was drawn into the work of the asylum, but she herself seemed proud. "William says I shall soon be a *great character* in this country."[26] The asylum was a channel for ambition, and that is where organization went tradition one better.

For the upper-middle-class women of Petersburg, there was nothing quite comparable to the asylum to give focus to that special combination of sisterhood and ambition, and that helps explain why the women launched the institution so rapidly, took it so seriously, and sustained it so loyally through the decades. Once established, the organization clearly heightened the women's sense of their own significance; the most prominent symptom of this was the development of an active mode of fundraising. In the beginning, the founders of the asylum collected dues from the membership but otherwise relied on men to raise their money for them. Local poet Martha Ann Davis made the point in "A PIECE In behalf of the Orphans Under the protection of the FEMALE ORPHAN ASYLUM":

> *And there stands a brother, whose trembling emotions*
> *Evince he ne'er turn'd from humanity's woes;*
> *He flies to the Orphans, he vows to befriend them,*
> *And on the Asylum donations bestows.* [27]

In public fundraising events, only men took the stage. Clergymen preached charity sermons, and for theatre-lovers there were benefit comedies and farces performed by the Thespian Society, a company of local male amateurs. [28] These sources were not abandoned as time went on, but beginning in the 1820s, the women took over most of the fundraising, discovering in the process their capacity to raise large sums of money. The first "fair" was held in 1829, a four-day sale of all kinds of handcrafted goods. "As we were all novices in the business, it has given us a good deal of trouble," wrote one of the managers. The trials of inexperience made success all the sweeter, however, and Mary L. Simpson reported the good news: "Why they cleared about Two thousand Dollars!!!" "We are informed," echoed a newspaper, "that the nett profits amount to about *Two Thousand Dollars.*" [29] Thereafter, periodic fairs and feasts testified to the women's commitment to an active and visible style of raising money.

The asylum itself, meanwhile, remained true to its origins in an intimate female network; in this there were both limitations and virtues. The asylum remained small. With only fifteen or at the outside twenty girls in residence, the institution could not have made much impact on the overall condition of the white poor. As for free blacks, the asylum had no impact at all, for the programs were for whites only. (No one ever said that blacks were to be excluded, but the few white girls bound out by the court after 1813 were all bound to the asylum while the black girls were bound to individuals as before.) [30] It may never have occurred to the organizers that it might be any other way. Petersburg's free black population had been growing fast, and by 1810, free blacks and slaves together outnumbered the whites four to three. Conscious or not, the decision to exclude black children may have been triggered by fear of contamination, an impulse to confine illiteracy, poverty, and sexual deviance to the other side of the color line. The prevailing assumption, in any case, was that for black women poverty was almost inevitable and licentiousness natural. It is not clear whether the organizing women of Petersburg believed this. It is clear that they failed to challenge it, that there was no personal identification strong enough to cut through or transcend racial barriers.

Personalism had its virtues, however, for the asylum never sank to severe regimentation or mere custodial care. Officers and members of the society maintained ongoing, personal relationships with the orphans. They made demands: "[I] heard Mary Price say her Collect; which she did, only tolerably," one volunteer informed another in 1842; "I gave her another, with strict injunctions, to get it with more care, as I would write you . . . about it." They searched out promising apprenticeship opportunities: "The Ladies have instructed Mrs. Damish to write Miss Benteen, to look out a suitable situation for Margaret Tucker, while she is in Baltimore: one in a Mantua Makers, or Milliners etablishment, if to be procured." And some of them remained personally involved for decades. Mary L. Simpson became active in the asylum's work in the 1820s. In the 1850s, she was as concerned as ever. "I am delighted to hear of the good condition of our Orphan Asylum," she wrote from England in 1858, "& pray daily for its encreased prosperity."[31] Simpson was abroad for weeks, and every letter home contained inquiries about the asylum's welfare.

As time went on, Petersburg's women undertook a number of other poor-relief efforts. In the 1830s, a House of Industry was established, probably to give work relief to poor women; in 1847, a second female orphan asylum was founded; and throughout the antebellum period, women's societies organized poor-relief endeavors within the churches. Because these activities are so sparsely documented, it is difficult to assess the women's total contribution. When the behavior of the women is contrasted with the behavior of men of the same class, however, even the feeblest of the women's efforts take on greater significance.

Until the 1850s, the men's collective response to the plight of the poor was typified by neglect, delay, and tightfistedness. Voluntary associations seem to have interested them not at all. An obligation to establish a charity school was foisted on them in 1812 by the will of David Anderson, merchant and town chamberlain, who left the bulk of his estate for "the education of Poor Boys and Girls (white Children). . . ." The town eventually placed an imposing marker over Anderson's grave "to mark their gratitude for his beneficence," but in the beginning there was something less than enthusiasm; "inactivity and slowth" were the words chosen by a local editor. Anderson's executors first attempted to have the will voided. That failing, they went forward, but the Anderson Seminary was not established until 1821, nine years after David Anderson's will was first admitted to probate. The school was organized on the Lancasterian plan, a system much in vogue at the time for its efficiency. In 1823, the *Republican* reported that 165 students were learning their three Rs under the supervision of just one instructor.[32]

The town government, meanwhile, could have given lessons to Ebenezer Scrooge. The panic of 1819 and the depression that surrounded it touched off a crisis in local government's relationship to its poor, and in Petersburg the official response was to get tough. From 1820 to 1823, the bill for poor relief averaged more than five thousand dollars a year, a sum triple or quadruple the normal expense. Radical cuts were called for. In 1823, the outdoor relief system was abolished; only persons who would go to live in the poorhouse were eligible for assistance. In 1824, it was ordered "that the Poorhouse establishment of this town be hereafter also considered & used as a Workhouse." These two moves set the policy for the remainder of the antebellum period and together created the standard irony of nineteenth-century poor relief: Inmates of the poorhouse were expected to work for their keep, but so dreary was the prospect of life in the poorhouse that only the very desperate—people who could not work to begin with—would let themselves be taken there. This problem did not go unnoticed by the Overseers of the Poor. In 1830, they reported that most of the twenty-seven paupers in residence were "wholly unable to perform any duty" due to old age and illness. The town was undaunted, however, and in the late 1830s, on the promise that in the future only a "small pittance" would be needed for the support of the poor, it invested several thousand dollars in transforming the poorhouse property into a working farm.[33]

The farm never did meet the expectations of its promoters (it was operated largely by hired slave labor), but its establishment apparently satisfied taxpayers that all due efforts had been made to put the poor to work. The real saving came from the continued refusal to assist "out paupers," poor people who would not live in the poorhouse. This was effective from the start. In 1825, just two years after the policy's adoption (and with some help from a partially revived economy), the total expenditure for the relief of the poor was only one-third what it had been in 1823. Even as late as the middle 1850s, despite substantial population growth, annual spending for the poor did not come close to the amounts spent in the crisis years of the early 1820s.[34]

How people got by is a mystery. Those most likely to find charity outside the poorhouse were Petersburg's most venerable poor—aging, respectable, white widows. "Kind Sir," one of them wrote to her pastor, "If you have any Wood please Send me Some, as I have not one whole Stick in the House." Most of the churches seem to have offered occasional aid, in cash or in kind, to their impoverished members, and fraternal associations also played some role in taking care of their own. The Petersburg Benevolent Mechanic Association, an organization of white artisans and manufacturers, was founded in 1825, in part to look after distressed widows and orphans. In the 1840s and 1850s, the mechanics made reasonably regular cash payments to six widows of deceased members; ". . . we have never let a deserving application pass unheeded," they claimed.[35]

For the less respectable poor, sources of charity were even fewer. The town government's refusal to expand or alter its poor-relief system seems particularly hardnosed given the growth of the new industrial working class— free blacks in the tobacco factories and whites in the cotton mills. By the late 1830s, hundreds of factory workers lost their jobs whenever financial panic struck. "The Manufacturers here are discharging all the free negroes," a Petersburg retailer reported in 1837, "and the number is said to be between 1200 and 2000." Another crisis in 1842 generated the same sort of dismal news. "The pressure of the times here is great and I believe increasing—but the suffering of the poor is much more to be deplored—There are many families now without the means of subsistence since some of the factories have stopped work."[36] How people got by, to repeat, is a mystery.

Until 1858, voluntary, organized charity was the exclusive province of women. Women were also the mainstays of the churches and of church-related organizations. In all parts of the country, the majority of church members were female, and in Petersburg the pattern held good. Membership statistics can be recovered from the records of five of Petersburg's white, Protestant churches. The proportion of members who were female ranged from a low of 65 percent to a high of over 80 percent.[37]

The appeal of the churches was enormous, and historians have done much to account for it. Through religious activity women found personal identity and a sense of order and larger purpose in life, at the same time that they found community, the chance to associate with like-minded, serious Christians. While religion could, of course, do the same for men, men had access to alternative sources of identity and community and were therefore less likely to turn to the churches. Religion also spoke to the particular needs of women as a subordinate group. It gave them psychological distance from male authority, and it offered a respectable space in which women could indulge in new kinds of assertion, from the quiet self-absorption of writing in a devotional diary to the assumption of visible leadership roles in benevolent organizations.[38]

The evidence from Petersburg confirms all of this and underscores the importance of still another bond between women and their churches, the economic bond. The standard cluster of women's benevolent organizations in any given white Protestant church included at least one mission society, a cent or mite society, an education society, and a Dorcas society for relief of the poor, and women taught in the Sunday schools as well. With the exception of the Sunday schools, the main activity of all of these groups was to raise and redistribute money. As time went on, moreover, congregations—white, black, Protestant, and Catholic—became increasingly dependent on the proceeds of women's fundraising events to pay for the construction and maintenance of church buildings.[39] The economic bonds tugged both ways; some women needed the churches as much as the churches needed the women. Church membership was the one means by which a woman, on her own initiative, could buy into a kind of social security system. In exchange for years of faithful giving and service, an elderly communicant could turn to her congregation for rent money, food, fuel, and medicine. Women who were still in a position to contribute, meanwhile, found satisfaction in working for the cause. Religious benevolence diminished the status gap between middle-class women and men by providing the women with opportunities to engage in productive, income-generating labor. For some women, organized benevolence was a career in itself.

The growth of religious activism among the women of Petersburg cannot be mapped with anything approaching accuracy; the women themselves worked quietly, and the written records left by men usually ignored women's societies altogether. We do know that organized benevolence preceded the revivals. Petersburg's first Sunday school was established in 1817. No one knows who organized it, but it was staffed by "the ladies." Two years later, sixteen Presbyterian women banded together to form the town's first mission society, and by 1821, a Dorcas society had gathered to aid the poor. Then came the revival. In 1822, Methodists and Presbyterians together succeeded in stirring up Petersburg's first dramatic religious awakening. William S. Simpson (Anglican) found the shrieking and groaning "quite appalling." Samuel Mordecai (Jewish) retained a certain dry detachment: "The town is half deserted and the remaining half so pious that I hear of nothing but preaching and Conversion – One of the religious characters is doing penance in jail for forgery . . . but faith will wipe away these trifling stains." To Methodist insider William W. Bennett, however, the revival launched "the era of a great moral revolution in Petersburg."[40]

Bennett claimed too much, but after 1822 there were indeed new indications that a substantial segment of the townspeople supported sterner standards of public moral behavior. When J. L. Roqueta brought his Grand Moving Theatre to town in the summer of 1823, he tendered his assurances: "Any ladies and gentlemen, of different sects of religion, may with propriety visit this theatre, as it contains nothing offensive to the feelings of moral people." The following summer, the common hall outlawed daylight skinnydipping in the river and passed ordinances requiring artisans and storekeepers to close on Sundays.[41]

Predictably enough, the revival also gave a boost to organized benevolence, as it generated scores of new church members, greater enthusiasm, and deeper concern for the remaining unchurched. In 1822, women of the Presbyterian church established the Education Society to raise money for the training of impoverished young candidates for the ministry. Year in and year out, it was Petersburg's most impressive benevolent association. New organizations proliferated with renewed revivals in 1827 and the early 1830s. By 1833, the list of Presbyterian women's organizations included a Young Ladies' Missionary Society, a Married Ladies' Missionary Society, a Tract Distribution Society, a Dorcas Society, and an Education Society. Presbyterian women also contributed to an interdenominational Female Bible Society.[42]

We will never know just how many of these organizations were begun, how active they were, or how long they survived. What is certain is that they made a great deal of money. The most commonplace means of raising funds was the "ladies' fair," and this was ordinarily a major undertaking. Most fairs ran for only three or four days, but since the women made by hand most of what they sold, the preparations could take months. The organizers also mobilized their country cousins when they could. In 1860, for example, the daughter of a Methodist minister passed word to her brother: "If the ladies about your neighborhood are not very busy, I wish you would get them to fix me up some little things for the fair." Susan Catharine Bott, directress and prime mover of the Education Society, sent the raw materials out first and asked for help later:

> I am induced by Yr former obliging readiness, to worke for the Ed. Society to request yr assistance in helping us to prepare for our annual meeting. . . . I have therefore taken the liberty of sending to you some Bobinett and Hop for the purpose of working infant Caps, also Scarlet Merino Cloth which I will thank you or your sisters to make up in Emery Strawberries such as was made at your House some years ago. . . . It will afford me pleasure if I can give you patterns to aid you in Yr labor of Love.

After all the months of stitching and crafting, the fair itself brought an intense burst of activity. The organizers of most fairs put on at least one public dinner—sometimes there were daily lunches and dinners—and they arranged for concerts and other kinds of entertainment as well. The prize for originality went to the Ladies' Benevolent Society of the High Street Presbyterian Church, whose 1843 fair featured a lecture on electricity, "in addition to which, the Electrical Shock will be administered to as many of the audience as may desire it."[43]

The main attraction for customers, meantime, was the opportunity for social interaction. Ronald G. Walters has aptly characterized the fairs staged by northern abolitionists as rituals of community. Although fairs were profitable, Walters suggests, their more important function was to reinforce commitment to the movement.[44] In Petersburg, the process was not so straightfoward, not for most of the men, anyway. It may well have been that fairs gave men the chance to show their good intentions while stopping short of thorough commitment. By spending money at a fair, one could contribute to religious causes without undergoing the public act of submission that was required for church membership. In any event, fairs certainly encouraged interaction of the boy-meets-girl variety, as sales of some items (and returns—boy buys and then returns the item; girl keeps the money) were converted into rituals of flirtation and courtship. Ann T. Davis described a particularly lucrative series of transactions at a Methodist fair of 1860:

> Alice undertook to sell a boquet for me the other night, and she got for it $2.01. She at first sold it for 50. cts, and it was given back to her; she sold it the second time for the same price, and it was again given to her; she afterward met with a spry old widower, who seemed to be much taken with her, he told her that he would give her for it all the money he had left in his purse, which amounted to $1.01. The next morning she handed back the boquet with the money. Several of the girls have resold their boquets, and made from $1. to $1.25 cts, and then brought back the flowers.

Note that Ann Davis, who was a married woman with grown children, was not in the business of selling bouquets. What was on sale here was youthful charm. The system must have been excruciating for the most bashful of the young saleswomen, but it was undeniably profitable. In 1859, the one year for which a number of totals happen to be available, the women of the Gillfield Church (black Baptist) made $328, the women of the Market Street Methodist Church made $750, the women of Grace Episcopal Church made $1,160, and the women of the Catholic church made $1,200.[45]

Ann Davis's close accounting of the flower sales suggests that for the organizers, the profits were at least as important as the rituals, something to be expected from women who were generally isolated from the experience of making money in a purely commercial context. For middle-class women as a group, the material significance of organized religious benevolence was that it blunted the impact of the economic forces that separated women's experience from that of men in the nineteenth century. For some time now, historians of women, particularly those who see the early nineteenth century as a time when women's status deteriorated, have emphasized the process by which economic modernization increased the status gap between men and women: Production moved out of the home; men moved with it and earned money; and women were left at home, unproductive and earning nothing. As the previous chapter suggests, we still have much to learn about the nature, timing, and meaning of this process. For the present, be it noted that religious benevolence did something to soften and obscure its force. The preparation of goods for a fair was in fact productive labor, and the sale of those goods did in fact yield a cash return. For most of those involved, the work was part-time and seasonal, but there were also those who worked overtime all of the time, women who made a career of religious benevolence.

In Petersburg, the outstanding example was Susan C. Bott, "a woman of admirable & rare qualities," as Edmund Ruffin put it. "I had an uncommon degree of respect for her," mused Anna Campbell, and in this her contemporaries were agreed. After Bott's death in 1853, her sister church women placed a headstone over her grave "as a tribute of affection and a memorial of her eminent piety," and the Presbyterian press in Philadelphia published her life story. A veteran of the founding of the Female Orphan Asylum and a charter member of the Female Missionary Society, Bott was active in organized benevolence from its beginnings. After she found herself widowed and nearly impoverished in 1824, she intensified her commitment, assuming leadership of the Presbyterian Education Society. From then on, Susan Bott never let up. She organized fairs, she found outlets for private sales in other cities, and she dedicated every spare minute to fashioning some salable article. Under her direction, the Education Society raised close to seven thousand dollars. When she died in 1853, so legend had it, sewing for the Education Society fell from her hands.[46]

How much the women had to say about how their money was spent is an open question. Control over allocation of funds varied enormously from one organization to another. Some societies exercised minute supervision over spending; this was most commonly the case when the stakes were small and the organization unaffiliated with any regional or national network. The Dorcas Society of the First Baptist Church (Washington Street), for example, had an annual budget of less than seventy-five dollars, funds derived from membership dues of twelve and a half cents a month. The minutes of a meeting of 1856 reveal the care with which each appropriation was made:

> The subject of disbursements coming next in order, the ladies were unanimously agreed, after deliberating; that the sum of 5.00, should be sent to Mrs. Holloway as a donation; but in view of Mrs. Hughes low state of health, and Mrs. Wells' frequent and violent attacks of illness, a regular appropriation shall be made monthly for their benefit on and after Nov 1st; of 1.50 to Mrs. Hughes and 1.50 to Mrs. Wells towards the payment of their rents.

Education societies, on the other hand, were generally auxiliaries to centralized boards in charge of ministerial training, and the women who raised the money locally lost control of it almost as fast as they made it. It had not always been that way. When Petersburg's Presbyterian women first organized their Education Society in 1822, they allotted money directly to ministerial candidates of their own choosing. In time, however (it is not clear exactly when), the Education Society threw in with the growing bureaucracy of benevolence, sending its earnings to a central Board of Education.[47]

For all its probable efficiency, the auxiliary system increased the distance between contributors and recipients, and this aggravated a problem inherent in Christian outreach efforts: It became all the more difficult for contributors to see the results of their labors. The numbers of clergymen trained, of new congregations gathered, and of Bibles and tracts distributed all could be added up and pored over, but the fundamental object of evangelism, the salvation of souls, remained stubbornly intangible. In the 1840s and 1850s, the women of Petersburg's churches made a decisive turn in the direction of the local, the specific, and the literally concrete, as they committed the greater part of their fundraising skills to the construction of new buildings for their own congregations.

The founding of Grace Episcopal Church provides a remarkably neat illustration of the inward turn. In 1840, the women of St. Paul's Church, Petersburg's only Episcopal congregation, proposed that the vestry hire a full-time missionary to work among the people of Petersburg's cotton mill district. As the women offered to pay the missionary's salary, the vestry had no cause for hesitation, and before the end of 1841, Reverend Churchill Jones Gibson had accepted the new post and begun his work. He met with a mixed reception. Forty or fifty children attended his Sunday school, but hardly any grownups would come to hear him preach. "As to my labors at the Factories," Gibson reflected, "I am sometimes disposed to be encouraged & at others to think that I am quite useless." With his middle-class sponsors, however, Gibson was an instant success, and a campaign was soon initiated to establish a second Episcopal church in Petersburg with Gibson as its pastor. The deed was done quickly; Grace Episcopal Church was consecrated in February 1843. Thereafter the women of Grace Church devoted their fundraising efforts to paying for the construction and repair of buildings.[48]

So, for that matter, did the women of St. Paul's and most of the other churches. To anyone who sees attempts to reach the unchurched as a critical Christian endeavor, the new concentration on buildings represents retreat and decline; investing in buildings—and there were some very fine buildings—was part of the larger process by which southern Protestantism made itself respectable. And yet there was an assertive quality to the women's participation. This was explicit in the case of Petersburg's oldest black Baptist church, the Gillfield Baptist Church. Late in 1858, all the constituent societies of the church were asked to turn over the contents of their treasuries so that lumber could be purchased for a new building. The church's main women's organization, the Good Samaritan Sisters, refused. The next month the Sisters made their report, but still released no funds. "We the sisters that hold the money thought it right to give you the Church an answer the money we hold was gotten up to enlarge or rebuild and when the Building is in progress we will come up with our mite." Six months later, the women relinquished several hundred dollars, making good on the promise that the church would see the Sisters' money when the Sisters saw some progress on the church.[49] Even when the women had very little to say about when and how construction funds were spent, there was an implicit assertiveness in their involvement in the building of a church. Every new building was a visible monument to the labor and values of women.

To see in benevolent activity motives and rewards of a material sort is not to disparage the quality of the women's piety. For Susan C. Bott, money and labor were of no value except as they advanced the cause of Christ, and if she was atypical in the exclusiveness of her preoccupation with the faith, she nonetheless symbolized a set of priorities that was most often found among women. The women's investments of money and time in benevolent causes cannot be compared precisely with those of men, but a count of gifts to church and charity by will reveals a clear difference between the sexes. With deathbed giving, family came first; very few testators of either sex left legacies to anyone but kin and close friends. Still, the women were twice as likely as the men to allot parts of their estates to churches, benevolent societies, and the relief of the poor.[50]

There was indeed an identifiable women's culture in Petersburg, and some of its components went hand-in-glove with nineteenth-century stereotypes. Women did inhabit a separate sphere, as they were told they must; except for attendance at church services, the organizational lives of women were almost entirely segregated from those of men. And through their organizational activities, women confirmed what the nineteenth century chose to believe of them: Woman was first in piety and benevolence. Life and ideology were remarkably well matched.

Men, of course, continued their dominion in commerce and politics, and, as Barbara Welter has pointed out, this was not a separate-but-equal arrangement. The ladies were permitted to amuse themselves with benevolent enterprises precisely because American men, by and large, did not think religion and charity mattered very much.[51] There are a number of ways to read this division of labor. One is to accept the judgment of nineteenth-century men as to what (and who) mattered; women's activities, for all the high-flying rhetoric, were second best. It is also possible to reverse the judgment of nineteenth-century men, as many women must have done at the time. Where was the riveting significance, after all, in managing a shoestore or in campaigning for the Whig who was nearly indistinguishable from the Democrat?

A third approach emerges from the recognition that living with separate spheres was not as comfortable as it looked. The creation of separate spheres was a temporary and uneasy solution to the continuing problem of how to distribute tasks and spaces under new conditions, and like most solutions, it brought problems of its own. Interestingly enough, the main problem was not so much that women thought they had been given too little, but rather that men thought they had conceded too much. The 1850s brought an intriguing sequence of convergences and trade-offs.

The first indications that men were not universally comfortable with woman's sphere came from within the white churches. While the majority of men seemed content to relegate religion to their wives, for the men on the inside, the clergy and the active laymen, the predominance of women in the churches was a source of chronic embarrassment. However churchmen may have handled this privately, they coped in public by inflating the importance of their own efforts and by minimizing those of the women. The most striking feature of the records left by the men of the white churches is their persistent failure to acknowledge women's collective contributions. This was not the case in the black churches. The records of the Gillfield Baptist Church are full of references to contributions from the Good Samaritan Sisters, the women of the Musical Society, and the Female Building Society, the result, perhaps, of long experience with female breadwinning and of the fact that for black men religious activity did not connote effeminacy.

The writings of white churchmen, meanwhile, are a study in significant silences. Consider William W. Bennett's account of the revival that swept Petersburg in 1822:

> One man, while sitting on a keg of nails in his store, was struck down with conviction, then prayed, and was forgiven; another was joyfully converted while reading Fletcher's Appeal to earnest seekers of salvation; a third while waiting on his customers, gave his heart to God, shouted his praise, then fell dead, and went to heaven.[52]

From Bennett's description, one would never suspect that the majority of converts in 1822 were female; he gives no hint that any of the converts were female. Editors of the early evangelical periodicals likewise opted for the ostrich approach. The *Christian Monitor* and its successor, the *Virginia Evangelical and Literary Magazine,* refrained from mentioning the women's benevolent societies that were forming in every part of Virginia. The men's organizations, such as they were, were the ones that got the publicity. More remarkable for their silences are the manuscript records of the governing bodies of the local churches. The women of the First Baptist Church (Washington Street) held fairs in 1857, 1858, and 1859 to furnish their new church and to speed "the liquidation of the Church debt," but not a word of recognition was entered in the church's minute book. The women of St. Paul's Episcopal Church organized fairs in 1852, 1854, 1856, and 1857. Except for the acknowledgment of a donation for painting the church recorded in 1853, the vestry book says nothing about the women's work.[53]

The churches were heavily dependent on their women, and since there was not very much the men could do about this, they chose to ignore it. With charity the story was different. In the 1850s, women lost their monopoly on organized charity, as men reclaimed voluntary poor relief as a legitimate male concern. The pivotal year was 1858 when, for the first time, some of the men of Petersburg created a voluntary association whose primary aim was the relief of the poor. For this, the panic of 1857 was partly responsible. In mid-October, the *Express* estimated that from five to six hundred cotton mill hands had been laid off. A month later, the estimate rose to a thousand unemployed. As winter set in, the *Express* reported that "little girls, barefoot and poorly clad," were to be seen begging in the streets, and by February, the city was "swarming with beggars" of all ages and both sexes.[54] The newspapers offered the usual remedies. To the unemployed, they counseled patience; to the city fathers, they recommended the building of a workhouse to employ beggars and relieve the crowding at the poorhouse; to everyone who could give, they urged acts of individual charity. Organized charity, it appears, was still considered the territory of the ladies. Two winters earlier, the *South-Side Democrat* had reported that "many" women were busy raising subscriptions for the relief of the poor, and with the approach of the winter of 1857, the *Democrat* suggested that the women organize once again.[55] It does not seem to have occurred to anyone that the men might organize as well.

The men did not in fact organize until the following winter, the winter of 1858–59, when economic conditions were somewhat less brutal. What motivated them to adopt a feminine cause is uncertain, but the revivals of 1858 and 1859 may have been important. In Petersburg, as in most of the nation, a revival of religion followed close on the heels of the economic disasters of 1857. Whatever the causal relationship between the panic and the quickening of religious faith, the two together seem to have intensified both the need and the desire for some practical godliness. The churches, in any case (white churches only, but Catholic as well as Protestant), provided the organizational base for Petersburg's new relief effort. In December 1858, lay representatives from each of the ten white churches met to draft a constitution and bylaws. They decided to adopt whole the constitution of a Baltimore organization, and by Christmas week, the Association for Improvement of the Condition of the Poor was functioning with considerable newspaper coverage, a paid agent, a president (Methodist), a vice president from each church, and a board of managers whose job was to canvass the city's four wards for contributors. In its first two months, the association gave assistance to more than two hundred families, almost all of them white. In his enthusiasm, the agent by spring had spent more than the organization had collected, but the financial crisis was surmounted, and the association survived to carry out a second winter of activity in 1859–60.[56]

The men of the white Methodist churches, meanwhile, were going farther still in adopting the feminine mode of public service. In a not altogether fathomable move of 1858, Methodist men got into the business of operating a female orphan asylum, or, more accurately, they assumed legal control over an institution their wives had been running for ten years. The known facts are these. There were two female orphan asylums in Petersburg in 1858 (there were none for boys). First was the asylum founded in 1812, managed by women of several different denominations but identified most strongly with the Episcopal churches. In 1847, women of the Methodist churches had founded a female orphan asylum of their own. The immediate cause had been the last request of a thirteen-year-old boy. Thomas Cooke Paul was the son of devout and wealthy Methodist parents; according to his biographer, he was also a model of youthful piety. In 1845, young Thomas was stricken with a serious illness, and just before he died, he asked that his parents establish a female orphan asylum.

Petersburg already had a female orphan asylum, of course, and that is probably why Thomas Paul asked his parents to build one: It was the only form of institutional charity in his experience. The new asylum, endowed by D'Arcy and Elizabeth Paul and run by Methodist women, was the virtual twin of what now came to be called the Episcopal asylum. In its corporate charter, its system of governance, and its program, the Thomas Cooke Paul Female Orphan Asylum was a nearly exact replica of its sister institution. And then in 1858 the Paul asylum was transformed. A new act of incorporation created a board of twenty-one trustees, all of whom were men, and in this board were vested all effective powers. The board held the property, the board made the bylaws, the board made personnel decisions.[57] Legally speaking, it was a thorough coup.

It is difficult to know for certain whether to read the events of 1858 as capitulation on the men's part or as an invasion. On the one hand, men's new interest in poor relief was a capitulation to female values. At long last, some men admitted that poor people sometimes suffered through no fault of their own and that the privileged bore collective responsibility for alleviating their suffering. Once men made that decision, their greater financial resources allowed them to collect more money, and to collect it more quickly, than was possible for women. For poor people themselves, most of whom were women and children, it was fortunate that the men got involved.[58]

On the other hand, poor relief was the one field that women had had entirely to themselves, and if the events of 1858 did not represent a conscious assault on female autonomy, they nonetheless paralleled a general move away from autonomous women's organizations. In the 1850s, Petersburg women came to participate in several new organizations. In every documentable case, the organizations were run by men, with the women playing well-defined auxiliary roles.

First there were the Sons of Temperance, who despite their name made the admission of women members a matter of local option. Petersburg's division roundly supported the attendance of "lady visitors," as they were called, adopted a formal ritual for their admission, and in 1859 urged other divisions to try it for themselves. The struggle against drunkenness, it was assumed, was the men's struggle; the task of the women was to cheer the men on, "to help us with their presence and encourage us by their smiles," as the *Virginia Conductor* put it.[59] In two other new organizations, women took on somewhat more active roles. Every year from 1854 on, the Union Agricultural Society sponsored a fair to foster the spread of modern farming techniques, and every year the society appointed two women's committees, one to decorate the exhibition halls and the other to judge the various domestic arts entries submitted by women exhibitors. Finally, there was the Library Association, founded in 1853 to provide Petersburg with a public library. Not many women joined initially; at the end of the first year, there were only 17 women among the 315 members. When it came time to raise the money to furnish the new library hall, however, dozens of women pitched in and organized a fund-raising fair.[60]

The new library hall was opened in 1859, and to mark the occasion, Thomas S. Gholson addressed a packed house on the subject of "Woman and Her Mission." Woman's mission, "in its highest and noblest sense," Gholson declaimed, was "that of helpmate to man, the kind consoler of his cares, the confiding sharer of his joys, the sweet counsellor, and always the fond, firm and abiding friend."[61] The women in the audience must have heard that message hundreds of times before, but by 1859, it had special resonance. By 1859, it not only conveyed an ideal of private behavior, but it also described the new structure of voluntary associations, with men at the center and women playing supporting parts. It was, as Natalie Zemon Davis has commented in another context, a case of "together but unequal."[62]

There was something in it for the women, of course. Through the new organizations, women were able to contribute to a wider range of causes; to church and charity were added temperance, the promotion of literary culture, and agricultural modernization, a cause increasingly associated with southern nationalism. They also got their names in the papers. The newspapers never reported the names of the managers of the female orphan asylums, nor did they list members or officers of the women's religious benevolent societies. The names of women active in the auxiliaries, however, were often meticulously listed; in 1859, for example, the *Intelligencer* printed the names of all thirty-eight members of the arrangements committee for the library fair.[63] Togetherness had its rewards.

Togetherness also exacted concessions, although it is not clear that the women saw it that way at the time. The rise of women's auxiliaries was accompanied by the establishment of two new rituals of female deference. First was the matter of names. When Mildred Walker Campbell signed the orphan asylum petition of 1812, she signed herself "M. W. Campbell." When she headed the library fair committee in 1859, the *Intelligencer* listed her as "Mrs. John W. Campbell," even though her husband had been dead for seventeen years. The new practice placed the husband at the center of female identity, at least on a symbolic level, and it must have made unmarried women feel their deviant status the more keenly. Before 1830, identifying the woman by the husband's first name was almost unheard of. In the 1840s and 1850s, it became commonplace.[64]

In the 1850s also, the question of public speaking was finally settled, and in the negative. Oratory had never been a routine female activity, but there were a few occasions in which women spoke in public before mixed audiences. Whenever a new militia company was raised, it was customary for a delegation of women to supply the company with a flag. A short speech was part of the presentation ceremony, and when new militia units were organized in 1825 and 1831, the women spoke for themselves. In 1847, however, a gentleman was designated to present the flag to the Petersburg Volunteers on the women's behalf, and this became the established practice, giving men yet another opportunity to hold forth on the nature of woman. "Weak and defenceless in herself," said Richard G. Pegram in a flag ceremony of 1852, "woman looks to man for protection; and, as she gazes upon your serried ranks, she feels a sense of security from the approach of danger, which entirely supercedes her natural timidity."[65]

In the early 1850s, opportunities for female oratory were revived with the movement to upgrade female education. The students in the new female "colleges" were subject to more rigorous requirements, including the obligation to compose their own commencement addresses. In the beginning, they also delivered their own addresses. After hearing the performances of Leavenworth's Female Seminary's class of 1853, a listener was inspired to write a letter to the editor: "In truth, I believe some of the ladies declaimed their pieces much better than half the young men in this city could do. . . . During the progress of these exercises, I was most forcibly struck with the reflection, that although man has always been regarded as the superior of woman, yet I became satisfied in my own mind of this fact, that the one has never invented or accomplished anything which the other could not have effected by a similar effort." There would not be many more opportunities for such reflections. In 1856, Petersburg Female College held its second annual commencement exercises. The featured speaker went on for an hour, telling his audience that the intellectual capacity of women was "equal to that of the opposite sex, in attaining and retaining the highest and noblest literary and scientific accomplishments." When the speaker sat down, it was time for the reading of the graduates' original essays. "Upon a point of delicacy arising, Professor Lupton and Rev. Mr. Coulling performed the part of readers for the fair authors." That, apparently, was that. If any of Petersburg's young women made speeches after 1856, no evidence of it survives.[66]

A final evaluation of the overall progress of women's organizations up to 1860 hinges, as do so many questions of progress and decline, on our point of reference. If we compare women's options in the 1850s with those available to them at the beginning of the century, there is no question that their organizational lives had grown immeasurably richer. If we compare women's options to those available to men, the women consistently come up short. In every decade, men had access to organizations that were closed to women. There were long-standing fraternal associations like the Masons; there were shorter-lived debating clubs; there were two mechanics' organizations; there were several single-sex temperance societies; and there were political parties, fire companies, and the militia. These last two were particularly important (and so were political parties after 1851, when propertiless white men got the vote) in that they engaged white men of the working class. For working-class white women, there appear to have been no formal organizations at all.

Comparing the organizational opportunities open to women with those open to men makes it clearer than ever that women's place was indeed mainly in the home. Once again, the cult of true womanhood turns out to be a closer description of social reality than we might like. It is time for a last look at the relations among the changing status of women inside the home, the cult of true womanhood, and the changing status of women outside the home.

The question of what a given ideology had to do with

social reality is usually a complicated one, and with the cult of true womanhood, a great deal of territory remains to be explored. A first hypothesis was suggested briefly by the historian who gave the cult its name. In a widely reprinted article of 1966, Barbara Welter proposed that the ideal of the true woman served as a kind of national tranquilizer: As men gave themselves over to the relentless pursuit of wealth, they assuaged their anxiety and guilt by assuring themselves that women, as long as they stayed home, would keep the country's religious faith vital and its moral virtue strong. After Welter's essay appeared, speculation on the cult's meaning shifted quickly away (perhaps too quickly) from the subject of male anxiety and refocused on the question of what the cult might tell us about how the status of women was changing.[67] Here the true woman revealed her full capacity for ambiguity. On the one hand, it can be argued that the rise of the cult of true womanhood reflected a real change for the better, that women did experience a significant increase in prestige and power within the home. On the other hand, the cult can be read as a sign of disaster: Never before had women been so rigidly confined; the insistence that women exercised "influence" through their domestic roles was merely a bribe, an attempt to buy women's compliance with their new confinement.

This debate is complicated by the fact that once the basic tenets of true womanhood were established, they could be, and were, used in diametrically opposite ways. The cult was invariably invoked by those who wished to repel some new female incursion on male prerogative. The horrified reaction of a number of clergymen to the spectacle of women abolitionists speaking in public to mixed audiences provides a well-known example. At the same time, the true woman's claim to superior virtue and piety could be used to justify the creation of new spheres of female activity outside the home.[68] The cult of true womanhood was sufficiently elastic in character to be used by different groups for different purposes, and this helps account for its longevity and force.

Insofar as the Petersburg evidence speaks to these issues,

it strongly suggests backlash. Or to phrase it more carefully, the cult of true womanhood was a selective, mainly conservative response to real changes in the status of women; while the cult may well have drawn strength from male anxiety over materialism run wild, it was also an acknowledgment of women's increased options and an attempt to contain those options. In 1780, it was not necessary to tell women to stay home and mind their husbands; with a very few exceptions, they had no place else to go. But by 1820 or so, some women had some choices. They could choose the church. They could choose participation in a number of voluntary associations. Many of them were sufficiently well educated to rival or surpass their husbands in learning. A few of them possessed property and income their husbands could not touch. It stands to reason that an ideology that tried to fix the boundaries of women's sphere should have become pervasive and urgent just as women began to exercise a few choices.

By the same token, it stands to reason that the further gains made by women in the antebellum period would provoke backlash in one form or another. This, perhaps, was the significance of men's encroachments on women's organizational territory in the 1850s and of the new rituals of deference. As women acquired new degrees of power and autonomy in the private sphere, they were confronted with new forms of subordination in the public sphere.

The statement that women acquired new autonomy and power in the decades before 1860 brings with it a trail of qualifiers. First, there were central aspects of life that we simply cannot see; sexuality, fertility, contraception, and abortion all are blind spots. Petersburg's women may well have followed the national trend of fewer pregnancies and fewer births, but there is no way to verify this. Second, there were cases where women's status improved in one respect but declined in another. Free black women increased their control over property, for example, but along with black men their status under the law deteriorated badly after 1831. Middle-class white women also increased their control over property, but their work as housewives became more burdensome as slave help became scarcer. In these cases, it can be difficult to judge whether there was net gain or loss. Third, what we call gain or loss depends in part on our frame of reference. We have just seen this with organizations; women's opportunities did increase absolutely over time, but compared to what was available to men, women's options were still relatively stunted. Business presented a parallel case. Women's roles as proprietors seem to have held steady over time. But relatively speaking, this was a loss, for women did not become officers in the new business corporations. Finally, we need to be careful about indicators; a high rate of gainful employment may indicate enhanced options for women, or it may indicate the opposite. The same goes for participation in productive labor. The surest statement that can be made about the experience of women in the nineteenth century is that it grew in complexity.

For all that, it is still possible to make a case for gain. What the women of Petersburg gained was greater autonomy in a very specific sense: They gained greater freedom from immediate and total dependence on particular men. This was achieved in part by staying away from marriage. The proportion of white women who never married went up, though by how much we cannot say, while free black women all along had special reasons for staying single. Widows, meanwhile, did not usually remarry if they could afford to remain as they were. The second face of the new autonomy was economic. Factories provided hundreds of new jobs for women workers, and even if they failed to pay subsistence wages, they made the women less dependent on male breadwinners than they would otherwise have been. Among the propertied, separate estates had the same effect. An increasing proportion of Petersburg's women owned property in one form or another, and as time passed, they became increasingly active in its disposition; they bought and sold more land, freed more slaves, lent and borrowed more money, pressed their dower rights more often, and executed more wills and deeds of gift.

Men, meanwhile, must have felt increasingly dependent

on a business cycle that could humiliate the most careful provider, that forced workingmen to rely on the earnings of their wives and daughters, and that threw proprietors back on their womenfolk's earnings and separate estates. Was it coincidence that men took over so many of women's causes in the 1850s? The assumption of voluntary poor relief as a male responsibility, the take-over of the female orphan asylum, the formation of women's auxiliaries, the injunction against women speaking in public, the use of the husband's name to identify the married woman—the motives behind these new moves cannot be assigned with any confidence. The effect, however, was the same as if there had been a deliberate campaign to compensate for women's growing autonomy. The effect was to erase, in symbol and in organizational structure, the appearance of autonomous action by women in the public sphere. This did not entail crushing female assertiveness or achievement wherever it arose. Rather it meant that women's roles were to be relational, that women were to act and achieve through men.

For the women of Petersburg, the story in the antebellum period was not one of linear progress or decline; in organizational terms, it was neither a permanent retreat into a separate sphere nor a steady march from the confines of the home to the riskier and more varied regions the nineteenth century called "the world." Instead, there was a trade of sorts. Women were experiencing growing autonomy in their personal lives. For this, they apparently paid a price; in their public lives, they lost both the symbols and structure of autonomy. The consolation, if there was one, was that the men who co-opted their causes had no choice but to adopt some of their values.

EPILOGUE

On Feminism, Slavery, and the Experience of Defeat

In 1841, Alexander Wells, who was white, sold his wife, who was also white. He literally sold her, to another man, for one dollar, and he got away with it. This happened in Petersburg, and it raises with particular vividness the possibility that for women the South was a distinctively dismal place, that in a society dedicated to the maintenance of chattel slavery, free women were degraded in much the same way that slaves were. But before proceeding with this line of inquiry, it is only fair to fill in the rest of the story. Alexander Wells and Saluda Ann Hastings were married in Petersburg in 1830. They lived together, not very happily, for eleven months. Suspecting that Saluda had not been faithful to him, Alexander ran off to Richmond to enlist in the army and was posted to Florida. He was gone eleven years. During the first year, he wrote one letter home. After that, he sent no word at all, and he sent no money to support Saluda or their child. Nonetheless, after eleven years, Alexander returned to Petersburg and took Saluda to the house of a relative, where he did his best to get her to live with him again as his wife. Saluda wanted no part of it. Since Alexander had been missing for more than seven years, Saluda had thought herself a widow, and three years before Alexander's unsettling return, she had married a man named George Patram. As for Alexander, Saluda "constantly rejected all his advances, and avowed her determination never to live with him as his wife. . . ."

One rebuff after another finally persuaded Alexander that he would never win Saluda back. Yet so far as he knew, he was still legally bound to support her, and he was not free to marry anyone else. It was at this point that Alexander sold Saluda. Witnesses were gathered, George Patram paid Alexander a dollar, and Alexander issued to Patram a receipt. That, Alexander hoped, was enough to dissolve his marriage to Saluda, and a few months later, Alexander married a woman named Judith B. Longworth. For Saluda, there was no happy ending; she eventually wound up in the poorhouse. For Alexander, the ending may ultimately have been happier. In June 1842, Alexander was tried for bigamy, convicted, and sentenced to two years in the penitentiary. Immediately after sentence was pronounced, however, counsel for the defense, the prosecuting attorney, the jury, and several local officials united in petitioning the governor for clemency. Alexander was pardoned on June 25, 1842.[1]

One hesitates to make too much of so bizarre a case, especially given the fact that in parts of England, wife sale was not unheard of as a means by which men divorced their wives.[2] (It is not known whether Alexander or any of the other actors in the Petersburg case knew about this. If Alexander did know, he perhaps deserves some credit for dispensing with the English practice of harnessing the wife like a heifer and leading her to a ritual auction.) And yet there must have been some significance in it. In all the petitions submitted on Alexander's behalf by some very prominent Petersburg men, there was no disapproval, not a hint of moral outrage at the fact that a free woman had been sold.

Perhaps this is what we should expect from a society in which human beings were routinely bought, sold, swapped, and mortgaged. It would be surprising indeed if there were no evidence that nonslave women were degraded by slavery. But it is by no means clear just how much and in what ways chattel slavery did shape the lives of free women. Nor is it yet clear how the lives of free women were reshaped by the war that brought slavery to an end. This epilogue is devoted to a speculative exploration of the problem.

This relatively new problem feeds into an old controversy, of course; to ask about the impact of slavery and its demise is to stir up the debate over southern distinctiveness. For decades, historians and others have reflected on what it was that made the South different from the North, whether the differences outweighed fundamental similarities, and whether the New South—the South that emerged from the rubble of war—was significantly different from the old.[3] The participants in the debate have not concerned themselves much with women. Historians of southern women, however, have had little choice but to concern themselves, if only indirectly, with southern distinctiveness, with the meaning of slavery and the impact of a war that for white men, at least, was a devastating defeat. The prevailing point of view is that for women the Civil War was a watershed. The war, as Anne Firor Scott phrased it, "speeded social change and opened Pandora's box"; the war weakened patriarchy and paved the way for a more complex social order that gave elite women more options in work, education, organizations, and politics.[4]

The war-as-watershed thesis may continue to carry the day as we gather more concrete evidence about the status of women both before the war and after. It is worth pointing out, however, that as it was originally formulated, the watershed thesis was based in part on a misconstruction of antebellum society: One of the reasons the war loomed so large was that the amount of social change that took place in the antebellum decades was assumed to be so small. It was explicitly noted (and correctly so, as far as subsequent research revealed) that the antebellum South permitted no public feminist protest and produced no organized feminist movement. The main explanation for this is that feminism was closely aligned with the movement to abolish slavery, and southerners would therefore have nothing to do with it.[5] The problem with war-as-watershed theory is that this same logic was applied to the status of women generally. That is, it was assumed that the maintenance of slavery required the strict subordination of women; in protecting slavery, the South was so defensive and so resistant to social change that nothing could alter the status of women, nothing short of the killing and maiming of massive numbers of men and the onset of widespread, desperate poverty.

The point should be obvious by now, but it is worth making explicitly: Positive change in the status of women can occur when no organized feminism is present. In Petersburg, there was considerable change, as we have seen, and much of it was change for the better. Antebellum women of both races made substantial gains in the acquisition and disposition of property; they formed organizations and built churches; they took up work in factories. White women made progress in education, and both white and black women displayed new varieties of personal assertiveness. It will be some time before we know the relative significance of these changes. We need comparative data, as precise as can be mustered, from the North, the rural South, and the New South. In the meantime, the evidence of change in antebellum Petersburg is sufficient to warrant some rethinking of the relations among feminism, changing status, slavery, and war.

It seems likely that the development of organized feminism was indeed inhibited by the slave system. It is not clear whether the determination to maintain slavery made southern men peculiarly intolerant of any signs of incipient feminism; nothing in the Petersburg evidence, for example, indicates that the abolitionist origins of northern feminism were particularly troublesome to southern men. But it does seem probable that living with slavery made it difficult for free women to grow into a feminist frame of reference. As Blanche Hersh has written, the abolition movement in the North was "the catalyst which transformed latent feminist sentiment into the beginnings of an organized movement."[6] Southern women simply did not have access to that abolitionist catalyst.

Insofar as feminism requires a consciousness that all women share similar problems, the women of the South faced an especially difficult task. White women could sometimes reach across class lines, as their charitable work demonstrated; it was relatively easy for white, middle-class women to identify with poorer whites, for middle-class women had cause to fear that they themselves might be thrown on charity someday. But this there-but-for-fortune attitude apparently stopped at the color line. We do not have any direct evidence on how black women regarded white women. As for white women's attitudes toward black women, it appears that identification came hard. An examination of slave emancipations for evidence of female bonding turns up some thought-provoking information: In Petersburg, white women emancipated more male slaves than female slaves. The local authorities, meanwhile, did what they could to prevent social contacts between white and black women of the lower classes. In 1857, a free black named Annie Nichols was charged with assaulting a white woman named Susan Turner. Nichols was sentenced to ten lashes. The white woman was "severely reprimanded . . . for degrading herself so far as to associate with the prisoner. . . ."[7] Racism cripples its perpetrators as well as its targets. It may have been that the single greatest barrier to the development of an indigenous southern feminism was the difficulty both white and black women had in seeing something of themselves in one another.

Nonetheless, though there were no signs of organized feminism, the mind of the South was at least occasionally open to new ideas about women's capacities and women's roles. In 1822, the young men of the Petersburg Franklin Society conducted a formal debate on the question, "Is the mind of man naturally superior to that of woman?" It was a split decision, and the women lost. "After discussion it was decided in the affirmative, 3 to 2." But two votes for intellectual equality was not bad, not for 1822, and subsequent newspaper editorials were supportive of improved education for young women. Some of these were written with real punch. A lengthy editorial of 1854 lauded writer and feminist Margaret Fuller for her courage as well as for her gifts, and an essay of 1855 laid down the conditions for the flowering of female genius. "The word *bluestocking* must lose its terrors, strength of mind must cease to be a reproach, ostracism must cease to hang over every female who dares to think and write, the arts must be opened in their classic grandeur to the hand and head of woman before the Dr. [*sic*] Staels and the Margaret Fullers cease to be prodigies or exceptions."[8]

The newspapers of the 1850s also advocated expanded opportunities for self-support. "We bring up our women to be dependent," the *South-Side Democrat* pointed out, "and leave them without any one to depend on. There is no one, there is nothing for them to lean upon, and they fall to the ground. Now, what every woman, no less than every man, should have to depend upon, is an ability, after some fashion or other, to turn labor into money. She may or may not be compelled to exercise it, but every one ought to possess it. If she belong[s] to the richer classes, she may have to exercise it; if to the poorer, she assuredly will." As we have seen, editorials made explicit pitches for widening the range of occupations open to women, and indirect support for the same cause was added when news columns reported progress in other locations. The *Intelligencer,* for example, made a significant statement in two short sentences. "There are in the United States eighty-one women holding the office of postmaster (?) thirty-one of whom are in Pennsylvania. Some of these are important offices."[9]

The newspapers were not uniform in their advocacy of female intellectual development and economic independence. The *South-Side Democrat* on one occasion carped that education in the classics and in higher mathematics was making women too "formal and distant," and another editor expressed doubt that women should study medicine.[10] There were, besides, countless subtle indications that the editors could do very well without any major changes in women's status. Yet the point stands that the editors were frequently willing to promote progressive ideas concerning women's sphere.

Organized feminism was another matter. When, from 1848 on, northerners began to engage in collective protest through women's rights conventions, there was no positive response from the Petersburg press. Still, it can be said for Petersburg's newspapers that they did not suppress news of the disturbing doings up north, and about half of the time, they printed reports of convention proceedings straight on, with no editorial venom and no wisecracks.[11] The other half of the time, the approach was ridicule, either locally composed or borrowed from some hostile northern paper. The *South-Side Democrat* remarked on the Syracuse convention of 1852, "They have resolved to do a thousand things and done nothing except make fools of themselves, which they have succeeded in doing very effectually. The correspondent of the Herald says that the most of them are in Bloomer costume. Why not go the whole figure? Breeches, ladies, by all means."[12]

Northern feminism, it is clear, did not escape southern notice. Would that we knew what Petersburg women thought when they read news of the conventions or when in 1854 they went to hear a library lecture on "Woman's Rights." (The speaker was humorist Oliver P. Baldwin; the *Democrat* promised that the speech "will raise many an anti-dyspeptic guffaw before it concludes.") The one hint that someone was taking feminism seriously came in 1856. A letter to the editor of the *South-Side Democrat* had asked, "Why not advocate woman's rights more?" The editor's reply was vague, but he made an intriguing statement along the way: "Even in this small burg we have noticed that the ladies or the women who have endeavored to throw off some of their bondage, have made the 'world' speak most unkindly of them."[13]

Throwing off their bondage? How, and how consciously? It would be foolish to argue that there was a significant amount of overt feminism in Petersburg—we simply do not have the evidence. Even so, what we do know about Petersburg suggests that for the majority of free women, North and South may not have been so very different after all. The North was itself no feminist paradise. Before 1860, converts were few, and agitation generally met with hostility from men and timidity or indifference on the part of women. In Petersburg, meanwhile, there was more open-mindedness and more actual change than we might have expected from a southern place, even a southern city. So it might be worth trying on a new thesis: The status of southern women did not diverge radically from that of northern women until after the Civil War; the war itself was in some respects a setback for the South's free women.

"Petersburgh has been a prety Place," a Yankee soldier wrote in 1865, "but it is a hard looking Place now." [14] Petersburg took a beating in the war. At first, there had been bustle and enterprise. Petersburg was a major railroad center, the most important link between the capital and the vast territory of the Confederacy to the south and west, and so in the beginning the town was alive with moving troops and supplies. The railroads also made the capture of Petersburg a major objective of the Union army. The Confederates knew this and in the summer of 1862 began construction of a ten-mile line of fortifications around the city. The work took a year to complete; the test came in 1864. In June and July, Union armies made repeated assaults on the Confederate line, and the city itself was shelled. But Petersburg was not taken, and both sides settled in for a seige. As fall came, and then winter, the soldiers' complaints of dust and hunger changed to complaints of cold and hunger. By March 1865, when the Union army renewed its concentrated attacks near Petersburg, the Confederates were already three-quarters beaten by sickness and starvation. The Yankees attacked Petersburg itself on April 2. It was not a prolonged battle. In an eleventh-hour attempt to join his forces with the remnants of Confederate troops in North Carolina, General Lee ordered the soldiers defending Petersburg to evacuate. The

Union army took quiet possession of the town on April 3, just before dawn. Richmond capitulated four hours later, and Lee himself surrendered within a few days.

Confederate women experienced the same sequence of energy, endurance, and defeat. At first, they rushed to war work with extraordinary intensity. "To be idle was torture," remembered one; "we lived on excitement," wrote another. Sewing for the war effort was organized instantly through the networks already existing in the churches, and the work was done quickly. "Rec'd 2 Bales cotton cloth (1456 yds) – to be made into sheets," read the minutes of the Washington Street Soldiers' Relief Society, "Made 145½ prs sheets & 60 Suits of Clothing for a Miss[issippi] Company." When troop trains approached Petersburg, the engineer whistled a signal, and the women appeared at the depots with food, flowers, and cheer. There was hospital work, and scores of women took recuperating soldiers into their homes.[15] And there was romance. A soldier from the Petersburg encampment wrote home in 1862: "I tuck a nice walk with a yong lady the other night to church and also friday night to the theater and yo may no I felt happy I have got the purties Sweetehart you ever saw in your Life you tell the ladies if they dont wright me I will bring me a wife from forginnia. . . ." "We are campt in the edge of Petersburg," another soldier wrote in 1863, "and we are having a glorious time. . . ."[16]

For some, disillusionment set in early. Mary Ann Whittle lost a son in the first months of the fighting. "This dreadful war," she wrote in 1861, "when o when will it be at an end." As time went on, war weariness was expressed in every hand and accent. Free blacks, women as well as men, suffered the special indignity of forced labor in the Confederate camps, hospitals, and fortifications.[17] Everyone was affected by inflation and profiteering. Some people managed to joke about it: "Eggs seemed to have been purposely kept for a rise," wrote one observer in 1863, "and so high too, that they lost their balance and fell from my top window." But the dizzy prices worked real hardships. So did the shortages of medicine and food. Then in

1864 the worst of war came to Petersburg. Civilians were killed in the shelling, and untold numbers became refugees. "The vandals are still throwing shell into the city," a diarist noted, "& it is very distressing to see the women & children leaving. It is hard on all; but to see the poor women with the children on one arm & their little budgets on the other seeking for a safe place – is enough to move the hardest heart." He added weakly, "Providence certainly will reward such a people." [18]

We know now that there were few rewards in store for the South's free people. The central facts of southern life after the war were poverty and troubled, volatile relations between the races, and it is worth inquiring how much the status of women could have improved under these conditions. For black women who had been free before the war, there were some important gains. All their relatives were at last free, and they did eventually gain the right to an elementary education. It must also be said that for some white women, the war brought a heightened sense of self-esteem as they carried out tasks vital to the war effort and as they learned to make do in a hundred ways. Bessie Callender was treasurer of a soldiers' relief society; "its a serious job," she wrote, "to cut out and distribute and see if its well done, then lastly but not the easiest to pay all the women. . . ." For Callender, there was satisfaction in announcing that she was too much needed in Petersburg to visit her family in the country: ". . . I must attend to my duties as treasurer of the society—or things will get into terrible confusion." Sarah A. Pryor had jumped right into sewing for the soldiers; she sacrificed her household linen for bandages; she overcame her faintness and learned to be a nurse in an army hospital; she moved her family several times without help from her husband; she supported her children by sewing after her husband was taken prisoner; and she drew up a flawless will for a dying man. She wrote about all of this forty years after the war ended, and she was still proud of what she had managed to do.[19] There is no question that in the war many women discovered in themselves new reserves of competence and daring.

The question is: How far did this take them when the war was over? This can only be answered through detailed research of the kind that informs the previous chapters, but preliminary indicators are not heartening. The credit ledgers kept by R. G. Dun & Company indicate that women's businesses in Petersburg suffered badly during the war. Credit reporting was suspended during the war itself, but agents were back at work by December 1865, and for several male proprietors, they reported, "Made money during the war." No woman was so fortunate. Of all the women proprietors rated in 1860–61, only one was back in business in 1865. One other eventually turned up as a milliner in a department store. The rest either disappeared completely or were listed as "out of business." It was true that a number of female proprietors appeared in 1865 for the first time and that some of them were able to stay in business for several years. But there was no net gain.[20]

The evidence from the wills, meanwhile, is mixed. During the period 1861 to 1870, the frequency with which husbands nominated their wives as executors went up. The frequency with which wives inherited some property in fee simple, however, went down. And there was a dramatic, puzzling decline in the proportion of wills written by women. In the 1840s and 1850s, nearly 45 percent of the wills recorded in Petersburg were written by women. During the war years, the proportion of women will writers declined only a little, to 41.4 percent (43 / 104). When the war was over, however, the proportion of wills left by women dropped to 22.4 percent (15 / 67). This was the lowest figure since the 1820s.[21] While the cause of the decline is unclear, it does not look like a good sign.

When the requisite research is done, we may in fact find that in the war and its aftermath, male authority was seriously weakened. But we may also find that male authority was wounded, and for women this had to be dangerous. White men returned from the war demoralized and exhausted. Some were cripples, some emotionally disturbed. There was hardly any money and there was very little credit. There was plenty of unemployment. The man's position as breadwinner was thus undermined, while his position as master of slaves was terminated. And his political world was turned upside down—black men were granted the vote while some white men had it taken away.

Losers are not inclined to be generous. It was after the war that the mythology of rape became a prominent feature of white southern thinking. What more efficient way to reestablish the dominance of white men? The belief that black men were bent on raping white women justified the suppression of any form of black male assertiveness. The claim that white women were in constant need of physical protection was a denial of all that the women had learned and accomplished in the emergencies of war and impoverishment. In the myth of rape, the suppression of blacks and the suppression of women came together with new and sickening clarity.

Once again, we need research—specific, comparative, and as attentive to domestic life as to the public realm. In the meantime, some qualifications are in order. Rather than labeling the Civil War an absolute setback for southern women, it may be wiser to cast the war and its aftermath in relative terms: The South may have improved for women in several respects, but the North improved faster. At the same time, it must be emphasized that a very narrow base of evidence underlies our impression that women in the postwar South were significantly worse off than women in the North. About all that is known is that feminism as an organized public movement came to the South comparatively late, that women's suffrage organizations remained small, and that southern feminists had short luck persuading legislatures that women deserved the vote. About the rest of women's experience we know very little. Can we assume that the sorry state of organized feminism was an accurate indicator of the status of southern women overall? Recall that in the 1850s, Petersburg's women gained power within the family even while their autonomy in the public sphere was curtailed. A similar pattern may have prevailed in the postwar era. It may be that for women, the distinctiveness of the South lay in the breadth of the gap between private power and public display: No one objected to a woman's acquisition of power as long as she did not ask that it be made obvious, official, or general.

The white women of Petersburg, meanwhile, channeled much of their collective energy into keeping alive the spirit and memory of the Confederacy. In October 1865, more than 600 Petersburg women signed a petition asking President Andrew Johnson to release from prison former Confederate president Jefferson Davis. The following spring, 278 women founded the Ladies Memorial Association. They began to raise money to move the remains of Confederate soldiers to Blandford Cemetery, and each ninth of June, they sponsored an observance of the battle of Petersburg, a battle in which a hometown guard of boys and old men had fended off the Yankee cavalry. As time went on, the women of the Ladies Memorial Association became more firmly convinced of the importance of their work. By the 1880s, there were young adults in Petersburg who could not remember the war, and the women could not abide the possibility that the rising generation would know nothing of what their parents had suffered. The women became interested in permanent memorials. Eventually they acquired the Old Blandford Church. They collected money from all over the South; they restored the building; and for every Confederate state, they installed a stained glass window, each window an original Tiffany production.[22]

Should you ever visit the Old Blandford shrine, recall the words of the women who built it: "We feel that the women who worked and suffered through that terrible war deserve to be called heroes and veterans as much as the men who stood behind the guns."[23] All across the South, the women who created monuments to the Lost Cause were building monuments to their own historic fortitude. The irony is that they spent so much of themselves in venerating a war that seems to have gained them little more than memories.

An Essay
on Sources

The contents of Virginia's local public records vary over time and from one jurisdiction to another. Nonetheless, I hope this description of Petersburg's records will be of use to those who are considering embarking on local-records research. Lists of newspapers and manuscripts consulted are appended; for printed primary and secondary sources, the notes should provide an adequate guide.

The following Petersburg records are available on microfilm in the Virginia State Library:

Account books 1–10, 1806–60
Circuit court chancery order books 1–5, 1831–65
Circuit court will books 1–2, 1831–60
Hustings court deed books 1–26, 1784–1862
Hustings court minute books, 1784–1860
Hustings court will books, 1784–1871
Marriage register (bonds), 1784–1865
Marriage register 1, 1854–65
Record of interments, Blandford Cemetery, 1843–60
Register of births, 1853–71
Register of deaths, 1853–71

United States, population schedules for Petersburg, 1810–
60

Other public records are:

Land books, 1788–1860, Virginia State Library
Legislative petitions, 1782–1863, Virginia State Library
Personal property books, 1788–1860, Virginia State Library
Petersburg common council minutes, 1784–1860, Office
of the Clerk of the City Council, City Hall, Petersburg
Petersburg common council ordinances, 1836–61, Office
of the Clerk of the City Council, City Hall, Petersburg
Register of interments in the Blandford Church Yard,
1824–53, Virginia State Library
Reports of the Overseers of the Poor, 1829–60, Auditors
Item 227, Virginia State Library

Of all the sources listed above, the minute books contain
information on the greatest variety of subjects. These literally are minutes, hastily written by the clerk of the hustings court as the justices proceeded through their various
chores. (For some Virginia locations, there are also order
books. The order book was a formal rendition of the minutes, written at leisure and therefore more legibly. Order
books are more likely than minute books to give the first
names of parties to lawsuits, an important feature for anyone who wants to learn about women's participation in
civil actions. Petersburg's books for the 1780s and 1790s
are order books, though they are labeled minute books.)
Considerable space in the minute books was devoted to
probate matters and to the care of orphaned and poor children. Appointments of administrators (on estates of
deceased persons) were recorded in the minutes, as were
occasional declarations by widows that they would not
accept the terms of their husbands' wills. The minutes also
noted appointments of curators to look after the property
of persons certified as insane. Assignments of guardians
for propertied children were routinely recorded in the
minute books, as were orders of apprenticeship for poor

children. Guardian assignments state the names of the minor and the guardian, the amount of bond required of the guardian, and, usually, the name of the minor's father. The mother's name is not often given, unless she was the guardian. In the antebellum period, guardians sometimes requested permission to spend the principal of the ward's estate for the ward's maintenance; these requests were also recorded in the minutes. Apprenticeship orders give the child's name and age and the master's name. Usually, the craft is specified, as is the race of the child. Parents' names are sometimes given. (Ordinarily, the name of a deceased father is given, but the name of the mother, living or deceased, was not usually recorded until 1839, when masters were required to pay parents for the services of their apprenticed children.) There were also very occasional complaints registered by apprentices, along with orders discharging abusive masters.

Petersburg's minute books for the 1780s and 1790s give detailed information on allocations to the poor. Entries usually include the name of the poor person, the amount allocated, how it was spent, and, where appropriate, the names of those who provided nursing, housing, or other benefits. Such entries are rare in the nineteenth-century minute books. Sporadic reports of the Overseers of the Poor are, however, collected in Auditors Item 227 in the Virginia State Library.

The minute books also provide evidence of the hustings court's role as an instrument of racial control, in the granting (and occasional denial) of applications for free papers and for permission to remain in Virginia. There are a few orders declaring applicants non-Negro by virtue of descent from Indians and whites only. These last orders contain some genealogical information; the other orders give names only. In general, the minutes are erratic in reporting the race of persons who appeared on routine business.

The clerks' inconsistency in specifying race also makes it difficult to analyze criminal proceedings systematically. The minutes do give the names and status (slave or free) of persons suspected of crimes; they also state the charge and the disposition of the case. These entries are especially interesting for the period before 1820, when the minutes contain testimony of witnesses in cases sent on to superior courts, testimony that conveys a considerable amount of useful social detail. Also in the minutes are grand jury presentments against violators of local ordinances; these concern fire and health hazards, gambling, illegal retailing of liquor, and insufficient attention on the court's part to the earlier presentments of the grand jury. Breach-of-the-peace proceedings also appear in the minutes. These give the names of accuser and accused, along with the disposition of the case. The cause of the complaint (wife beating, for example, or threatening to burn down a house) sometimes appears but often does not. There are also a few paternity suits noted; these give the names of the mother, the alleged father, and the disposition of the case.

Other entries located in the minute books include: licenses granted to liquor dealers, importers, tobacco manufacturers, butchers, lawyers, and ministers; declarations of foreigners' intentions to become United States citizens (here names and countries of origin are given); oaths of insolvency; occasional affidavits supporting pension claims (these contain mainly genealogy); and exemptions of slaveholders from paying taxes on infirm slaves, along with other tax adjustments.

The deed books are organized chronologically; if one wants to read only a particular kind of deed (say, marriage contracts), it is still necessary to skim all the other deeds in order to distinguish which is which. All sales of real estate were recorded, along with certificates of relinquishment of dower. Long-term leases were also routinely recorded. Not routinely recorded were rental agreements, sales of personal property, and sales of slaves, although a few deeds of each kind do appear. Gifts of real estate and of personal property were generally recorded, as were deeds establishing separate estates for married women (marriage contracts, separation agreements, deeds of gift, and deeds of purchase and sale). Another large class of deeds were those concerning debts. Among these were deeds of trust, entered

into to secure loans. Stipulated here are the names of the
parties and the date payment was due; the collateral put up
by the debtor, the amount of the debt, and the cause of
indebtedness may or may not be given. There are also deeds
of release for debtors who managed to pay on schedule
and, after 1840, accounts of trust sales—sales of the property of debtors who did not pay on time. In the deed books
of the 1850s, loans from the new building and loan associations appear. Other deeds include powers of attorney,
agreements among heirs on the division of inheritances,
subscription sheets for new organizations like fire and theatre companies, and slave manumissions. Manumissions,
as they are short, are relatively easy to spot. After about
1820, they typically give the first and last name of the slave,
along with age, height, skin color, and any other distinguishing physical characteristics. Before 1820, information
of this kind is less often given, but the motives for manumission are stated somewhat more often. In deeds of all
kinds, race is stipulated only if the person drawing up the
deed saw fit to do so; the clerks did not take it upon themselves to insert this information.

The same is true of the wills; race is specified only if the
writer of the will chose to specify it. Besides wills, the will
books contain inventories of the personal property
(including slaves) of deceased persons. Some of these are
extremely detailed and could be put to good use by a student of material culture. This is also true of the account
books. The account books contain lists of income and
expenditures of estates, as rendered by administrators,
executors, guardians, and trustees. These are uncommonly good sources for identifying gainfully employed
women.

The circuit court chancery order books consist of decrees
issued as the result of actions in equity; from the decrees,
it is possible to learn something about conflicts over inheritance and about the complications attending separate
estates for married women. From 1835 on, these order
books contain divorce decrees. (Other sources on divorce
are separation agreements, recorded in the deed books, and

legislative petitions, which are organized first by place and second chronologically.)

The land books are annual lists of those paying taxes on real estate. They do not identify the race of the taxpayers. The personal property books, however, do identify taxpayers by race. The personal property books are annual lists of those who paid taxes on slaves and other personal property. They do not stipulate whether the taxpayer was the owner or the hirer of the slaves enumerated. Until 1842, taxable property consisted of slaves over twelve years of age, horses, and carriages. (The exception was in 1815, when special taxes were placed on a variety of household items; the 1815 personal property book could thus be another very useful source for a study of material culture.) In 1842 and 1843, a number of items were added to the tax lists, including watches, clocks, pianos, and portions of income from dividends and professional fees. There was another major addition of taxable items in 1852, including many forms of income and the total value of household furnishings. Some of the personal property books also contain lists of licensed business owners.

Beginning in 1853 and 1854, Virginia jurisdictions began to keep vital records. The birth register gives the child's name, sex, race, birth date, and birthplace. Also given are the mother's name and the name and occupation of the father (for free children) or owner (for slave children). Finally, the birth register states whether the child was born alive or dead and whether the birth was multiple, also leaving room for comments on birth defects or other unusual circumstances. The death register gives the name, race, status (slave or free), sex, and age of the deceased, along with the date, place, and cause of death. The following additional information was also recorded, but for whites only: the birthplace and occupation of the deceased (occupations are given for women as well as for men), the names of the deceased's parents and spouse, the name of the person furnishing the foregoing information, and the relationship of that person to the deceased. I have not run a statistical check, but my impression is that the death register's reporting was very poor for Petersburg's free black population. The marriage register, meanwhile, did not stipulate race at all. The marriage register did give the names of both bride and groom, their ages, places of birth and residence, and the names of their parents and the minister who performed the ceremony. Also noted was the previous marital status of both bride and groom (single or widowed—there was no column for divorce). Occupations were listed for grooms, but not for brides.

In addition to the public records listed above, manuscripts of private institutions were located as follows:

Bristol Parish Vestry Book, 1788–1901, St. Paul's Episcopal Church, Petersburg

Church Records, Tabb Street Presbyterian Church, Union Theological Seminary, Richmond

Dorcas Society Minutes, 1856–59, Minutes, 1854–84, Sunday School Society of Market Street Baptist Church Minutes, 1850–52, First Baptist Church (Washington Street), Petersburg

Gillfield Baptist Church Records, Alderman Library, University of Virginia

Grace Church Minutes of Vestry Meetings, 1843–93, Parish Register, 1841–92, Christ and Grace Episcopal Church, Petersburg

Hanover Presbytery Minutes, Union Theological Seminary, Richmond

Minutes of the Dorcas Society of the Washington Street M. E. Sabbath School—Established 1844, Keiley Family Papers, Virginia Historical Society

Petersburg Benevolent Mechanic Association Records, 1825–36, Virginia Historical Society

Petersburg Benevolent Mechanic Association Records, 1825–1921, Alderman Library, University of Virginia

Petersburg Franklin Society Minutes, William R. Perkins Library, Duke University

Record of Inquisitions taken by James Davidson Coroner of the Town of Petersburg Commencing 16th of September, 1825, William R. Perkins Library, Duke University

R. G. Dun & Co. Credit Ledgers, Virginia, Vol. 11 (Dinwiddie County), Baker Library, Harvard University Graduate School of Business Administration

Second Baptist Church Records, Virginia Baptist Historical Society, Richmond

Stewards and Leaders Record, Sept. 21, 1810 to Aug. 31, 1827, Washington Street United Methodist Church, Petersburg

Upper Appomattox Company Records, Virginia Historical Society

Among personal, family, and business papers, the richest for this study were the papers of the Cameron, Mordecai, Ruffin, and Beckwith families, along with the Craig Letters, the Beale-Davis Papers, and the papers of Charles Campbell (College of William and Mary) and William S. Simpson. Full citations for these are given below. Also listed are the names of all manuscript collections that provided some useful information.

WILLIAM R. PERKINS LIBRARY, DUKE UNIVERSITY

Fletcher Harris Archer Papers
William T. Bain Letters
Thomas Baxter Papers
John G. Brodnax Letters and Papers
Charles Campbell Papers
Winifred A. Cowand Letters
Alexander Cunningham Letters and Papers
Asa G. Fowlkes Papers
Fuller-Thomas Family Papers
Hiram Haines Letters
William E. Hardy Papers
Joseph Jones Papers
Daniel William Lassiter Papers
Abner Johnson Leavenworth and Frederick P. Leavenworth Papers
Robert Leslie Papers

Ellis Malone Papers
David May Papers
John L. Mertens Papers
B. and Y. M. Moody Letters
Jacob Mordecai Letters and Papers
Mary Ann Peabody Papers
Peebles Family Papers
Snow Family Papers
William F. Spotswood Papers
Rosalia E. Taylor Papers
Paul Turner Vaughan Papers
James King Wilkerson Papers

SOUTHERN HISTORICAL COLLECTION, UNIVERSITY OF
NORTH CAROLINA—CHAPEL HILL

James W. Albright Diary and Reminiscences
Beale-Davis Papers
Edmund Ruffin Beckwith Papers
James Payne Beckwith, Jr. Papers
Thomas Bragg Diary
Cameron Family Papers
Harrison Henry Cocke Papers
Margaret Mordecai Devereux Papers
John Early Diary
Ferebee-Gregory-McPherson Papers
Heartt and Wilson Family Papers
Hubard Papers
Drury Lacy Papers
Thomas Muldrop Logan Papers
Mordecai Family Papers
George W. Mordecai Papers
Ruffin-Meade Papers
White Hill Plantation Books
Lewis Neale Whittle Papers
Joseph H. Young Papers

VIRGINIA HISTORICAL SOCIETY

Margaret Stanly Beckwith, "Reminiscences, 1844–1865"
William Bolling Diary

Carrington Family Papers
Chamberlayne Family Papers
David Dunlop Tobacco Company Account Book, 1847–56
James Minor Holladay Papers
Keiley Family Papers
George Bolling Lee Papers
Ida (Spooner) Lownes Commonplace Book
Massie Family Papers
Nisbet Family Papers
Ridley Family Papers (Southampton County, Virginia)
Edmund Ruffin Papers
Skipwith Family Papers
Spotswood Family Papers

ALDERMAN LIBRARY, UNIVERSITY OF VIRGINIA

Baxter Family Papers
Bernard Family Papers
Margaret and Mary Craig Letters
Gilliam Family Papers
Anne Fontain Maury Diary
Jacob W. Morton Papers
Prentis Family Papers
Papers of the Spooner and Lownes Families

EARL GREGG SWEM LIBRARY, COLLEGE OF WILLIAM AND MARY

John Thompson Brown Papers
Cabaniss Papers
Charles Campbell Papers
Dorsey and Coupland Papers
Leavenworth Papers

ARCHIVES BRANCH, VIRGINIA STATE LIBRARY

Bolling Family Records, 1747–1843
Gibson Papers
Henry McClaren Collection
William S. Simpson Papers

Dandridge Spotswood Collection
Martha Spotswood Papers

NORTH CAROLINA DIVISION OF ARCHIVES AND HISTORY

James B. Clifton Diary
Little-Mordecai Collection
Pattie Mordecai Collecton
Rice Letters
Alfred M. Scales Papers

PETERSBURG NEWSPAPERS

American Constellation, 1834–35, 1838
American Star, 1817
American Statesman, 1841
Country Advertiser, 1839
Daily Courier, 1814–15
Daily Express, 1852–53, 1855–60
Farmers' Journal, 1860
Intelligencer,★ 1788, 1791, 1793, 1796–97, 1799–1801,
    1804–1809, 1811–16, 1819–21, 1824–29, 1834–36,
    1840–41, 1843–60
Little Cockade, 1841
Morning Advertiser, 1825
Old Dominion, 1830
Press, 1858–60
Republican, 1801–1804, 1808–1809, 1815–16, 1818–22,
    1826, 1843–44, 1846–50
Southern Farmer, 1856
South-Side Democrat, 1852–58
Times, 1831
Virginia Conductor, 1859
Virginia Index, 1860
Virginia Mercury, 1817
Virginia Star and Petersburg Advertiser, 1795

★ Title varies.

Notes

INTRODUCTION

1. The original idea for this book took shape after a study of the statutory law of married women's property made it clear that some women were able to escape their common-law disabilities through the use of separate estates; a reading of Philip J. Greven, Jr., *Four Generations: Population, Land, and Family in Colonial Andover, Massachusetts* (Ithaca: Cornell University Press, 1970), and Jackson Turner Main, *The Social Structure of Revolutionary America* (Princeton: Princeton University Press, 1965), led to the hunch that the significance of separate estates might be assessed through the use of local public records. Mary P. Ryan, *Cradle of the Middle Class: The Family in Oneida County, New York, 1790–1865* (Cambridge: Cambridge University Press, 1981), is an excellent recent example of how local records may be used to illuminate the history of women and the family.

2. Dexter, *Colonial Women of Affairs: Women in Business and the Professions in America before 1776* (2nd ed.; Boston: Houghton Mifflin, 1931), pp. 182–92; Dexter, *Career Women of America, 1776–1840* (Francestown, N. H.: Marshall Jones Company, 1950), pp. 219–20; Welter, "The Cult of True Womanhood: 1820–1860," *American Quarterly*, XVIII (Summer 1966), 151–74.

3. Mary Cumming to Margaret Craig, 25 November 1811,

Margaret and Mary Craig Letters, Public Record Office of Northern Ireland, No. T1475/2, Virginia Colonial Records Project, Supp. Reel 46, University of Virginia (hereafter cited as Craig Letters); Anna Campbell to cousin, 20 April 1856, Charles Campbell Papers, College of William and Mary.

4. Culture, of course, has many definitions; for controversy over the meanings of "women's culture," see Ellen DuBois et al., "Politics and Culture in Women's History: A Symposium," *Feminist Studies,* VI (Spring 1980), 26–64. This book concentrates on certain limited aspects of culture—on attitudes, values, and some of the behavior that grew out of those attitudes and values. I do not mean to suggest that women's culture encompassed only these things.

5. Lerner, "Placing Women in History: Definitions and Challenges," *Feminist Studies,* III (Fall 1975), 5–6.

CHAPTER 1 PETERSBURG: THE SETTING

1. Quoted in the *New-England Historical and Genealogical Register and Antiquarian Journal,* XXVII (July 1873), 251–52.

2. Davis, *Three Centuries of an Old Virginia Town: The Story of Petersburg, Its History and Memorials* (Richmond, 1942), p. 1.

There were also several technical reasons for settling on Petersburg. The point of departure for this study was the realization that through separate estates married women could acquire considerable power over property and that this power could be measured and plotted over time. It made sense to study a Virginia community for two reasons. First, Virginia required the documents establishing separate estates to be publicly recorded. Second, Virginia did not remove married women's common-law disabilities as to property until 1877. Thus, for an unusually long period of time, persons who wished married women to own property would have to resort to separate estates, in the process leaving a record of their intentions. Petersburg itself had two additional virtues—a full run of records and a population that remained small enough to allow one person to read all the documents.

For scholarly histories of Petersburg, see William D. Henderson, *The Unredeemed City: Reconstruction in Petersburg, Virginia: 1865–1874* (Washington, D.C.: University Press of America,

1977) and *Gilded Age City: Politics, Life, and Labor in Petersburg, Virginia, 1874–1889* (Washington, D.C.: University Press of America, 1980).

3. James G. Scott and Edward A. Wyatt, IV, *Petersburg's Story: A History* (Petersburg: Titmus Optical Company, 1960), pp. 3–31; Writers' Program of the Work Projects Administration in the State of Virginia, *Dinwiddie County: "The Countrey of the Apamatica"* (Richmond: Whittet & Shepperson, 1942), pp. 9–59; J. Pinckney Williamson, *"Ye Olden Tymes": History of Petersburg, Va., for Nearly 300 Years* (Petersburg: Frank A. Owen, 1906), pp. 3–17; Edward Pollock, *Historical and Industrial Guide to Petersburg, Virginia* (Petersburg: n. p., 1884), pp. 6–21.

4. In 1800, the sex ratio among whites aged sixteen and above was 157.4 (males per 100 females); in 1820, it was 145.5.

5. Jedidiah Morse, *The American Gazetteer* (Boston, 1797); Duke de la Rochefoucault Liancourt, *Travels Through the United States of North America, the Country of the Iroquois, and Upper Canada, in the Years 1795, 1796, and 1797; With an Authentic Account of Lower Canada* (4 vols.; London: R. Phillips, 1799), III, 110–11; Isaac Weld, Jr., *Travels Through the States of North America and the Provinces of Upper and Lower Canada, During the Years 1795, 1796, and 1797* (London: John Stockdale, 1799), p. 106.

6. Respectively, Morse, *Gazetteer;* Thomas Fairfax, *Journey from Virginia to Salem Massachusetts 1799* (London: Private printing, 1936), p. 2; J. F. D. Smyth, *A Tour in the United States of America* (2 vols.; London: G. Robinson, 1784), I, 62.

7. William Prentis to Joseph Prentis, 6 July 1800, Prentis Family Papers, University of Virginia; Mary Cumming to Margaret Craig, 17 November 1812, 24 November 1814, Craig Letters.

8. Emily Ellsworth Ford Skeel, ed., *Notes on the Life of Noah Webster* (2 vols.; New York: Privately printed, 1912), I, 143; Benjamin Henry Latrobe, *The Journal of Latrobe, Being the Notes and Sketches of an Architect, Naturalist and Traveler in the United States from 1796 to 1820* (New York: D. Appleton and Company, 1905), pp. 22–23.

9. Weld, *Travels,* p. 106; *Intelligencer,* 23 April 1805, 21 June 1808; quotations from "Reminiscences of Petersburg," *Index,* 10 October 1868.

10. Edward A. Wyatt, IV, "Three Petersburg Theatres," *William and Mary Quarterly,* 2nd Series, XXI (April 1941), 83–110; Susanne K. Sherman, "Thomas Wade West, Theatrical Impressario, 1790–1799," *William and Mary Quarterly,* 3rd Series, IX (January 1952), 10–28; James H. Dorman, Jr., *Theater in the Ante*

Bellum South, 1815–1861 (Chapel Hill: University of North Carolina Press, 1967), pp. 23–25.

11. *Republican,* 30 December 1805; *Intelligencer,* 14 March 1806.

12. Mary Ann Cameron to Thomas D. Bennehan, 12 February 1821, Cameron Family Papers, in the Southern Historical Collection, University of North Carolina—Chapel Hill; Minutes I, 355 (1791); "Reminiscences of Petersburg," *Index,* 3 October 1868.

13. *Ibid.*

14. Mary Cumming to Margaret Craig, 6 December 1811, Craig Letters.

15. Calculated from the land and personal property books for 1790. Taxable property consisted of land (taxed according to its annual rental value), slaves over twelve years of age (taxed by the head), horses, and carriages. The tax books did not distinguish between those who owned slaves and those who hired slaves. This calculation includes all taxes paid by living individuals except for the taxes paid on tobacco warehouses, there being no comparable taxes levied on other businesses.

16. The population figures come from United States, *Return of the Whole Number of Persons within the Several Districts of the United States, . . .* (Philadelphia: Childs and Swaine, 1791) and *Aggregate Amount of Persons within the United States in the Year 1810* (Washington, D. C.: n. p., 1811). Figures on taxpayers are calculated from the land book and personal property book for 1810.

17. "Reminiscences of Petersburg," *Index,* 24 October 1868 (first quotation); *Republican,* 13 September 1816 (second quotation); Morris Birkbeck, *Notes on a Journey in America, from the Coast of Virginia to the Territory of Illinois* (2nd ed.; London: Severn & Co. for James Ridgway, 1818), pp. 15–16; *Niles' Weekly Register,* 29 July, 15 August 1815.

18. *Republican,* 20, 24, 27 September 1816; Anne Fontain Maury Diary, 28 March 1832, University of Virginia; Joseph Martin, *A New and Comprehensive Gazetteer of Virginia, and the District of Columbia* (Charlottesville, Va.: Joseph Martin, 1835), p. 163.

19. Philip Slaughter, *A History of Bristol Parish, Va., with Genealogies of Families Connected Therewith, and Historical Illustrations* (2nd ed.; Richmond: J. W. Randolph & English, 1879), pp. 36–37; Luther P. Jackson, *A Short History of the Gillfield Baptist Church of Petersburg, Virginia* (Petersburg: Virginia Printing Co., 1937), pp. 6–14; William S. Plumer, *Manual for the Members of*

the Presbyterian Church in Petersburg, Virginia (Petersburg: Yancey & Wilson, 1833), pp. 4–6; *Literary and Evangelical Magazine,* VII (1824), 212.

20. Minutes, April 1809 to February 1810; *Republican,* 12 December 1815, 9 January 1816, 30 May 1817. The story in question was the lead item in a new literary publication, *The Aeolian Harp, and Young Ladies' and Gentlemen's Literary Repository,* 4 August 1821.

21. Samuel Mordecai to Ellen Mordecai, ? September 1828, Jacob Mordecai Letters and Papers, Duke University; Ellen Mordecai to Samuel Mordecai, 5 April 1829, Mordecai Family Papers in the Southern Historical Collection, University of North Carolina—Chapel Hill.

22. William S. Simpson to William Colquhoun, 1 July 1830, William S. Simpson Papers, Accession 23886, Personal Papers Collection, Archives Branch, Virginia State Library; *Niles' Weekly Register,* 5 October 1833; Philip Morrison Rice, "Internal Improvements in Virginia, 1775–1860," (Unpublished Ph.D. dissertation, University of North Carolina, 1948), pp. 303–8; Peter C. Stewart, "Railroads and Urban Rivalries in Antebellum Eastern Virginia," *Virginia Magazine of History and Biography,* LXXXI (January 1973), 3–22.

23. United States, Manuscript Census Schedules, Industry, 1850; *Ibid.,* 1860; United States, *Statistics of the United States, (Including Mortality, Property, &c.,) in 1860. . . .* (Washington, D.C.: Government Printing Office, 1866), p. xviii; Edward A. Wyatt, IV, "Rise of Industry in Ante-Bellum Petersburg," *William and Mary Quarterly,* 2nd Series, XVII (January 1937), 1–36.

24. Mary Cumming to Andrew Craig, 29 January 1813, Craig Letters. Statistics on taxpaying were calculated from the land and personal property books for the years given. The list of taxable items had expanded considerably by 1860; I have counted only those taxes paid on land, slaves, horses, and carriages, for purposes of comparison with the earlier period.

25. *Express,* 2 December 1859.

26. *South-Side Democrat,* 10 November 1853; *Press,* 18 October 1858.

27. *South-Side Democrat,* 31 December 1853; *Intelligencer,* 8 April 1859.

28. *South-Side Democrat,* 21 November 1853, 25 September 1854; *Express,* 31 March 1858; R. G. Dun & Co. Credit Ledger, Virginia, Vol. 11, pp. 404, 432, Baker Library, Harvard University Graduate School of Business Administration. Hereafter

cited as Dun Credit Ledger. In all quotations from the credit ledger, abbreviations have been spelled out.

29. Henry A. Murray, *Lands of the Slave and the Free: or, Cuba, the United States, and Canada* (London: G. Routledge & Co., 1857), p. 216. See also Charles Mackay, *Life and Liberty in America: or, Sketches of a Tour in the United States and Canada in 1857–8* (New York: Harper & Brothers, 1859), p. 221; John Shaw, *A Ramble Through the United States, Canada, and the West Indies* (London: J. F. Hope, 1856), p. 198.

30. Quoted in the *New-England Historical and Genealogical Register and Antiquarian Journal*, XXVII (July 1873), 252.

CHAPTER 2 THE POLITICAL ECONOMY OF MARRIAGE

1. *Republican,* 22 June 1801.

2. The chief proponents of this point of view are, for England, Lawrence Stone, *The Family, Sex and Marriage in England, 1500–1800* (London: Weidenfeld and Nicolson, 1977), pp. 325–404, and for America, Carl N. Degler, *At Odds: Women and the Family in America from the Revolution to the Present* (New York: Oxford University Press, 1980).

3. Eliza K. Myers to Caroline Plunkett, 21 March 1830, ? April 1830, Jacob Mordecai Letters and Papers; Maria Antoinette Morton to Elizabeth C. Carrington, 5 November 1841, Carrington Family Papers, Virginia Historical Society.

4. Eliza Selden to Martha Douglas, 8 February 1791, Robert Fitzgerald to Eliza Selden, 8 April 1789 [misdated], Gibson Papers, Virginia State Library; Eliza Selden to Robert Fitzgerald, 21 April 1791, Eliza (Selden) Macmurdo Letter, Virginia Historical Society. Eliza Selden was married within a few months and died the following year, apparently from complications attending childbirth.

5. Fanny Bernard to George S. Bernard, 3 March 1856, Bernard Family Papers, University of Virginia.

6. Dun Credit Ledger, 494h.

7. Ann Eliza (Pleasants) Gordon to Thomas E. Massie, 30 November, 22 December 1854, Massie Family Papers, Virginia Historical Society; William S. Simpson to Walter McIndoe, 29 April 1833, William S. Simpson Papers.

8. Mary L. Simpson to Jane E. Levick, 30 January 1823, William S. Simpson to Sophy Hooper, 11 November 1826, William S. Simpson Papers; Mary D. Smith to Mary Jones, 18 August 1842, Joseph Jones Papers, Duke University; W. R. Drinkard to Fletcher H. Archer, 30 November 1847, Fletcher Harris Archer Papers, Duke University; S. B. Parker to Daniel Lassiter, 13 January 1854, Daniel William Lassiter Papers, Duke University.

9. E. W. Goodwyn to William B. Goodwyn, 1 February 1808, Ridley Family Papers (Southampton County, Virginia), Virginia Historical Society; Herbert Gregory to Francis R. Gregory, 15 March 1831, Ferebee-Gregory-McPherson Papers, in the Southern Historical Collection, University of North Carolina—Chapel Hill.

10. If the husband died without having made any disposition of the wife's real estate, then the real estate reverted to the wife. Otherwise, the wife's real estate was treated as though it belonged to the husband. A more benign interpretation of the law's effects on women can be found in Joan R. Gundersen and Gwen Victor Gampel, "Married Women's Legal Status in Eighteenth-Century New York and Virginia," *William and Mary Quarterly,* 3rd Series, XXXIX (January 1982), 114–34.

11. Margaret Stanly Beckwith, "Reminiscences, 1844–1865," I, 1 (first quotation), 26 (second quotation), Virginia Historical Society; *Intelligencer,* 5 October 1852; *South-Side Democrat,* 1 October 1853, 19 September 1854; Marriage register, 1857; Deeds XXIV, 493 (1858).

12. In this count, the women classified as not remarrying were those who a) remained unmarried until death, death occurring at least five years after the death of the husband (women who remained single but died within five years of the death of the husband were not counted one way or the other), and b) women who remained single for at least five years and then disappeared from the records. The decision to count these disappearing women as not remarrying is based on the fact that of those women who documentably did remarry, over three-quarters did so within five years of the death of the first husband.

13. The numbers are much larger if we include women for whom ages are not known, and they confirm the relationship of wealth to remarriage. For the entire period 1784 to 1850, only 25.7 percent (18 / 70) of the women in the wealthiest group (bonds ten thousand dollars or more) remarried, while 47.4 percent (36 / 76) of the women in the poor to middling group (bonds nine thousand dollars or less) remarried.

Meanwhile, it looks as though the tendency of wealthy widows to remain unmarried was a new development that began shortly after 1800 and grew more pronounced thereafter. (This is suggested tentatively because the numbers for the period before 1800 are so small.) As the table shows, wealthy women were as likely as their poorer sisters to remarry in the period before 1800; by the antebellum period, class differences in remarriage patterns were substantial.

Year widowed	Number remarried	Number not remarried	% remarried
Bonds $9,000 or less			
1784–1800	6	5	54.5
1801–20	10	16	38.5
1821–50	20	19	51.3
Bonds $10,000 or more			
1784–1800	5	4	55.6
1801–20	6	14	30.0
1821–50	7	34	17.1

The presence or absence of children and the status of the widow as an executor (or administrator) were also tested for their possible influence on the widows' remarriage decisions. Controlling for both wealth and age (the numbers here include only those women widowed at age forty or younger), the numbers were too small to warrant any firm conclusions. Desire to retain one's position as executor or administrator, however, seems to have had little effect, even after the statutory reform of 1824–25. After 1825, widows in the wealthiest group tended not to remarry, whether they were in control of their deceased husbands' estates or not. Among widows who were not executors or administrators, nonremarriers outnumbered remarriers six to zero. Among those who were executors or administrators, nonremarriers outnumbered remarriers four to one. Among poorer widows, meanwhile (estate bonds nine thousand dollars or less), remarriage was more commonplace; among those who were executors or administrators, remarriers outnumbered nonremarriers seven to two.

The class pattern held good for widows with children. Among widows with children in the wealthiest group, only four of sixteen remarried. Among poorer widows with children (estate bonds nine thousand dollars or less), five of eight remarried. The number of widows who were demonstrably childless was too small to permit worthwhile comparison. It could be argued that the widows as a group were motivated less by concern with personal autonomy than by the desire to protect the interests of their children. Numbers do not help us distinguish one from the other: The only women who had real choices were the rich, and for them, both ends—autonomy and protecting their children's legacies—were served by staying single.

14. Mary Cumming to Margaret Craig, 9 January, 24 February 1812, Craig Letters.

15. Mary Cumming to Margaret Craig, 24 June 1812, 6 January 1814, n. d. [1812–13], to Andrew Craig, 20 December 1813, to William Cumming, 24 March 1815, Craig Letters.

16. Anna Campbell Diary, 14 April, 23 April, 13 July 1851, Charles Campbell Papers, College of William and Mary.

17. *Ibid.*, 18 March 1854.

18. Anna Campbell to Charles Campbell, ca. 1859 (XI, 81), Anna Campbell to cousin, 7 February 1859, Charles Campbell Papers, College of William and Mary.

19. Anna Campbell Diary, 18 March 1854.

20. Beginning in 1854, the marriage register became more informative than before, containing information on parentage, age, and the men's occupations. The figures given here are derived from the marriage register for 1854 to 1860. The three largest groups of workingmen were carpenters (35), laborers (29), and machinists (18); of these men, thirteen (15.9 percent) married women older than themselves, and the average age gap between groom and bride ranged from 2.4 years for the machinists to 3.4 years for the laborers. The next largest workingmen's groups were blacksmiths (8), housepainters (8), brickmasons (7), and cabinetmakers (7); four of these men (13.3 percent) married older women, and the average age gap ranged from 4.1 years among the blacksmiths to 5.3 years for the brickmasons.

21. According to the federal manuscript census schedules for 1860, 10.1 percent (242 / 2,401) of white women aged twenty-one and above were illiterate, while among white men 6.2 percent (152 / 2,466) were illiterate.

22. Newspapers in the 1850s frequently mentioned that "ladies" were to be seen in numbers only in fair weather; meetings and (indoor) performances were sometimes rescheduled so that the rain would not prevent women from attending. The observation that escorts were required at night comes from the

Misses Mendell and Hosmer, *Notes of Travel and Life* (New York: Published for the authors, 1853), p. 182. It is not clear when either of these restraints became customary.

23. Minutes, 19 August 1824, 21 May, 17 September 1840; *South-Side Democrat,* 5 November 1857. Several factors conspire against our discovering how commonplace wife beating was. One, of course, is that a great deal of domestic violence must have gone unreported. Second, many wife-beating incidents were recorded (in the minute books) only as breach of the peace complaints; the precise character of the breach was not stated, a serious omission given the fact that many kinds of misbehavior, including verbal threats of harm to a person or to property, were handled through breach of the peace proceedings. Third, in the 1850s the newspapers became the chief sources of information on domestic violence, and their reporting was erratic.

24. Minutes, 21 November 1844, 19 June 1845; Works Progress Administration of Virginia Historical Inventory of Blandford Cemetery Epitaphs (1937), no. 1624. Hereafter cited as WPA Blandford Cemetery.

25. *Express,* 26 August 1852, 3 April 1855, 23 July 1856; *South-Side Democrat,* 23 July, 16 September 1856, 27 November 1857; Register of deaths, 1859.

26. Wills II, 130 (1816).

27. Virginia, *The Code of Virginia* (Richmond: William F. Ritchie, 1849), tit. 38, ch. CXXX, sec. 8, pp. 541–42. Hereafter cited as *Revised Code* (1849). For the sake of simplicity, I use the generic terms "executor," "administrator," and "testator," rather than the feminine forms "executrix," "administratrix," and "testatrix."

28. This count includes only those wills for which an executor's bond was recorded. In a few cases, wills were publicly recorded many years after they were written. Here the wills are grouped according to the year in which they were written. For data on the terms of widows' inheritances in two earlier periods, see Lois Green Carr and Lorena S. Walsh, "The Planter's Wife: The Experience of White Women in Seventeenth-Century Maryland," *William and Mary Quarterly,* 3rd Series, XXXIV (October 1977), 555–58, and Daniel Blake Smith, *Inside the Great House: Planter Family Life in Eighteenth-Century Chesapeake Society* (Ithaca, N.Y.: Cornell University Press, 1980), pp. 237–42.

29. In the category of greatest wealth (bonds ten thousand dollars or more), all six widows who were documentably in their

twenties were excluded from executorship. In the same category of wealth, women in their thirties and forties were named executors in eight of fourteen cases.

30. Virginia, *Revised Code* (1849), tit. 38, ch. CXXX, sec. 9, p. 542.

31. From 1784 to 1830, 28.2 percent (11 / 39) of poor to middling testators (bonds nine thousand dollars or less) excluded their wives from executorship. For the period 1831 to 1860, the figure rose to 40.6 percent (13 / 32).

The wild card in all this is a set of wills for which no bond was recorded. When these wills are added in, we find that the nomination of wives as executors declined somewhat over time. From 1784 to 1830, 55.3 percent (57 / 103) of the testators named their wives executors. From 1831 to 1860, the figure was 48.1 percent (52 / 108).

32. From 1831 to 1860, a quarter (4 / 16) of the testators in the poorest group (bonds two thousand dollars or less) excluded their wives, 56.3 percent (9 / 16) of the middling group excluded their wives, and half (23 / 46) of the wealthiest groups (bonds ten thousand dollars or more) excluded their wives.

33. Eleven of the sixteen nominated the wife as guardian. Nominations of guardians by will did become more commonplace with time. From 1784 to 1830, only 9.4 percent of married male testators with minor children nominated guardians (5 / 53). For the period 1831 to 1860, the figure was 25 percent (11 / 44).

34. From 1784 to 1840, in the wealthier group, the mother was passed by in nineteen of thirty-one cases. From 1841 to 1860, in the same category of wealth, the mother was passed by less often, in nine of nineteen cases. In three cases before 1840, no bond was stipulated.

35. From 1841 to 1860, the number of modestly endowed children for whom guardians were appointed was double that of the previous twenty years. One consequence of this greater tendency to appoint guardians for relatively poor children was an increase in the number of guardians who appeared in court asking permission to spend the principal of the ward's estate on the ward's support and education.

36. Wills I, 356 (1803).

37. *Ibid.,* 231 (1795).

38. Childless testators also tended to give the bulk of their estates to their wives. For the entire period 1784 to 1860, 78.7 percent (48 / 61) of childless testators gave the entire estate to the wife.

39. From 1784 to 1830, 9.3 percent (11 / 118) of married male testators included remarriage clauses; from 1831 to 1860, the figure rose to 15 percent (18 / 120). The majority of those who included remarriage restrictions (15 / 21; bonds were not recorded in several cases) were in the upper income bracket. In many cases, it is difficult to tell whether the portion allotted the wife was equivalent to dower. Educated guesswork produces these figures: From 1784 to 1830, 71.4 percent of testators with children (45 / 63) gave their wives more than the legal minimum. For the period 1831 to 1860, the figure fell somewhat to 64.4 percent (38 / 59).

40. Wills II, 74 (1813), IV, 322 (1856).

41. Wills III, 141 (1837); Minutes, 17 March 1838.

42. Wills II, 256 (1827), III, 377 (1846), 477 (1848); Minutes, 20 September 1827, 21 May 1846, 18 August 1848.

43. The most important early proponent of a thesis of decline was Dexter, *Colonial Women of Affairs*. Among the more recent works subscribing to the thesis of decline (most of these works contain refinements and qualifications not adequately summarized here) are Barbara Leslie Epstein, *The Politics of Domesticity: Women, Evangelism, and Temperance in Nineteenth-Century America* (Middletown, Conn.: Wesleyan University Press, 1981); Ann D. Gordon and Mari Jo Buhle, "Sex and Class in Colonial and Nineteenth-Century America," in Berenice A. Carroll, ed., *Liberating Women's History: Theoretical and Critical Essays* (Urbana: University of Illinois Press, 1976), pp. 278–300; Gerda Lerner, "The Lady and the Mill Girl: Changes in the Status of Women in the Age of Jackson," *Midcontinent American Studies Journal*, X (Spring 1969), 5–15; Mary P. Ryan, *Womanhood in America: From Colonial Times to the Present* (New York: New Viewpoints, 1975); Roger Thompson, *Women in Stuart England and America: A Comparative Study* (London: Routledge & Kegan Paul, 1974); Joan Hoff Wilson, "The Illusion of Change: Women and the American Revolution," in Alfred F. Young, ed., *The American Revolution: Explorations in the History of American Radicalism* (DeKalb: Northern Illinois University Press, 1976), pp. 383–445.

44. Norton, "The Myth of the Golden Age," in Carol Ruth Berkin and Mary Beth Norton, eds., *Women of America: A History* (Boston: Houghton Mifflin, 1979), pp. 37–46, and *Liberty's Daughters: The Revolutionary Experience of American Women, 1750–1800* (Boston: Little, Brown, 1980), pp. xiii–xiv and *passim;* Koehler, *A Search for Power: The "Weaker Sex" in Seventeenth-Century New England* (Urbana: University of Illinois Press, 1980).

45. Daniel Scott Smith, "Family Limitation, Sexual Control, and Domestic Feminism in Victorian America," in Mary S. Hartman and Lois Banner, eds., *Clio's Consciousness Raised: New Perspectives on the History of Women* (New York: Harper & Row, 1974), pp. 119–36; Degler, *At Odds*.

46. *Ibid.*, p. 18. While the stated theme of Degler's book is that the family has all along been at odds with women's equality and individuality, the portions of the book that deal with the nineteenth century do not sustain this assertion. In studying variations in women's status over time or from one culture to another, it may be more useful to ask under what circumstances the family has expanded women's opportunities and under what circumstances the family has circumscribed them.

47. *Ibid.*, p. 43; "Family Limitation," p. 132.

48. Smith, however, suggests that upper-class women may have lost status in the nineteenth century when the practice of paying deference to high-status families was eroded.

CHAPTER 3 LOOPHOLES: SEPARATE ESTATES

1. Beard, *Woman as Force in History: A Study in Traditions and Realities* (New York: MacMillan, 1946), pp. 144, 158.

2. Marylynn Salmon, "Women and Property in South Carolina: The Evidence from Marriage Settlements, 1730 to 1830," *William and Mary Quarterly*, 3rd Series, XXXIX (October 1982), 655–85, is among the first works to give equity its due. For works emphasizing the limitations of equity, see Carol Elizabeth Jenson, "The Equity Jurisdiction and Married Women's Property in Ante-Bellum America: A Revisionist View," *International Journal of Women's Studies*, II (March-April 1979), 144–54; Joan Hoff Wilson, "Hidden Riches: Legal Records and Women, 1750–1825," in Mary Kelley, ed., *Woman's Being, Woman's Place: Female Identity and Vocation in American History* (Boston: G. K. Hall, 1979), pp. 11–15. See also the very apt comments of Berenice A. Carroll, "Mary Beard's *Woman as Force in History:* A Critique," in Carroll, *Liberating Women's History*, pp. 26–41; and see too Carl N. Degler, "*Woman as Force in History* by Mary Beard," *Daedalus*, 103 (Winter 1974), 67–73, and Norma Basch, *In the Eyes of the Law: Women, Marriage, and Property in Nineteenth-Cen-*

tury New York (Ithaca, N.Y.: Cornell University Press, 1982), pp. 30–36. Basch's book is the best state study of married women's property law. For additional commentary on Beard's work and life, see Ann J. Lane, ed., *Mary Ritter Beard: A Sourcebook* (New York: Schocken Books, 1977).

3. Dun Credit Ledger, pp. 377, 410, 466, 477, 499.

4. *Intelligencer,* 9 April 1859.

5. See Carroll, "Mary Beard's *Woman as Force,*" and Lane, *Mary Ritter Beard,* p. 65, for analysis of Beard's complex, perhaps contradictory, views on women's roles in history.

6. James T. Hubard to Susanna Wilcox, 3 November 1806, Hubard Papers, in the Southern Historical Collection, University of North Carolina—Chapel Hill.

7. For a more detailed discussion of the workings of separate estates in Virginia, see M. P. Burks, *Notes on the Property Rights of Married Women in Virginia* (Lynchburg: J. P. Bell Company, 1894). When no trustee was appointed, the husband was assumed to be the trustee. In Virginia, the conveyances were generally publicly recorded; a conveyance that was not publicly recorded was binding on the parties to it, but did not protect the property from other parties—from the husband's creditors, for example.

8. Recapturing the exact intentions of grantors of separate estates is complicated by ambiguities in Virginia law. Some high court decisions suggested that a conveyance granting the woman no explicit powers over her separate estate nonetheless gave her, implicitly, the same powers as a single woman or a man. If, however, the woman was granted one explicit power, say, the power to make a will, then she was to have this power and no others. As late as the 1890s, these rulings were still open to question. (See Burks, *Property Rights of Married Women,* p. 35.) Meanwhile, we do not know how aware grantors of separate estates were of the courts' various rulings. I have decided to follow the local courts' decisions, to assume that women had only those powers that were explicitly granted.

9. More specifically, 61 separate estates were established in the 1820s, 85 in the 1830s, 174 in the 1840s, and 264 in the 1850s. The count is based on an examination of all deeds and all wills publicly recorded in Petersburg from 1784 to 1860.

10. Edmund Ruffin Diary, pp. 2, 21–22, 59–60, 120–21, 141–42, 203–4 (1857), 274 (1858), Library of Congress microfilm. This reconstruction of the Ruffin-Beckwith feud is also based on the following: Samuel Mordecai to George W. Mordecai, 19 September 1845, George W. Mordecai Papers, in the Southern Historical Collection, University of North Carolina—Chapel

Hill; *Republican,* 28 October 1846; Deeds XXIV, 148 (1857); Agnes R. Beckwith to Edmund Ruffin, 9 January 1863, Edmund Ruffin to Agnes R. Beckwith, 13 January 1863, Edmund Ruffin Papers, sec. 25, Virginia Historical Society; Beckwith, "Reminiscences, 1844–1865," I, 1–2, 23, II, 34–35. The feud is also treated in Betty L. Mitchell, *Edmund Ruffin: A Biography* (Bloomington: Indiana University Press, 1981).

11. Frederick P. Leavenworth to A. J. Leavenworth, 5 September 1855, Abner Johnson Leavenworth and Frederick P. Leavenworth Papers, Duke University; Deeds XXIII, 458, 529 (1857). Of all the separate estates established by deed of gift from friends, relatives, and husbands, more than a third (119/334 = 35.6 percent) went to women whose husbands were in documentably serious financial trouble. That is, either the deed itself indicated financial difficulty, or the deed books contained some record of a sale of mortgaged property to pay off debts. The actual proportion of financially troubled husbands were probably a good deal higher than one-third, but no worthwhile estimate can be made from the available evidence.

12. Wills III, 45 (1831); William S. Simpson to James C. McKendrick, 3 October 1828, William S. Simpson Papers; Deeds IV, 142 (1812); *Intelligencer,* 2 April 1813, 22 July 1814; *Index,* 22 August 1868.

13. Deeds VIII, 237, 300 (1830), IX, 173 (1834), X, 510 (1838), XI, 154 (1839); Samuel D. Morton to Jacob Morton, 11 April 1837, Jacob W. Morton Papers, University of Virginia; Mary L. Simpson to Frederick Levick, 29 October 1823, William S. Simpson Papers.

14. Deeds XI, 258 (1839); Samuel D. Morton to Jacob Morton, 11 April 1837, Jacob W. Morton Papers. On the incidence of default in this period, see Peter J. Coleman, *Debtors and Creditors in America: Insolvency, Imprisonment for Debt, and Bankruptcy, 1607–1900* (Madison: The State Historical Society of Wisconsin, 1974), p. 287.

15. Mildred W. Campbell to Charles Campbell, 15 January 1827, Charles Campbell Papers, College of William and Mary; William S. Simpson to self, 22 October 1827, William S. Simpson to Sophy Hooper, 14 December 1827, William S. Simpson Papers.

16. William Waller Hening, *The New Virginia Justice, Comprising the Office and Authority of a Justice of the Peace in the Commonwealth of Virginia* (2nd ed.; Richmond: Johnson & Warner, 1810), pp. 602–3, secs. 26–29.

17. Deeds V, 253, 266 (1818).

18. Deeds IX, 145 (1834), VIII, 118 (1828).

19. The precise number cannot be calculated, because conveyances did not always stipulate how many slaves were being placed in trust.

20. Samuel Mordecai to Ellen Mordecai, 26 January 1845, Jacob Mordecai Letters and Papers.

21. Hening, New Virginia Justice, p. 601, sec. 11; Virginia, The Code of Virginia. Second Edition, Including Legislation to the Year 1860 (Richmond: Ritchie, Dunnavant & Co., 1860), p. 532, tit. 31, ch. 110, sec. 7. Hereafter cited as Revised Code (1860).

22. Intelligencer, 27 December 1811.

23. Legislative petitions, 11 December 1809, 15 December 1823. The petition that failed was submitted by a woman whose main complaint was that her husband had taken a slave mistress. That may have been insufficient grounds in the eyes of the legislature, or the committee may not have believed her. Divorce petitions were always written in florid phrases, but this one read more like a sentimental novel than most and may not have had the requisite ring of truth. Legislative petitions, 31 December 1820. This petition is quoted in full in James Hugo Johnston, Race Relations in Virginia and Miscegenation in the South, 1776–1860 (Amherst: University of Massachusetts Press, 1970), pp. 241–43.

24. Virginia, Supplement to the Revised Code of the Laws of Virginia: Being a Collection of All the Acts of the General Assembly, of a Public and Permanent Nature, Passed Since the Year 1819, with a General Index (Richmond: Samuel Shepherd & Co., 1833), ch. 165, pp. 222–23.

25. Virginia, Revised Code (1860), pp. 530–31, tit. 31, ch. 109, secs. 6, 14. On divorce law and its interpretation throughout the South, see Jane Turner Censer, " 'Smiling Through Her Tears': Ante-Bellum Southern Women and Divorce," American Journal of Legal History, XXV (January 1981), 24–47.

26. Of the twenty-five women who signed separation agreements or won divorces from the courts, nine were documentably in business and seven others owned substantial amounts of property.

27. Wills I, 202 (1794), 274 (1798); Minutes II, 118, 136 (1794), 154 (1795); Marriage register, 1794; Deeds II, 579 (1798) (quotation).

28. Minutes, 5 July 1802; Wills II, 130 (1816); Marriage register, 1818; Deeds VI, 6, 54, 56 (1819); Register of Interments in the Blandford Church Yard, 1841.

29. Circuit court orders I, 169 (1835) (first quotation); *Intelligencer,* 29 October 1819, 3 April 1825; Marriage register, 1820; Deeds VII, 108 (1823); Jean M. Syme to Margaret Cameron, 12 May 1842, Cameron Family Papers; Dun Credit Ledger, 394 (second quotation).

30. This count is based on the culling of all deed books (for separation agreements) and the Petersburg circuit court order books (for divorce decrees).

31. The count of marriage agreements is based on a search of the deed books. The number of marriages is calculated from entries in the marriage register.

32. Wills I, 76 (1787); Deeds I, 263 (1788); Minutes II, 25 (1792); *Intelligencer,* 1 August 1806; Chesterfield Wills VIII, 145 (1814); Francis Earle Lutz, *Chesterfield—An Old Virginia County* (Richmond: William Byrd Press, 1954), p. 100.

33. Edward A. Wyatt, IV, *John Daly Burk, Patriot – Playwright – Historian* (Charlottesville, Va.; Historical Publishing Co., 1936), p. 15; Deeds III, 479 (1809), 537 (1810); Land books, 1810–18; Minutes, 7 September 1812.

34. Deeds IV, 134 (1810, 1812); Accounts I, 53 (1813), 79 (1818); Wills II, 115 (1815) (quotations); WPA Blandford Cemetery, no. 1421. The fourth woman of affairs to sign a marriage contract in this period was Jane Bradley, an innkeeper who had lived as a widow for seventeen years.

35. Deeds II, 533 (1798), III, 429 (1808).

36. Deeds I, 492 (1789).

37. Deeds V, 288 (1818).

38. Deeds XII, 309 (1842), XIII, 254–58, 272–75 (1843); Wills III, 415 (1847); *Republican,* 8 February 1847.

39. The actual number may have been much higher; there may have been a good many "gifts" from husband to wife that were in fact compensation for relinquishment of dower, but that were not so defined by the conveyance itself.

As with other separate estates, it is not always clear whether the wife was asserting her interests against those of her husband or whether husband and wife conspired together to defeat the interests of the husband's creditors. Two factors suggest that these dower-substitution cases for the most part resulted from assertion of the wife against the husband. First, separate estates that were compensation for relinquishment of dower tended to give the wife more power than did other separate estates conveyed from husbands to wives. In dower compensation cases, two-thirds of the conveyances (17/25 = 68 percent) empowered the wife to write a will and two-fifths ($10/25 = 40$ percent) empowered her to sell. In other conveyances from husband to wife, only 13.8 percent ($16/116$) authorized the writing of a will, and less than a quarter ($27/116 = 23.3$ percent) empowered the wife to sell. Second, the available information on length of marriage suggests that the wives had generally reached an assertive age; of the nine couples for whom length of marriage is known, all had been married for more than 10 years, and the average was 19.1 years.

40. Not included in this count of deeds of gift are deeds from husbands to wives, fourteen deeds in which the estate was a joint gift from a married couple, and nine deeds from groups of unnamed friends.

41. Carroll Smith-Rosenberg, "The Female World of Love and Ritual: Relations between Women in Nineteenth-Century America," *Signs: Journal of Women in Culture and Society,* I (Autumn 1975), 1–29; Nancy F. Cott, *The Bonds of Womanhood: "Woman's Sphere" in New England, 1780–1835* (New Haven, Conn.: Yale University Press, 1977), pp. 160–96; Lillian Faderman, *Surpassing the Love of Men: Romantic Friendship and Love between Women from the Renaissance to the Present* (New York: William Morrow, 1981). Among the grantors in conveyances in which the relationship of grantor to recipient is known, there were forty-one mothers, ten mothers-in-law, eight aunts, six sisters, two grandmothers, and one stepdaughter.

42. Wills II, 94 (1814) (first quotation); Legislative petitions, 6 January 1824 (second quotation), 23 December 1839; Deeds V, 284 (1818) (third quotation).

43. Legislative petitions, 6 January 1824, 23 December 1839 (quotations); Deeds VII, 284, 288 (1825).

44. Circuit court orders V, 388 (1860).

45. Wills II, 102 (1814); Deeds VI, 235 (1820).

46. The proportion of conveyances authorizing sale, with the proceeds to remain part of the separate estate, rose from 13.3 percent ($23/173$) from 1784 to 1840 to 27.2 percent ($108/397$) from 1841 to 1860.

47. Circuit court orders III, 206 (1845), IV, 370, 416 (1854), V, 167 (1857), 305, 357 (1859).

48. *Ibid.,* II, 333 (1843), IV, 210 (1851), 248 (1852), 425 (1854), V, 25, 34 (1855), 205, 216 (1858).

49. Deeds XVI, 168 (1847); Circuit court orders IV, 238 (1851). This case also illustrates one of the ironies of nineteenth-century married women's property litigation: The married women who

were among the most active economically were also the most likely to appear in court arguing incapacity.

50. *Woman as Force in History,* pp. 132 (first quotation), 159, 166 (second quotation), 165–69.

51. For a more detailed version of this argument, see Suzanne D. Lebsock, "Radical Reconstruction and the Property Rights of Southern Women," *Journal of Southern History,* XLIII (May 1977), 195–216. See also Norma Basch, "Invisible Women: The Legal Fiction of Marital Unity in Nineteenth-Century America," *Feminist Studies,* V (Summer 1979), 346–66; Basch, *In the Eyes of the Law;* John D. Johnston, Jr., "Sex and Property: The Common Law Tradition, the Law School Curriculum, and Developments toward Equality," *New York University Law Review,* XLVII (December 1972), 1033–92; Peggy Rabkin, "The Origins of Law Reform: The Social Significance of the Nineteenth-Century Codification Movement and Its Contribution to the Passage of the Early Married Women's Property Acts," *Buffalo Law Review,* XXIV (Spring 1975), 683–760; Albie Sachs and Joan Hoff Wilson, *Sexism and the Law: A Study of Male Beliefs and Legal Bias in Britain and the United States* (Oxford, Eng.: Martin Robertson, 1978), pp. 75–80; Kay Ellen Thurman, "The Married Women's Property Acts" (Unpublished LL.M. thesis, University of Wisconsin School of Law, 1966).

CHAPTER 4 FREE WOMEN OF COLOR

1. *South-Side Democrat,* 29 November, 12 December 1853 (first quotation), 17 March, 18 March, 20 March 1854; Minutes, 15 December 1853, 16 March, 17 March 1854 (second quotation).

An earlier version of this chapter was published as "Free Black Women and the Question of Matriarchy: Petersburg, Virginia, 1784–1820," *Feminist Studies,* VIII (Summer 1982), 271–92.

2. E. Franklin Frazier, *The Negro Family in the United States* (Chicago: University of Chicago Press, 1939); Daniel P. Moynihan, *The Negro Family: The Case for National Action* (Washington, D. C.: Office of Policy Planning and Research, United States Department of Labor, 1965). More extensive summaries of these works may be found in the articles by Gutman, Lammermeier, and Shifflett, cited below.

3. John W. Blassingame, *Black New Orleans, 1860–1880* (Chi-

cago: University of Chicago Press, 1973), pp. 79–105; Frank F. Furstenberg, Jr., Theodore Hershberg, and John Modell, "The Origins of the Female-Headed Black Family: The Impact of the Urban Experience," *Journal of Interdisciplinary History,* VI (Autumn 1975), 211–33; Herbert G. Gutman, "Persistent Myths about the Afro-American Family," *ibid.,* pp. 181–210; Crandall A. Shifflett, "The Household Composition of Rural Black Families: Louisa County, Virginia, 1880," *ibid.,* pp. 235–60; Herbert G. Gutman, *The Black Family in Slavery and Freedom, 1750–1925* (New York: Pantheon Books, 1976), pp. 432–60; Paul J. Lammermeier, "The Urban Black Family of the Nineteenth Century: A Study of Black Family Structure in the Ohio Valley, 1850–1880," *Journal of Marriage and the Family,* XXXV (August 1973), 440–56; Elizabeth H. Pleck, "The Two-Parent Household: Black Family Structure in Late Nineteenth-Century Boston," *Journal of Social History,* VI (Fall 1972), 3–31. Pleck, however, does point out the value-laden nature of terms like "family disorganization," and in *Black Migration and Poverty: Boston 1865–1900* (New York: Academic Press, 1979), she has reevaluated the significance of two-parent households. The importance of the mother-headed family has been recognized by George Blackburn and Sherman L. Ricards, "The Mother-Headed Family among Free Negroes in Charleston, South Carolina, 1850–1860," *Phylon,* XLII (March 1981), 11–25.

4. For a summary of changing legislation regarding free blacks in Virginia, see Luther Porter Jackson, *Free Negro Labor and Property Holding in Virginia, 1830–1860* (New York: D. Appleton-Century Company, 1942), pp. 3–33 and *passim.* For general works on the changing status of southern free blacks, see Ira Berlin, *Slaves Without Masters: The Free Negro in the Antebellum South* (New York: Pantheon Books, 1974); Leonard P. Curry, *The Free Black in Urban America, 1800–1850: The Shadow of the Dream* (Chicago: University of Chicago Press, 1981); Eugene D. Genovese, "The Slave States of North America," in David W. Cohen and Jack P. Greene, eds., *Neither Slave Nor Free: The Freedman of African Descent in the Slave Societies of the New World* (Baltimore, Md.: Johns Hopkins University Press, 1972), pp. 258–77.

5. Calculated from *Aggregate Amount of Persons within the United States in the Year 1810,* p. 55a. According to this census, Petersburg contained 1,089 free blacks, 2,173 slaves, and 2,404 whites. In reading these figures, allowance should be made for probable undercounting of free blacks.

6. Legislative petitions, 11 December 1805.

7. According to the *Census for 1820* (Washington, D.C.: Gales & Seaton, 1821), p. 24, the town's free black population grew from 1,089 in 1810 to 1,165 in 1820.

8. Common council minutes, 11 June 1810; Petersburg, *Acts of the General Assembly of Virginia, Relative to the Jurisdiction and Powers of the Town of Petersburg. To Which Are Added, the Ordinances, Bye-laws and Regulations of the Corporation* (Petersburg: Edward Pescud, 1824), pp. 43–44; *Republican,* 26 September 1823.

9. Robertson to Lelia Skipwith, 27 August 1831, Skipwith Family Papers, Virginia Historical Society.

10. Additional discriminatory statutes included a law of 1853 barring free blacks from obtaining liquor licenses and an 1858 law forbidding the purchase of slaves altogether.

11. This procedure was used sporadically from the 1820s on. By the 1850s, minute book entries show that from 6 to 30 free blacks were jailed annually for lack of free papers. Like other mechanisms of racial control, registration requirements were relaxed at times and at other times were enforced in vigorous campaigns. In 1850 and 1851, for example, 827 free blacks were registered in Petersburg; during the ten previous years, a total of only 565 had registered. Likewise in 1850–51, 106 blacks emancipated in Petersburg (some of whom had been free for many years) applied for permission to remain in Virginia. Only 20 had bothered to do so in the ten previous years. All figures are from the minute books.

12. *South-Side Democrat,* 10 September 1856. Similar cases were reported in the *Express,* 10 September 1852, 4 December 1856. In another instance, however, a free black woman who had been sentenced to ten lashes for insulting a white had the sentence reversed on appeal. Minutes, 24 January 1853.

13. *South-Side Democrat,* 21 July, 9 August 1855.

14. *Press,* 14 January 1859.

15. Minutes, 4 February 1806, 2 July 1810, 18 March 1820, 22 October 1830, 17 December 1831, 16 August 1832, 20 November 1834, 15 January 1852, 17 February 1853, 20 January 1854, 26 January 1855, 22 February 1856, 16 June 1859, 17 May 1860.

16. Common council ordinances, 1 September 1860.

17. Wills II, 229 (1826), III, 7 (1828); Circuit court wills I, 9 (1834).

18. This count of manumissions is derived from a culling of all deeds and all wills recorded in Petersburg from 1784 to 1860. This may be a slight overcount; of the relatively few slaves directed freed by will, some may have remained enslaved due to litigation or to the owner's indebtedness.

In absolute terms, the rate of emancipation remained stable over time. Before 1806, the rate was 7.9 emancipations per year; after 1806, the rate was 7.7 per year. In relative terms, the rate of emancipation declined, since Petersburg's slave population doubled from 1790 to 1820 and nearly doubled again from 1820 to 1850.

19. Tommy L. Bogger, "The Slave and Free Black Community in Norfolk, 1775–1865" (Unpublished Ph.D. dissertation, University of Virginia, 1976), p. 49, also found a female advantage in emancipation. Of fifty-nine adults (ages sixteen to forty-five) manumitted by will from 1790 to 1806, thirty-six were women.

The loss of the female advantage in emancipation by whites may also have been related to an increase in the incidence of self-purchase; since women who hired themselves out could not generally earn as much as men could, an increase in self-purchase would have favored men. Very few deeds of emancipation indicated whether or not the slave had paid the master, however, so this remains a matter of speculation.

20. Neither a decline in antislavery ideology nor a change in sexual ethics should have affected the decisions of black emancipators, and it was indeed the case that black emancipators, both male and female, continued to manumit more women than men after 1806. Black female emancipators set free seventeen women and ten men, while black male emancipators manumitted nineteen women (seven of whom were designated as the emancipator's wife) and seven men. All figures on the gender of manumitted adults are undercounts, since the ages of persons freed were not always stipulated.

21. Deeds II, 157 (1792), III, 58, 74 (1802), 236 (1805).

22. Deeds VII, 267 (1825), X, 438 (1838), XI, 517, 518 (1840), XII, 200 (1841), XIII, 57 (1842), XVII, 263 (1848). The fact that Minor freed so many slaves in so short a time suggests that more than one emancipation mechanism was at work. Some of the slaves may have hired themselves out and thus paid their own purchase price. In other cases, as Luther P. Jackson suggested in *Free Negro Labor,* p. 191, Minor may have acted as an agent for white persons who did not wish to be known as emancipators.

23. Deeds III, 78 (1802). Similar statements were made in Deeds VII, 184 (1823), X, 541 (1838).

24. At least forty-six women were freed with their children (this does not include those freed by husbands or other kin from whom they could expect financial assistance). Twenty-one were

freed with a single child, thirteen were freed with two children, and twelve were freed with three or more children.

Ages of children were not usually stipulated in the period before 1806. Of the mothers who were freed with children after 1806, two-thirds (17 / 24) had at least one child under the age of twelve. Only ten of the mothers had a child aged twelve or above.

25. THE AGE DISTRIBUTION OF MANUMITTED ADULTS, 1784–1860

Age	Women	Men
21–30	23	16
31–40	19	17
41–50	28	18
51–60	8	13
61 and older	1	2

While the relatively advanced ages of the persons manumitted might be taken as evidence that white owners were dumping their most unprofitable slaves, it should be noted that free black emancipators were just as prone to emancipate slaves over the age of forty.

26. Minutes, 1 June 1801, 6 January 1806, 16 June, 15 December 1859.

27. Deeds XI, 518 (1840); Phebe Jackson Account Book, University of Virginia.

28. Wills II, 161 (1819); *Republican,* 18 April, 7 July 1820, 23 May, 22 August 1823.

29. Minutes, 5 November 1804.

30. The imbalance may also have been due to a higher rate of male migration to the free states. After 1830, the extreme imbalances in the sex ratio in the upper age brackets suggest that men suffered from higher mortality rates. In 1840, for example, the sex ratio (number of males per 100 females) for free black persons aged fifty-five and above was 57.5, while the sex ratio for persons aged twenty-four and above was 70.0. In 1860, the sex ratio for persons aged fifty-five and above was 61.7, while the sex ratio for persons aged twenty-one and above was 66.5. Discussions of the free black sex ratio can be found in Curry, *The Free Black in Urban America,* pp. 8–10; Jane Riblett Wilkie, "The Black Urban Population of the Pre–Civil War South," *Phylon,* XXXVII (September 1976), 250–62; Wilbur Zelinsky, "The Population Geography of the Free Negro in *Ante-Bellum* America," *Population Studies,* III (March 1950), 386–401.

31. The 1810 census listed the names of free black heads of households, but the only further information given was the total number of free blacks (with a separate total for slaves) living in each household. The census of 1820 is somewhat more informative, supplying the number of persons of each sex in each of four age categories (under fourteen, fourteen to twenty-five, twenty-six to forty-four, and forty-five and above). It appears that 87 of 289 free black households were composed of one woman and her children. This figure is the total of all households in which one female from fourteen to twenty-five was listed along with one or more children under fourteen and in which one female of twenty-six or above was listed along with one or more persons under age twenty-six. The second most commonplace household arrangement in 1820 (51 / 289) appears to have been the male-headed household containing an adult couple and their children.

32. Figures for whites in 1860 are based on a 20 percent sample. All free black households were analyzed. Women counted as mothers with resident children were those women aged sixteen and above whose names were immediately followed by one or more persons who had the same surname and who were from fifteen to forty years younger than the "mother." Again in 1860, the second most commonplace household arrangement (114 / 874) appears to have been the male-headed household containing an adult couple and their children.

33. Bills and receipts, 1830s, 1840s, Robert Leslie Papers, Duke University; Minutes, 16 January 1840. It is not clear from the apprenticeship orders whether the mothers' consent was either sought or required before their children were bound out.

34. *Press,* 23 February 1859. According to surviving reports of the Overseers of the Poor for the early 1850s (Auditors Item 227, Virginia State Library), free black females were 18.3 percent (50 / 273) of the inmates of the poorhouse over a three-year period. According to the census of 1850, free black females were 15.6 percent of the free population of Petersburg.

35. Figures on taxable property were calculated from the land books and personal property books. Figures on real estate ownership were calculated from the land books. By 1860, property other than land, slaves, horses, and carriages was taxed, but I have counted only these four in order to make a worthwhile comparison with the earlier period. Personal property books designated the race of the taxpayer; Land books, unfortunately

did not. Racial identification of real estate owners was made by reference to the census schedules.

36. Slaveholding is not used here as a measure of wealth because of the special character of free black slave ownership. In 1820, free blacks controlled 5.9 percent of Petersburg's slaves (91 / 1,548); in this period, when it was still uncertain whether freed people would be forced to leave the state, some free blacks chose to keep enslaved relatives in bondage. By 1860, free blacks had divested themselves of slave property almost entirely; only 0.8 percent (18 / 2,278) of Petersburg's slaves were controlled by free blacks. These numbers are derived from the personal property books. The word "controlled" is used here because the personal property book did not stipulate whether the taxpayer owned or only hired the slave.

37. More precisely, in the census schedules for 1860, 35 percent of free black males who were listed as having occupations (256 / 731) were listed as laborers, and 200 (27.4 percent) were listed as tobacco factory hands. The other relatively large categories of free black male employment were carpenter (42), bricklayer (23), drayman (23), fireman (19), blacksmith (16), barber (14), fisherman (13), and shoemaker (12).

38. Minutes, 3 September 1800; Wills II, 192 (1822).

39. Deeds IX, 60 (1833); Minutes, 18 January 1833 (quotation). At least five other free black women emancipated their husbands. Liddy Bailey owned her husband for more than three years before she freed him, and Louisa Minge also waited three years before freeing her husband. Deeds X, 52 (1836), 508 (1838). See also Deeds XXI, 754 (1855), XXV, 538, XXVI, 129 (1860).

40. Legislative petitions, 8 January 1839.

41. Deeds VIII, 405 (1832); Legislative petitions, 14 January 1847.

42. Deeds V, 124 (1817); Minutes, 21 November 1806; Wills II, 182 (1821).

43. Deeds III, 376 (1807); Land books, 1809–20.

44. Minutes, 27 January 1802; Deeds V, 197 (1817).

45. Minutes, 6 April 1811 (first quotation), 6 May 1812 (second quotation).

46. Land books, 1806–12; Deeds IV, 330 (1815) (quotation).

47. Gillfield Baptist Church Record Book 3, 2 October, 16 October 1859, 29 January 1860, University of Virginia.

48. *South-Side Democrat,* 22 May 1856.

CHAPTER 5 WOMEN ALONE: PROPERTY AND PERSONALISM

1. See Lee Chambers-Schiller, "The Single Woman: Family and Vocation among Nineteenth-Century Reformers," in Kelley, ed., *Woman's Being, Woman's Place,* pp. 334–50.

2. Amelia County Wills 2X, 28 December 1769; Francois-Jean, Marquis de Chastellux, *Travels in North America in the Years 1780, 1781 and 1782* (2 vols.; Chapel Hill: University of North Carolina Press, 1963), II, 422, 426; Charles Campbell, "Reminiscences of the British at Bollingbrook," *Southern Literary Messenger,* VI (January 1840), 85–88.

3. Will of Robert Bolling (1777), Bolling Family Records, 1747–1843, Virginia State Library; Deeds I, 1 (1784), 55 (1785), 240 (1786), 304, 305, 320 (1787), 351 (1788); Deeds II, 145 (1791), 342, 345 (1794), 442, 450 (1796), 563 (1798); Deeds III, 462, 478 (1809); Deeds IV, 262 (1814); Wills II, 102 (1814); Minutes I, 64 (1785), 290 (1789), 363 (1791); Minutes, 2 March, 6 April 1807 (quotation), 1 April 1811; Legislative petitions, 3 November 1785, 5 December 1812; Accounts III, 48 (1815 / 1833).

4. Nottoway County Wills III, 129 (1811); Wills II, 102 (1814).

5. The estimate of the proportion of white women who were single and widowed comes from a one in five sample of the federal manuscript census schedules for 1860; in the sample, 37.1 percent of white women aged twenty-one or above either headed households or were listed directly beneath persons to whom they could not have been married.

Tax figures were calculated from the land books and personal property books for 1790 and 1860 and cover all taxes paid by living individuals on real estate, slaves, horses, and carriages.

6. Eliza Ruffin to Edmund Ruffin, 18 February 1828, sec. 7, Edmund Ruffin Papers.

7. Mary Read Anderson to Duncan Cameron, 4 March, 29 December 1813, Cameron Family Papers.

8. *Ibid.,* 18 April 1819.

9. *Ibid.,* 15 May, 19 December 1813 (quotation), 21 February 1814.

10. *Ibid.,* 18 April 1819, 27 March 1821.

11. Virginia, *A Collection of All Such Acts of the General Assembly of Virginia, of a Public and Permanent Nature, As Are Now in Force; with a New and Complete Index* (Richmond: Samuel Plea-

sants, Jun. and Henry Pace, 1803), ch. XCII, sec. 28, p. 164.

12. Ages are known for twenty-two of the widows who made decisions for or against administration from 1808 to 1830. Of the seven widows in their twenties, six accepted administration. For the period 1831 to 1860, ages are known for sixteen of the women who accepted administration; six of them were in their twenties.

The "upper income bracket" is defined by an administrator's bond of ten thousand dollars or more. Altogether, forty-two of the sixty-eight widows who had the choice from 1808 to 1830 (61.8 percent) accepted.

13. Minutes, 7 October 1816; *Republican,* 11 October 1816; Edward A. Wyatt, IV, ed., *Preliminary Checklist for Petersburg, 1786–1876* (Virginia Imprint Series, Number 9; Richmond: Virginia State Library, 1949), pp. 230–31; Register of deaths I, 7 (1853); quotations from Accounts I, 84 (1820).

14. Wills I, 197 (1800); Deeds III, 258 (1801 / 1805); WPA Blandford Cemetery, no. 3151.

15. Minutes, 5 June 1809, 17 December 1818; *Republican,* 10 June 1809, 12 January 1819; Accounts I, 37 (1813).

16. *Republican,* 13 October 1815, 23 July 1816; Accounts I, 78 (1818) (quotation), 68 (1816), 73 (1817).

17. The Petersburg figures on the nomination of women other than wives as executors are too small to warrant any conclusions, but they suggest that a larger group of wills might provide evidence that women were more likely than were men to entrust large estates to other women. None of the unmarried or widowed men in the upper-income bracket named a woman as sole executor, but two upper-income women did. All together, 11.3 percent of single and widowed male testators (18 / 159) named women as executors; 12.4 percent of female testators (15 / 121) named other women as executors.

18. Deeds XXI, 159, 160, 241, 242, 319, 459, 485, 486, 494, 509, 545, 549, 565 (1854), 593, 635, 637, 639, 660, 666, 704, 769 (1855); Deeds XXII, 1, 57, 101, 186 (1855), 464, 482, 483, 489, 505, 603, 620 (1856); Deeds XXIII, 6, 11, 45, 60, 94 (1856), 710 (1857); Deeds XXIV, 161 (1857); Deeds XXV, 358 (1860).

19. Deeds XXI, 18, 235 (1854).

20. This count includes only those transactions made by individual women; it does not include joint transactions such as sales of undivided inheritances by coheirs. When we add sales and purchases made by trustees who held separate estates for married women, the sale to purchase ratio becomes 266 to 574.

21. Of 278 purchases made from 1784 to 1850, the subsequent disposition of the property could be traced in 209 cases. In 75 cases, the property was sold; in 12 other cases, sold for debt. In 13 cases, the property was conveyed by gift to another person; in 7 cases, it was reduced to possession by the husband on remarriage. In 63 cases, the woman kept the property until her death, and in 39 more, the woman kept the property for at least ten years (with final disposition uncertain).

22. Only 177 deeds of trust were executed by women for the entire period from 1784 to 1860.

23. There were 281 women named as creditors in Petersburg's deeds of trust. It should be pointed out that one reason there were more creditors than debtors was that a single deed of trust was often used to secure several creditors at once.

24. Deeds VIII, 162 (1828); Deeds XXI, 687, 747 (1855).

25. Deeds V, 230 (1817), 303 (1818); Deeds XXIV, 161 (1857).

26. Of those women who made their first real estate purchase in the years from 1784 to 1830, only 8 subsequently made a second purchase. Seventeen of the women who made an initial purchase in the 1830s, however, were able to make a second purchase by 1860; likewise, 17 of the women who made an initial purchase in the 1840s made second purchases by 1860; 16 women who made initial purchases in the 1850s made second purchases by 1860. The growth in the proportion of real estate owned by women may be accounted for in part by the declining sex ratio. The sex ratio among free adults (white and black) fell from 113.7 (males per 100 females) in 1820 to 92.1 in 1860. Figures on the proportion of real estate owners who were women are calculated from the land books.

In order to give the most accurate assessment of women's participation in credit dealings, I have counted the number of women named in deeds of trust rather than the deeds themselves. Counting the deeds would result in an underestimate of women's participation as creditors, since many of the deeds listed more than one creditor.

27. There were, in addition, forty deeds of gift executed by married couples; in almost all cases, these were gifts of real estate, with the wife's signature required for relinquishment of dower. In most instances, it is not clear whether the real estate initially belonged to the husband or to the wife.

28. Deeds II, 567 (1798); *Republican,* 11 January 1805.

29. Deeds XXIII, 665 (1857).

30. Deeds V, 138 (1817); Minutes, 17 August 1817.

31. Deeds IV, 335 (1815); Marriage register, 1814.

32. "Propertied" in this instance means those persons who left wills along with those who had sufficient estate to warrant the appointment of an administrator (the latter were located in the minute books). The actual intestacy rate for women was probably even lower than that given here, as administrators were occasionally appointed for married women who did not have the legal capacity to write wills. The rise of will writing among women was due in part to the rise of separate estates. This was reflected in an increase in the number of married women who wrote wills; from 1784 to 1840, only 6.8 percent (3 / 44) of the women who wrote wills and whose marital status can be determined were married; from 1841 to 1860, the figure was 18.5 percent (12 / 65). The more significant effect of separate estates was probably hidden: Some of the property willed by widows was theirs to will because it had been preserved during their marriages as separate property. For the entire period 1784 to 1860, the substantial majority of women will-leavers (75 / 109 = 68.8 percent) were widows; smaller proportions were single (19 / 109 = 17.4 percent) and married (15 / 109 = 13.8 percent).

33. John Cameron to Duncan Cameron, 23 October, 25 October 1806, Cameron Family Papers; Wills II, 73 (1813).

34. Wills II, 232 (1826); Wills IV, 25 (1850).

35. It could be argued that women were more often discriminatory because they were on the average older than the men who wrote wills; the older testator would have a clearer idea of the children's varying needs and deserts. The available numbers suggest otherwise, however. Among men in their twenties and thirties, those calling for equal divisions outnumbered the discriminators eight to two. Among men in their sixties and seventies, those calling for equal divisions still outnumbered the discriminators twelve to four.

36. Wills III, 367 (1845); Wills IV, 322, 336 (1856), 580 (1859).

37. Wills III, 153 (1838).

38. See, for example, Anne Firor Scott, "Women's Perspective on the Patriarchy in the 1850s," *Journal of American History*, LXI (June 1974), 52–64; Donald G. Mathews, *Religion in the Old South* (Chicago: University of Chicago Press, 1977), pp. 118, 184.

39. These figures on the treatment of slaves by will are derived from all wills written from 1841 to April 1865 and probated by the end of 1870. By will and deed together, in the years 1841 to 1860, 23.8 percent (20 / 84) of white emancipators were women.

Unfortunately, we cannot tell for certain whether white women emancipated slaves out of proportion with their numbers as slaveowners; the tax books do not say whether the taxpayer owned or was hiring the slave. For what it may be worth, women were 15.1 percent (87 / 578) of the whites who paid taxes on at least one slave in 1840; for 1860, the figure was 16.5 percent (139 / 843).

40. Wills IV, 316 (1855).

41. Circuit court wills I, 293 (1856).

42. Letter of Kate Spaulding quoted in Beckwith, "Reminiscences, 1844–1865," I, 36; Mary Cumming to Margaret Craig, 25 November 1811, Craig Letters; Anna Campbell to cousin, 5 March 1855, Charles Campbell Papers, College of William and Mary; Eliza K. Myers to Caroline Plunkett, 30 December 1832, Pattie Mordecai Collection, North Carolina Division of Archives and History.

43. Edmund Ruffin Diary, Library of Congress microfilm.

44. Ann T. Davis to Robert Davis, 5 December 1859, Beale-Davis Papers in the Southern Historical Collection, University of North Carolina—Chapel Hill.

45. Mary L. Simpson to Sophy Hooper, 31 December 1821, William S. Simpson Papers. For an insightful analysis of the diaries of female slaveholders, see Sudie Duncan Sides, "Women and Slaves: An Interpretation Based on the Writings of Southern Women" (Unpublished Ph.D. dissertation, University of North Carolina—Chapel Hill, 1969).

46. See Aileen S. Kraditor, *The Ideas of the Woman Suffrage Movement, 1890–1920* (New York: Columbia University Press, 1965); William L. O'Neill, *Everyone Was Brave: The Rise and Fall of Feminism in America* (Chicago: Quadrangle Books, 1969).

47. Temma Kaplan, "Female Consciousness and Collective Action: The Case of Barcelona, 1910–1918," *Signs: Journal of Women in Culture and Society,* VII (Spring 1982), 545–66, makes a fascinating beginning.

CHAPTER 6 WOMEN WORKING

1. Glasgow, *Virginia* (London: William Heinemann, 1913). Quotations from pp. 331, 339.

2. Scott, *The Southern Lady: From Pedestal to Politics, 1830–1930*

(Chicago: University of Chicago Press, 1970), pp. 28–37. The point is underscored by Norton, *Liberty's Daughters,* which provides extremely useful descriptions of women's work in the late eighteenth century.

3. Gordon and Buhle, "Sex and Class in Colonial and Nineteenth-Century America," pp. 279–83; Thompson, *Women in Stuart England and America,* p. 60 and *passim.*

4. Norton, "Myth of the Golden Age," p. 42.

5. This point, along with a number of important points about the relation of housework to other forms of work, is made by Joan M. Jensen, "Cloth, Butter and Boarders: Women's Household Production for the Market," *Review of Radical Political Economics,* XII (Summer 1980), 14–24, and Elizabeth H. Pleck, "Two Worlds in One: Work and Family," *Journal of Social History,* X (Winter 1976), 178–95.

6. Mary L. Simpson to mother, 5 November 1821, William S. Simpson Papers; *Republican,* 19 September 1817; E. C. Baxter to nephew, 19 May 1858, Thomas Baxter Papers, Duke University.

7. Mary Cumming to Margaret Craig, 31 March 1812, to Andrew Craig, 6 December 1811, 20 December 1813, Craig Letters.

8. Mary Cumming to Andrew Craig, 20 December 1813, Craig Letters; Lizzie Partin to sister, 22 May 1857, William T. Bain Letters, Duke University; Anna Campbell to Charles Campbell, ca. 1859 (Box XI, 80), Charles Campbell Papers, College of William and Mary; Mary Read Anderson to Duncan Cameron, 5 June 1817, Cameron Family Papers.

9. Anne Dade Bolling to George Washington Bolling, 6 June 1840, George Bolling Lee Papers, Virginia Historical Society; *Intelligencer,* 8 March, 3 June 1859; *Press,* 10 December 1859.

10. Mary L. Simpson to mother, 5 November 1821, William S. Simpson Papers; Mary Read Anderson to Duncan Cameron, 10 November 1817, Cameron Family Papers; Eliza K. Myers to R. Mordecai, 14 February 1836, Jacob Mordecai Letters and Papers.

11. *South-Side Democrat,* 4 May 1854 (quotation); *Express,* 4 August, 12 September 1856, 31 December 1857, 1 June 1858, 26 June 1860.

12. Accounts I, 8 (1798), 83 (1819), 122 (1824), 128, 129 (1825); Deeds IV, 241 (1814), 335 (1815), VI, 73 (1819).

13. *Republican,* 8 July 1809.

14. P. M. Drewry, *The Story of a Church: A History of Wash-*

ington Street Church (Methodist Episcopal Church, South) at Peters-burg, Virginia, 1773–1923 (Petersburg: Plummer Printing Co., 1923), p. 101.

15. Eliza K. Myers to R. Mordecai, 14 February 1836, Jacob Mordecai Letters and Papers; M. Ligon to M. Virginia Harris, 28 March 1850, Charles Campbell Papers, Duke University; Anna Campbell Diary, 18 January 1851.

16. Figures on the number of slaves per slaveholding household are derived from the personal property books and therefore do not include slaves under the age of twelve. It should be kept in mind that there is no telling whether the slaves counted worked for the person who paid the tax, nor do we know how many slaves were primarily engaged in domestic labor. The total number of households was derived from the federal manuscript census schedules. Free black households are left out of this analysis on the assumption that most free black slaveholding was familial.

17. Anna Campbell Diary, 14 April 1851.

18. *Ibid.,* 19 November 1854, 15 March 1857; Anna Campbell to cousin, October 1854 [?], Charles Campbell Papers, College of William and Mary.

19. Ann T. Davis to son, 18 January 1860, Ann T. Davis Diary, 13 November 1859, Beale-Davis Papers.

20. The high demand for domestic management manuals in the 1840s and 1850s also suggests that the frustration experienced by Davis and Campbell was typical for middle-class women. See Kathryn Kish Sklar, *Catharine Beecher: A Study in American Domesticity* (New Haven: Yale University Press, 1973), pp. 151–55. See also Sklar's introduction to the reprinted edition of Beecher's *A Treatise on Domestic Economy* (New York: Schocken Books, 1977).

21. *South-Side Democrat,* 25 October 1854, 24, 25 October 1856; *Express,* 25 October 1859. It would be interesting to know whether northern fairs also drew participation from the elite. It may have been that for southern women in the 1850s, engaging in household manufacturing was a political act, a stand against Yankee colonialism comparable to the stand against British colonialism during the Revolution and the War of 1812. If this was the case, then fairs provided elite women with a special opportunity to exert social and political leadership.

22. Quoted in Beckwith, "Reminiscences, 1844–1865," I, 71, 73.

23. Margaret Mordecai to Ellen Mordecai, 18 November 1840,

Margaret Mordecai Devereux Papers, in the Southern Historical Collection, University of North Carolina—Chapel Hill; Mary Cumming to Rachel Craig, 29 January 1813, Craig Letters; Eliza K. Myers to Caroline Plunkett, 10 August 1828, Jacob Mordecai Letters and Papers.

24. Bernard Wishy, *The Child and the Republic: The Dawn of Modern American Child Nurture* (Philadelphia: University of Pennsylvania Press, 1968); Cott, *The Bonds of Womanhood,* p. 46; Mary P. Ryan, *Womanhood in America: From Colonial Times to the Present,* 2nd ed. (New York: New Viewpoints, 1979), pp. 98–101. For eighteenth-century developments of the same order, see Daniel Blake Smith, *Inside the Great House,* pp. 25–54.

25. The quality of fathers' relations to their children is more difficult to gauge. An interesting observation comes from Jean Syme, who in 1804 wrote of having caught a neighbor in the act of cuddling his newborn son: "You cant think how much ashamed he was, of being caught so efeminately imployed, he instantly put it down, & cleared himself." Jean Syme to Duncan Cameron, 16 December 1804, Cameron Family Papers.

26. Mary Cumming to Margaret Craig, 2 May, 26 May, 24 June, 17 November 1812, Craig Letters.

27. Mary Read Anderson to Duncan Cameron, 8 November 1801, 10 September 1805, Cameron Family Papers.

28. Fanny Bernard to David M. Bernard, September 1837, Bernard Family Papers; Anne Dade Bolling to George Washington Bolling, 6 June 1840, George Bolling Lee Papers.

29. Anne Dade Bolling to George Washington Bolling, 6 June 1840, George Bolling Lee Papers.

30. *Republican,* 4 February 1809, 8 February 1820.

31. See David M. Katzman, *Seven Days a Week: Women and Domestic Service in Industrializing America* (New York: Oxford University Press, 1978).

32. Campbell figured Eliza Wilson's board at only twenty-four dollars for three months, "as she sleeps in my room." It is not clear where Charles Campbell was sleeping. Anna Campbell Diary, 24 May 1854. Ann T. Davis to son, 18 January 1860, to John W. Davis, 13 June 1860, to son, 5 July 1860, Beale-Davis Papers.

33. *American Constellation,* 12 August 1834. The article was taken from the *Ladies Magazine.*

34. *South-Side Democrat,* 8 February 1855 (first quotation), 11 November 1854 (second quotation), 23 August 1854 (third quotation).

35. *Express,* 6 May 1858.

36. For a model treatment of what can be done with personnel records, see Thomas Dublin, "Women Workers and the Study of Social Mobility," *Journal of Interdisciplinary History,* IX (Spring 1979), 647–65. For a laudable attempt to make the census speak to the question of female occupational mobility, see Clyde and Sally Griffen, *Natives and Newcomers: The Ordering of Opportunity in Mid-Nineteenth-Century Poughkeepsie* (Cambridge, Mass.: Harvard University Press, 1978), pp. 228–54.

37. *South-Side Democrat,* 20 August 1855; Accounts II, 141 (1825).

38. Harriette Smith Kidder Diary, V, 193 (18 March 1850), Daniel P. Kidder Papers, Rutgers University; Minutes, 21 September 1810, July 1823; Deeds VII, 278 (1825).

39. Jane B. Donegan, *Women and Men Midwives: Medicine, Morality, and Misogyny in Early America* (Westport, Conn.: Greenwood Press, 1978); Gerda Lerner, *The Majority Finds Its Past: Placing Women in History* (New York: Oxford University Press, 1979), pp. 21–22; Catherine M. Scholten, " 'On the Importance of the Obstetrick Art': Changing Customs of Childbirth in America, 1760 to 1825," *William and Mary Quarterly,* 3rd Series, XXXIV (July 1977), 426–45; Richard W. Wertz and Dorothy C. Wertz, *Lying-In: A History of Childbirth in America* (New York: Free Press, 1977).

40. *Intelligencer,* 12 February 1808; James T. Hubard Day Book, Hubard Papers; William Cumming to Margaret Craig, 2 May 1812, Craig Letters.

41. William S. Simpson to mother, 3 December 1823 (quotation), to mother-in-law, 19 April 1826, to Sophy Hooper, 27 April 1828, to mother-in-law, 10 April 1829, William S. Simpson Papers.

42. Physicians' price list, 29 April 1800, Hubard Papers; James T. Hubard Day Book, 24 April, 16 October 1800, Hubard Papers; John F. Peebles Account Book, Peebles Family Papers, Duke University. Fees for midwifery were given in Accounts I–IX. It should be noted that most account book entries were for attendance on slave mothers; it is possible that fees were higher for free women.

43. In the 1850s, three midwives of the nine known to be practicing appeared in the deed books as purchasers of real property. At the beginning of the century, one of four known midwives owned real property.

44. Wyndham B. Blanton, *Medicine in Virginia in the Nine-*

teenth Century (Richmond: Garrett & Massie, 1933), p. 186; *Press,* 28 February 1860; Deeds VII, 267 (1825). Accounts II, 141 (1825), III, 27 (1829), 218 (1835), IV, 29 (1838), 47 (1839), 74 (1836), 160 (1839), 266 (1840), V, 40 (1843), 380 (1844), VII, 150 (1852), IX, 118 (1857).

45. *Press,* 21 January 1860. Further evidence concerning a woman healer appeared in the coroner's report on the death of free black Simon Ruffin in 1845. "The deceased had been for some time taking physic from a white woman called Nancy Clay. . . ." The death was ruled a "Visitation of God." James Davidson, "Record of Inquisitions taken by James Davidson Coroner of the Town of Petersburg Commencing 16th of September 1825," no. 163 (manuscript), Duke University.

46. Legislative petitions, 4 May 1852.

47. William S. Simpson to M. Scales, 20 November 1820, William S. Simpson Papers.

48. *Intelligencer,* 29 November 1808; William S. Simpson to M. Scales, 20 November 1820, William S. Simpson Papers.

49. *Intelligencer,* 9 December 1806, 30 December 1808, 17 December 1811; *Republican,* 31 December 1816, 5 September 1820; Andrew Syme to Duncan Cameron, 29 December 1824, Cameron Family Papers. French was another esteemed skill, but in this period it was evidently taught mainly by men from the mother country.

50. William S. Simpson to Sophy Hooper, 11 November 1826, William S. Simpson Papers; Unidentified newspaper clipping, William F. Spotswood Papers, Duke University.

51. William S. Simpson to Sophy Hooper, 11 November 1826, to A. C. Simpson, 11 November 1828, William S. Simpson Papers; Mary Ann Peabody to Nathaniel Peabody, 19 January 1843, Mary Ann Peabody Papers, Duke University.

52. Petersburg common council minutes, 3 June 1851, Petersburg common council ordinances, 1 March 1855, Office of the Clerk of the City Council, City Hall, Petersburg; *Express,* 29 April 1852; *South-Side Democrat,* 15 July, 7 October 1856. One of the free schools did have a female cosuperintendent, however.

53. *Catalogue of the Petersburg Female College* (Petersburg: "Express" Print, 1858), p. 13; Broadside, 1854 [?], Abner Johnson Leavenworth and Frederick P. Leavenworth Papers.

54. Virginia, *Acts of the General Assembly of Virginia* (Richmond: William F. Ritchie, 1856), pp. 197–98; Legislative petitions, 16 December 1859; *Express,* 21 September 1860; *Catalogue of the Petersburg Female College* (1858), p. 3.

55. Minutes, 18 November 1803, 8 May, 5 June 1804, 6 March 1805; Accounts I, 79 (1818); Land books, 1789–1814.

56. The figures are derived from license lists of 1805, 1806, 1809, 1817, 1818, and 1819 located in the personal property books.

57. These numbers are gathered from scattered entries in the minute books.

58. Minutes I, 244 (1788), 306 (1790), II, 67 (1793), 114 (1794). The numbers here are also derived from scattered entries in the minute books.

59. "Reminiscences of Petersburg," *Index*, 12 September 1868.

60. *South-Side Democrat*, 11 December 1855 (second quotation), 21 February 1856, 21 February 1857 (first quotation); *Express*, 15 December 1856 (third quotation).

61. Minutes, 19 October 1843, 21 March 1850, 19 April, 16 June 1853, 12 January 1857. One earlier instance of a woman applying for citizenship was the case of Mary Alexander. Alexander was given to understand in 1815 that because her husband had died intestate and because she had not applied for citizenship, her husband's real estate would escheat. Alexander took the oath of citizenship and petitioned the legislature to stop the escheat process. Minutes, 7 August 1815; Legislative petitions, 6 December 1815.

62. James H. Bailey, *A History of Catholicism in Historic Petersburg: A History of St. Joseph's Parish* (Petersburg: n. p., 1942), p. 9.

63. Dun Credit Ledger, 410, 448, 477. More precisely, in W. Eugene Ferslew, comp., *First Annual Directory for the City of Petersburg. To Which Is Added a Business Directory for 1859* (Petersburg: Geo. E. Ford, [1858]), 8 of 174 retail grocers were women. In Ferslew, comp., *Second Annual Directory for the City of Petersburg, To Which Is Added a Business Directory for 1860* (Petersburg: George E. Ford, n.d.), 9 of 159 retail grocers were women.

64. Minutes, 5 November 1804 (quotation), 1 July 1805; *South-Side Democrat*, 25 September 1857.

65. Legislative papers, #271, North Carolina Division of Archives and History; *South-Side Democrat*, 20 September 1856; *Express*, 20 September 1856.

66. *Express*, 4 October 1856; *Intelligencer*, 1 May 1827. The count is from the city directories.

67. *Intelligencer*, 27 May 1808; Minutes, 3 October 1808; Deeds VI, 83 (1819), VIII, 184 (1828); Land book, 1820; Personal property books, 1819, 1820.

68. *Intelligencer,* 29 October 1819; Marriages, 1820; Circuit court order book I, 169 (1835); Dun Credit Ledger, 394.

69. *Ibid.,* 512, 498, 458, 478, 394, 408.

70. The census schedules for 1860 listed twenty-nine free black women and ninety-seven white women as seamstresses. Because "seamstress" was sometimes used as a euphemism for prostitute, these figures are even less reliable than most of the numbers derived from the census.

71. United States, Manuscript Census Schedules of Industry, 1850, 1860; Wyatt, "Rise of Industry in Ante-Bellum Petersburg"; Martin, *A New and Comprehensive Gazetteer of Virginia, and the District of Columbia,* p. 162.

72. Harriette Kidder Diary, 18 March 1850. On the tobacco industry in Petersburg see John M. Webb, "Robert Leslie— Merchant Manufacturer" (Unpublished Ph.D. dissertation, Duke University, 1954).

73. *Express,* 16 December 1856. The *Press,* 28 January 1859, reported without editorial comment that a girl had gotten her arm caught in some machinery; this is the only additional instance I have seen of newspaper commentary on conditions in the mills.

74. *Express,* 26 May 1858 (quotation), 1 June, 5 June 1858, 4 May 1859; *South-Side Democrat,* 28 August 1858. In the 1850s, there was also an attempt to substitute white for black domestics; numerous newspaper ads specified a desire to hire white domestic servants (a few said that either white or black would do). This, as with the tobacco factories, was in part a response to the high cost of slave labor in the 1850s. If there was an invasion of white women into domestic service, however, the census did not show it. The census schedules for 1860 listed only seven white washerwomen, two houseservants, three housemaids, and six housekeepers.

75. *Express,* 26 May, 1 June 1858, 19 March 1859.

76. In evaluating these figures, it should be kept in mind that for 15 percent of males aged fourteen and above, no occupation was listed. In this respect, there was no difference between whites and free blacks. The figure comes from a one-in-five sample of all households.

77. Mildred W. Campbell to Anna Campbell, 31 July 1856, Charles Campbell Papers, College of William and Mary. This is the earliest case I have seen of a woman implying that "work" meant only gainful employment.

78. *Intelligencer,* 12 August 1806; *Times,* 3 January 1831; *American Constellation,* 10 August 1838.

79. *Republican,* 15 April, 18 July 1817; Wills II, 145 (1817), 153 (1818).

80. Wills II, 140 (1817) (first quotation); *Republican,* 5 December 1815, 22 March 1816 (second quotation), 17 February, 18 March 1817, 20 March 1818 (third quotation); Minutes, 18 April 1817.

81. More precisely, 68.6 percent (85 / 124) of the free blacks were heads of households, as were 53.3 percent (49 / 92) of the whites. Women counted as "mothers" were those women aged sixteen and above whose names were immediately followed by one or more persons who had the same surname and who were from fifteen to forty years younger than the "mother." Among the free blacks, 50.8 percent (63 / 124) were mothers. Among the whites, 37 percent were mothers (34 / 92). Meanwhile, 31.5 percent of the whites (29 / 92) appear to have been boarders, as compared with a smaller 7.3 percent (9 / 124) of the blacks.

82. Among white factory hands, 46.5 percent (125 / 269) apparently lived with parents (of these, 57 were living with both parents, 61 with their mothers only, and 7 with fathers only); 30.1 percent (81 / 269) appear to have been boarders; 17.1 percent (46 / 269) appear to have been mothers; and 13.8 percent (37 / 269) headed households of their own. Many cotton mill workers lived outside of Petersburg proper. Of the 269 workers counted here, 100 appeared on the Petersburg schedules, and the remaining 169 were located in the schedules for the Southern District of Chesterfield County. All other figures taken from the census are from Petersburg only. The census did not specify what sort of work millhands did. The figures for free blacks are for 293 workers, all residents of Petersburg; 41.6 percent headed households, 35.2 percent were mothers, 17.1 percent appear to have been boarders, and 9.9 percent were living with parents, usually mothers.

83. Claudia Goldin, "Female Labor Force Participation: The Origin of Black and White Differences, 1870 and 1880," *Journal of Economic History,* XXXVII (March 1977), 87–108; Elizabeth H. Pleck, "A Mother's Wages: Income Earning among Married Italian and Black Women, 1896–1911," in Michael Gordon, ed., *The American Family in Social-Historical Perspective,* 2nd ed. (New York: St. Martin's, 1978), pp. 490–510.

84. Samuel Mordecai to Ellen Mordecai, 16 October, 27 November 1842, Jacob Mordecai Letters and Papers. On eighteenth-century patterns, see Julia Cherry Spruill, *Women's Life and Work in the Southern Colonies* (New York: W. W. Norton, 1972), pp. 276–92.

85. *Intelligencer,* 5 February 1805; *Republican,* 14 April 1818; *South-Side Democrat,* 10 December 1855, 11 August 1856.

86. Hiram Haines to Mary Ann Currie Haines, 21 November 1836, Hiram Haines Letters, Duke University; Minutes, 18 April, 22 November 1822; *South-Side Democrat,* 19 May 1856, 30 May 1857; *Express,* 11 May 1859; *Press,* 9 May 1860; Dun Credit Ledger, 431, 393.

87. Wills II, 149 (1818); *Intelligencer,* 5 September 1828; Minutes, 20 June 1822, 21 December 1848; *Republican,* 13 April 1821; Accounts I, 108 (1821–24); Dun Credit Ledger, 505.

88. *South-Side Democrat,* 11 May 1855, 17 May 1856. Unfortunately, no copies of the *Kaleidoscope* seem to survive.

89. *Intelligencer,* 8 November 1808, 9 April 1819; *Republican,* 26 April 1816, 22 August 1817; Dun Credit Ledger, 377, 524; Manuscript census schedules, 1860, Households nos. 2774, 2830; *South-Side Democrat,* 21 July 1854, 21 May 1855.

90. MARITAL STATUS OF WOMEN IN SELECTED OCCUPATIONS

	Teachers		Store / Innkeepers		Boarding-house		Millinery	
	#	%	#	%	#	%	#	%
Single	67	58.3	2	3.1	4	9.8	17	36.2
Married	28	24.3	24	37.5	18	43.9	24	51.1
Widowed	19	16.5	34	53.1	19	46.3	6	12.8
Divorced	1	.9	4	6.3	0	0	0	0
Total known	115		64		41		47	
Total unknown	64		64		59		17	

In this analysis, women who changed marital status are counted as married if they were married during any part of their years of gainful employment.

91. *Republican,* 20 September 1816; Minutes, 20 July 1826; *Intelligencer,* 3 October 1826; Deeds IX, 157 (1834); Dun Credit Ledger, 394, 458, 512; Minutes, 18 March 1858.

92. *Republican,* 3 April 1821; Wills V, 308 (1844 / 1865); Dun Credit Ledger, 382; Mary [?] to Eleanor B. Meade, 20 April 1850, Ruffin-Meade Papers, in the Southern Historical Collection, University of North Carolina—Chapel Hill.

93. Jean Syme to Duncan Cameron, 29 April [?], Cameron Family Papers; Anna Campbell to Charles Campbell, 22 March 1853, Charles Campbell Papers, College of William and Mary; William S. Simpson to mother, 7 June 1823, Mary L. Simpson

to George Levick, 4 January 1825, William S. Simpson Papers.

94. Mildred W. Campbell to Anna Campbell, 20 September 1858, Charles Campbell Papers, College of William and Mary. For discussion of the relations between unpaid work in the home and gainful employment, see W. Elliot Brownlee, "Household Values, Women's Work, and Economic Growth, 1800–1930," *Journal of Economic History*, XXXIX (March 1979), 199–209; Alice Kessler-Harris, "Women's Wage Work as Myth and History," *Labor History*, XIX (Spring 1978), 287–307.

95. *Press*, 23 February 1859.

CHAPTER 7 WOMEN TOGETHER: ORGANIZATIONS

1. Wills I, 291 (1800), punctuation added.

2. Legislative petitions, 10 May 1782, 21 May 1784, 24 October 1787. Raymond C. Bailey, *Popular Influence upon Public Policy: Petitioning in Eighteenth-Century Virginia* (Westport, Conn.: Greenwood Press, 1979), p. 44, found that petitions on matters of public concern were most likely to include women's signatures when the subject at hand was religion.

3. The first position was taken by Keith Melder, "Ladies Bountiful: Organized Women's Benevolence in Early 19th-Century America," *New York History*, XLVIII (July 1967), 231–54. The contrary position is strongly implied by Ellen DuBois in DuBois et al., "Politics and Culture in Women's History," pp. 28–36. The compromise is in Cott, *The Bonds of Womanhood*, pp. 197–206. In "The Power of Women's Networks: A Case Study of Female Moral Reform in Antebellum America," *Feminist Studies*, V (Spring 1979), 66–85, and *Cradle of the Middle Class*, Mary P. Ryan makes significant departures from this frame of reference.

4. One early but little known article did call attention to organizational activity among southern women. See Virginia Gearhart Gray, "Activities of Southern Women: 1840–1860," *South Atlantic Quarterly*, XXVII (July 1928), 264–79. See also Guion Griffis Johnson, *Ante-Bellum North Carolina: A Social History* (Chapel Hill: University of North Carolina Press, 1937), pp. 155, 163–64, 171, 418, 419, 423–26, 702–3.

5. *Intelligencer*, 13 March, 27 March 1812.

6. A lot was given to the academy's trustees in 1813, but the academy apparently did not thrive and was probably defunct before 1830. Deeds IV, 175 (1813); Legislative petitions, 14 February 1835; Edward A. Wyatt, IV, "Schools and Libraries in Petersburg, Virginia, Prior to 1861," *Tyler's Quarterly Historical and Genealogical Magazine,* XIX (October 1937), 65–66.

7. Legislative petitions, 9 December 1812.

8. Virginia, *Revised Code* (1849), tit. 36, ch. 126, sec. 2, p. 530; *Acts Passed at a General Assembly of the Commonwealth of Virginia* . . . (Richmond: Samuel Pleasants, 1813), pp. 85–86.

9. Land book, 1814, under Hector McNeill; *Republican,* 9 February 1816 (quotation).

10. Melder, "Ladies Bountiful," pp. 232–34 and *passim.* Even though Petersburg's churches were not yet in a position to spawn benevolent societies, personal piety may have played a role in the asylum's founding. Unfortunately, there is little evidence one way or the other. Letters written by two of the asylum's early activists (both of whom were clergymen's daughters) convey a serious and dutiful attitude toward religion, but certainly no preoccupation with it. They also bear added testimony to the problems experienced by the Anglican congregation. Mary Cumming, for example, called the rector "as bad an orator as I would wish to hear," but resolved to attend church regularly anyway. Mary Cumming to Andrew Craig, 6 December 1811, Craig Letters. See also Mary Read Anderson to Duncan Cameron, 24 March 1799, Cameron Family Papers.

Mary Bosworth Truedley, "The 'Benevolent Fair': A Study of Charitable Organization among American Women in the First Third of the Nineteenth Century," *Social Service Review,* XIV (September 1940), p. 510, noted that the organizing idea was contagious, and indeed, Petersburg's women may have drawn inspiration from other organizations in or beyond Virginia. A Female Orphan Asylum was founded in Norfolk in 1804, a boarding school for poor girls was established in Fredericksburg in 1803, and a similar school was opened in 1807 by the Richmond Female Humane Association. Female Orphan Society of Norfolk Minute Book, 1816–53, University of Virginia; Fredericksburg Legislative Petitions, 21 December 1803, 24 December 1807; Julia Cuthbert Pollard, *Richmond's Story* (Richmond: Richmond Public Schools, 1954), p. 98. Still, contagion is only a partial explanation; we need to know why Petersburg women were receptive to the ideas that came from other places.

Finally, there is the question of social control, which has at least two meanings. First, it means an attempt by the middle or upper classes to impose their values or behavior on the lower orders. Of this the founders of the asylum were certainly guilty; they instructed their orphans in Protestant piety and Victorian morality as a matter of course. Social control also refers to attempts to impose order and stability on a society undergoing rapid social change; the mainspring behind social action was generalized anxiety about the consequences of economic expansion, westward migration, religious diversity, and political democracy. This latter thesis is difficult to prove or disprove for Petersburg or any other location. Melder, in "Ladies Bountiful," saw social control of the latter kind as having motivated the formation of women's organizations; David J. Rothman, *The Discovery of the Asylum: Social Order and Disorder in the New Republic* (Boston: Little, Brown, 1971), saw both forms of social control at work in asylums generally. On orphan asylums in particular, Rothman posits an "explosion" in their numbers after 1830; this probably needs revision. For his count of the numbers of institutions founded, Rothman relied on Homer Folks, *The Care of Destitute, Neglected, and Delinquent Children* (New York: Johnson Reprint Corporation, 1970), first published in 1900. Because few of the early institutions published reports, Folks badly undercounted them; he missed at least five in Virginia alone, all of them founded before 1820. The problem for the 1830s and beyond is not why so many more asylums were built, but why public authorities became interested in their operation.

11. Allocations to poor individuals before 1798 were recorded in the minute books. The figure on taxpayers is calculated from the land books and personal property books of 1790 and 1810.

12. In the minute books, the clerk recorded seventeen indentures of female orphans from 1789 to 1800 and twenty-one from 1801 to 1812.

13. Linda K. Kerber, "Daughters of Columbia: Educating Women for the Republic, 1787–1805" in Stanley Elkins and Eric McKitrick, eds., *The Hofstadter Aegis: A Memorial* (New York: Alfred A. Knopf, 1974), pp. 36–59. See also the following two works by Kerber: "The Republican Mother: Women and the Enlightenment—An American Perspective," *American Quarterly,* XXVIII (Summer 1976), 187–205; *Women of the Republic: Intellect and Ideology in Revolutionary America* (Chapel Hill: University of North Carolina Press for the Institute of Early American History and Culture, 1980), pp. 265–88. See also Ruth H. Bloch, "American Feminine Ideals in Transition: The Rise of the

Moral Mother, 1785–1815," *Feminist Studies,* IV (June 1978), 117–19; Ann D. Gordon, "The Young Ladies Academy of Philadelphia," in Berkin and Norton, eds., *Women of America,* pp. 68–87; Norton, *Liberty's Daughters,* pp. 256–94.

14. Minutes I, 352, 353, 355 (1791), 1 July 1805, 6 April 1807.

15. Norton, *Liberty's Daughters,* pp. 287–94, discusses links between improved education and nineteenth-century reform.

16. John Hall, ed., *Forty Years' Familiar Letters of James W. Alexander, D.D., Constituting, with the Notes, a Memoir of His Life* (2 vols. in 1; New York: Charles Scribner & Co., 1870), I, 114–15; Mary Cumming to Margaret Craig, 6 January 1814, Craig Letters; W. M. Paxton, *The Marshall Family* (Cincinnati, Ohio: R. Clarke & Co., 1885), p. 77; Edward A. Wyatt, IV, "George Keith Taylor, 1769–1815, Virginia Federalist and Humanitarian," *William and Mary Quarterly,* 2nd Series, XVI (January 1936), 16–17.

17. Edward A. Wyatt, IV, *Charles Campbell, Virginia's "Old Mortality"* (Charlottesville, Va.: Historical Publishing Co., 1935), p. 4; "Reminiscences of Petersburg," *Index,* 24 October 1868 (grammatical error his); Edmund Ruffin Diary, 6 June 1858.

18. Mary Cumming to Andrew Craig, 20 December 1813, Craig Letters. Mary L. Simpson, who came to Petersburg from London in 1820, was likewise impressed with women's interest in politics; after writing about European politics at some length in a letter to her sister, Simpson remarked, "It is no uncommon thing in America for a Lady to be a Politician & you must not therefore be surprised at what I have been writing." Mary L. Simpson to Mrs. Hooper, 4 September 1821, William S. Simpson Papers.

19. Wills II, 71 (1812); *Intelligencer,* 28 August 1812; Minutes, 2 August 1813. It is possible that there is name confusion here; there were other Goodwyn families in Petersburg, and I have not been able to determine the names of all the Goodwyn wives.

20. Information on who was married to whom was patched together from the marriage register (which is of limited value, since many Petersburg residents were married in other jurisdictions), newspaper notices, genealogies, wills, and deeds in which the wife relinquished her dower rights in property conveyed by her husband.

Information on the numbers and ages of children was drawn from wills, deeds, genealogies, tombstone inscriptions, and personal correspondence. Reasonably useful information is available for twenty-two of the subscribers. Of these, only two had raised all their children to adulthood; eighteen were rearing children under the age of twelve. The twenty-two subscribers averaged 2.6 children of their own. Many of the subscribers were also responsible for apprentices or the children of relatives, as well as slave children; in the census schedules for 1810, the average subscriber's household contained 3.6 white children (ages were not stipulated for blacks).

21. More precisely, there were twenty-eight merchants, at least four of whom combined commerce with banking, milling, or manufacturing. There were also four attorneys, two physicians, one clergyman, and the clerk of the hustings court. Figures on slaveholding are derived from the personal property book of 1810 and are available for the households of thirty-seven subscribers; these households averaged 1.9 adult female slaves each.

22. Surviving correspondence of three asylum activists suggests that stillbirths, miscarriages, and infant deaths were all too commonplace. Jean M. Syme's first pregnancy ended in miscarriage, Mary Cumming suffered one infant death and a stillbirth, and Mary Read Anderson lost three infant sons. The absence of vital records makes it impossible to calculate infant mortality rates.

Information on the geographic origins of the subscribers comes from newspaper marriage notices, genealogies, wills, and deeds and is available for thirty-one subscribers. Eight of them—mostly the younger women—were natives of Petersburg; twenty were from a variety of Virginia counties; one came from Pennsylvania; and two were foreign born, one English and one Irish.

Information on ages comes mostly from tombstone inscriptions and cemetery records; like figures on length of marriage, definite information on ages is available mostly for the younger women and is therefore unreliable for the subscribers as a group.

23. Mary Cumming to Margaret Craig, 9 January 1812, Craig Letters.

24. *Ibid.*, 17 November 1812, 17 November 1814.

25. This perspective was also suggested in Cott, *The Bonds of Womanhood*, pp. 181, 185, and was elaborated by Susan Porter Benson, "Business Heads and Sympathizing Hearts: The Women of the Providence Employment Society, 1837–1858," *Journal of Social History*, XII (Winter 1978), 302–12, while Ryan, *Cradle of the Middle Class*, pp. 136–44, identifies important links between family and voluntary associations. Barbara J. Berg, on the other hand, sees organization as an antidote to domestic monotony and isolation. See *The Remembered Gate: Origins of American Fem-*

inism, The Woman and the City, 1800–1860 (New York: Oxford University Press, 1978).

26. Mary Cumming to Rachel Craig, 9 March 1814, Craig Letters.

27. *The Poems of Laura; An Original American Work* (Petersburg: Whitworth & Yancy, 1818), p. 88.

28. *Intelligencer,* 24 April, 2 June 1812, 23 April 1813; *Republican,* 23 April 1816; *American Star,* 21 October 1817.

29. Jean M. Syme to Duncan Cameron, 8 May 1829, Cameron Family Papers; Mary L. Simpson to Jane E. Levick, 12 May 1829, William S. Simpson Papers; *Religious Herald,* 15 May 1829.

30. Minutes, 3 January, 7 June 1814, 6 March 1815, 4 March, 5 March, 5 August 1816, 22 May, 15 July 1819. Manuscript census schedules later confirmed the whites-only policy.

31. P.M.S. [?] to Ellen Mordecai, 7 August 1842, Mordecai Family Papers; Mary L. Simpson to [?], 9 December 1858, William S. Simpson Papers.

32. Wills II, 70 (1812); WPA Blandford Cemetery, no. 27; Wyatt, "Schools and Libraries," pp. 69–70; *Republican,* 13 February 1821, 6 June 1823.

Actual attendance was closer to eighty. The trustees also tried to economize by charging tuition, but it is not clear how long this policy was in force or whether it violated the spirit of Anderson's will. *South-Side Democrat,* 15 July 1856.

33. Report of the Overseers of the Poor, 1829, Auditors Item 227, Virginia State Library; Minutes, 16 September 1824; Deeds VIII, 278 (1830), IX, 239 (1835).

34. Reports of the Overseers of the Poor, 1829, 1830–44, 1851–54, Auditors Item 227, Virginia State Library.

35. S. M. Poythress to Mr. Keiley, n.d., Keiley Family Papers, Virginia Historical Society; Petersburg Benevolent Mechanic Association, Minutes, 11 January 1858, University of Virginia microfilm.

36. Samuel D. Morton to Jacob W. Morton, 11 April 1837, Jacob W. Morton Papers; Samuel Mordecai to George W. Mordecai, 24 July 1842, George W. Mordecai Papers.

37. Percentages are calculated from the following: Plumer, *Manual for Members of the Presbyterian Church;* First Baptist Church Minutes, 2 April 1856, First Baptist Church (Washington Street); Second Baptist Church Records, 1856–1860, Virginia Baptist Historical Society; Grace Church Parish Register, 1843–61, Christ and Grace Episcopal Church; Bristol Parish Vestry Book, 1850 List of Communicants, St. Paul's Episcopal Church.

38. Nancy F. Cott, "Young Women in the Second Great Awakening in New England," *Feminist Studies,* III (Fall 1975), 15–29, and *Bonds of Womanhood,* pp. 126–59; Mathews, *Religion in the Old South,* pp. 101–23, 238–40; Mary P. Ryan, "A Women's Awakening: Evangelical Religion and the Families of Utica, New York, 1800–1840," *American Quarterly,* XXX (Winter 1978), 602–23, and *Cradle of the Middle Class,* pp. 83–98; Anne M. Boylan, "Evangelical Womanhood in the Nineteenth Century: The Role of Women in Sunday Schools," *Feminist Studies,* IV (October 1978), 62–80.

39. The first Jewish congregation in Petersburg was formed in 1858; a house was purchased for conversion into a synagogue in 1859, but was later advertised for sale because it was too small. There was also a Hebrew Benevolent Society by 1859. It is not clear what the roles of women were in these efforts. *Press,* 1 March 1859; *Express,* 24 August 1859; Louis Ginsberg, *History of the Jews of Petersburg, 1789–1950* (Richmond: Williams Printing Company, 1954), p. 28.

40. Sarah Osborne, "A Short Sketch of the Women's Society of Tabb Street Presbyterian Church, Petersburg, Va.," typescript, 1922, Church Records, Tabb Street Presbyterian Church, Union Theological Seminary, Richmond; William S. Simpson to mother, 31 March 1821, 13 November 1822, William S. Simpson Papers; Samuel Mordecai to Solomon Mordecai, 10 August 1822, Jacob Mordecai Letters and Papers; William W. Bennett, *Memorials of Methodism in Virginia, From Its Introduction into the State, In the Year 1772, To the Year 1829* (Richmond: Published by the author, 1871), p. 697.

41. *Republican,* 15 July 1823; Petersburg, *Acts of the General Assembly of Virginia, Relative to the Jurisdiction and Powers of the Town of Petersburg. To Which Are Added, the Ordinances, Bye-laws and Regulations of the Corporation* (Petersburg: Edward Pescud, 1824), p. 46.

42. Plumer, *Manual for Members of the Presbyterian Church,* pp. 48–49.

43. Olin Davis to Robert Davis, 21 April 1860, Beale-Davis Papers; Susan C. Bott to Frances [Robertson?], n.d., Dandridge Spotswood Collection, Virginia State Library; *Republican,* 29 March 1843.

44. *The Antislavery Appeal: American Abolitionism after 1830* (Baltimore: The Johns Hopkins University Press, 1976), pp. 23–25.

45. Ann T. Davis to [?] Davis, 25 May 1860, Beale-Davis

Papers; Gillfield Baptist Church Record Book 3, 19 June 1859; *Intelligencer,* 17 May 1859; *Express,* 30 May, 7 November 1859.

46. Edmund Ruffin Diary, 28 December 1857; Anna Campbell Diary, 7 March 1853; WPA Blandford Cemetery, no. 2390; A. B. Van Zandt, *"The Elect Lady,"* A Memoir of Mrs. Susan Catharine Bott, of Petersburg, Va. (Philadelphia: Presbyterian Board of Publication, 1857).

47. Dorcas society minutes, 6 October 1856, First Baptist Church (Washington Street); Van Zandt, *"The Elect Lady,"* pp. 102–3.

48. Bristol Parish Vestry Book, 17 June 1840; Churchill Jones Gibson to Mrs. Hobart M. Bartlett, 23 December 1841, Chamberlayne Family Papers, Virginia Historical Society; *Express,* 13 November 1856, 12 January 1859.

49. Gillfield Baptist Church Record Book 3, 19 December 1858, 16 January, 17 July 1859.

50. There were 543 wills recorded in Petersburg from 1784 to 1860. Of the 394 male testators, 13 (3.3 percent) made religious or charitable donations; of the 149 female testators, 10 (6.7 percent) did so. There was no great difference in the amounts given. If David Anderson's unusually large bequest for the school is excepted, the men's gifts averaged $420, the women's $475. Lawrence M. Friedman, "Patterns of Testation in the 19th Century: A Study of Essex County (New Jersey) Wills," *American Journal of Legal History,* VIII (January 1964), 47, found similarly low numbers of charitable gifts by will.

51. "The Feminization of American Religion: 1800–1860," in Hartman and Banner, eds., *Clio's Consciousness,* p. 138.

52. Bennett, *Memorials of Methodism,* pp. 696–97.

53. *Express,* 22 June 1852, 24 October 1857, 20 July 1858, 18 October 1859; *South-Side Democrat,* 21 April 1854, 21 May 1856, 2 May 1857; Bristol Parish Vestry Book, 25 July 1853. On the clergy's ambivalence toward women, see Ann Douglas, *The Feminization of American Culture* (New York: Alfred A. Knopf, 1977), pp. 109–17.

54. *Express,* 17 October, 16 November, 27 November 1857; *South-Side Democrat,* 1 February 1858.

55. *South-Side Democrat,* 12 January 1856, 27 October 1857, 1 February 1858; *Express,* 16 November, 19 November, 27 November 1857.

56. *Express,* 25 November, 23 December 1858, 21 November 1859; *Press,* 14 December, 16 December, 23 December 1858, 5 January, 23 February, 22 March 1859; *Intelligencer,* 22 March 1859.

57. E. D. Sanders, *Sketch of the Life and Character of Thomas Cooke Paul, Son of D'Arcy Paul, of Petersburg, Va.* (Philadelphia: American Sunday School Union, 1849), pp. 181–94; Virginia, *Acts of the General Assembly of Virginia, Passed at the Session Commencing December 6, 1847, and Ending April 5, 1848, in the Seventy-Second Year of the Commonwealth* (Richmond: Samuel Shepherd, 1848), ch. 248, pp. 272–73; Virginia, *Acts of the General Assembly of Virginia, Passed in 1857–8, in the Eighty-Second Year of the Commonwealth* (Richmond: William F. Ritchie, 1858), ch. 375, p. 222.

The founding of the Methodist asylum may have been a means by which Methodists asserted a claim to greater social prestige; the founding of a Methodist female college in 1856 could be read this way also. One leader of the Episcopal asylum did, in any case, express a touch of competitiveness: ". . . Mrs. Paul is so sharp that she picks up all [the orphans] she can for the other school, and in consequence our number is rather small." Mary L. Simpson to Ellen Mordecai, 18 April [?], Mordecai Family Papers.

58. The *Press*, 23 February 1859, reported that the Association for Improvement of the Condition of the Poor had assisted 94 men, 259 women, and 469 children.

59. *Virginia Conductor,* 20 January 1859.

60. *South-Side Democrat,* 11 March, 22 September, 25 October 1854, 14 October 1856, 20 October 1857; *Intelligencer,* 26 May 1859; *Express,* 25 October 1859.

61. *Express,* 14 June 1859.

62. "City Women and Religious Change," in *Society and Culture in Early Modern France: Eight Essays by Natalie Zemon Davis* (Stanford, Calif.: Stanford University Press, 1975), p. 84.

63. *Intelligencer,* 26 May 1859. Similar lists appeared in the *South-Side Democrat,* 22 September 1854, 24 October, 25 October 1856, and in the *Express,* 25 October 1859.

64. For speculation on the meaning of the new naming practice, see Una Stannard, *Mrs Man* (San Francisco: Germainbooks, 1977).

65. *Morning Advertiser,* 1 August 1825; William S. Simpson to Sophy Hooper, 26 October 1831, William S. Simpson Papers; *Republican,* 1 February 1847; *Intelligencer,* 9 March 1850; *Express,* 16 June 1852.

66. *South-Side Democrat,* 6 December 1853; *Intelligencer,* 18 July 1856.

67. Barbara Welter, "The Cult of True Womanhood: 1820–

1860," *American Quarterly,* XVIII (Summer 1966), 151–74. For a similar typology and a very useful bibliography, see Cott, *The Bonds of Womanhood,* pp. 197–99.

68. Sklar, *Catharine Beecher,* was among the first to point this out.

EPILOGUE ON FEMINISM, SLAVERY, AND THE EXPERIENCE OF DEFEAT

1. Executive Papers, June 1842, Virginia State Library (quotation); Minutes, 16 June 1842; Annual Report of the Overseers of the Poor (1851–53), Auditors Item 227, Virginia State Library.

2. Stone, *The Family, Sex and Marriage in England,* pp. 40–41. See also the forthcoming work of John R. Gillis on the history of conjugality in England.

3. Recent work on this issue includes Carl N. Degler, *Place over Time: The Continuity of Southern Distinctiveness* (Baton Rouge: Louisiana State University Press, 1977); I. A. Newby, *The South: A History* (n.p.: Holt, Rinehart and Winston, 1978), pp. 1–34; Edward Pessen, "How Different from Each Other Were the Antebellum North and South?" *American Historical Review,* 85 (December 1980), 1119–49.

4. Scott, *The Southern Lady,* p. 79. For concurring interpretations, see Mary Elizabeth Massey, *Bonnet Brigades* (New York: Alfred A. Knopf, 1966), pp. 366–67; Bell Irvin Wiley, *Confederate Women* (Westport, Conn.: Greenwood Press, 1975), pp. 178–79. For examples of the incorporation of this point of view into the general literature, see Emory M. Thomas, *The Confederacy as a Revolutionary Experience* (Englewood Cliffs, N.J.: Prentice-Hall, 1971), pp. 105–107 and *The Confederate Nation: 1861–1865* (New York: Harper and Row, 1979), pp. 225–29. Dissenting points of view can be found in Lebsock, "Radical Reconstruction and the Property Rights of Southern Women"; Newby, *The South,* pp. 166–71, 320–22; H. E. Sterkx, *Partners in Rebellion: Alabama Women in the Civil War* (Rutherford, N.J.: Fairleigh Dickinson University Press, 1970), pp. 200–201; Jonathan M. Wiener, "Female Planters and Planters' Wives in Civil War and Reconstruction: Alabama, 1850–1870," *Alabama Review,* XXX (April 1977), 135–49.

5. Massey, *Bonnet Brigades,* pp. 19–20; Scott, *The Southern Lady,* p. 170; Sterkx, *Partners in Rebellion,* p. 20.

6. Blanche Glassman Hersh, *The Slavery of Sex: Feminist-Abolitionists in America* (Urbana: University of Illinois Press, 1978), p. 1.

7. *South-Side Democrat,* 16 October 1857. By my count, white women freed twenty-one male slaves and fifteen female slaves.

8. Petersburg Franklin Society Minutes, 22 March 1822, Duke University; *South-Side Democrat,* 23 March 1854, 19 July 1855.

9. *South-Side Democrat,* 3 July 1857; *Intelligencer,* 3 September 1852.

10. *South-Side Democrat,* 27 July, 22 November 1855.

11. *Intelligencer,* 31 May, 10 September 1852; *Express,* 19 February 1858.

12. *South-Side Democrat,* 14 September, 16 September 1852 (quotation); *Intelligencer,* 1 May 1851.

13. *South-Side Democrat,* 16 March 1854, 13 March 1856.

14. Joseph H. Young to Ann Eliza Young, 10 April 1865, Joseph H. Young Papers, in the Southern Historical Collection, University of North Carolina—Chapel Hill.

15. Mrs. Roger A. [Sarah Agnes Rice] Pryor, *Reminiscences of Peace and War* (New York: The MacMillan Company, 1904), p. 131 (first quotation); Beckwith, "Reminiscences, 1844–1865," II, 9 (second quotation); Minutes of the Ladies Club of Washington Street Church, Petersburg, for Soldiers Relief, Charles Campbell Papers, College of William and Mary.

16. J. J. Cowand to "cosin," 16 June 1862, Winifred A. Cowand Papers, Duke University; W. D. Hardy to father, 7 August 1863, William E. Hardy Papers, Duke University.

17. Mary Ann Whittle to Lewis Neale Whittle, 20 September 1861, Lewis Neale Whittle Papers, in the Southern Historical Collection, University of North Carolina—Chapel Hill. The impressment of free blacks is mentioned in "Petersburg During War-Time," *The Old Guard* (November 1868), pp. 858–59; Thomas Bragg Diary, 2 August 1862, in the Southern Historical Collection, University of North Carolina—Chapel Hill; James K. Wilkerson to A. H. Wilkerson, 15 October 1864, James King Wilkerson Papers, Duke University.

18. S. H. Kettlewell to James Minor Holladay, 21 September 1863, James Minor Holladay Papers, Virginia Historical Society; James W. Albright Diary, 21 June 1864, in the Southern Historical Collection, University of North Carolina—Chapel Hill.

19. Bessie Callender to John E. Meade, 17 October 1861,

8 January 1862, Ruffin-Meade Papers; Pryor, *Reminiscences of Peace and War*, pp. 131–33, 180–87, 309–13, and *My Day: Reminiscences of a Long Life* (New York: The MacMillan Company, 1909), pp. 286–88.

20. The combined evidence from the Dun credit ledgers and city directories suggests that millinery as an independent women's enterprise underwent a major decline; the city directory for 1877 listed only four milliners. Benjamin R. Sheriff, comp., *Sheriff & Co.'s Petersburg Directory, 1876–77* . . . (n.p.: Sheriff & Co., 1877). The decline in millinery may have been offset by an increase in women in the retail grocery business. Nine new women grocers appeared in the credit ledgers in 1865, four of them surviving into the 1870s. In Sheriff's directory for 1877, 11.5 percent of the retail grocers listed (17 / 148) were women.

21. The 22.4 percent figure is for the years 1866 to 1870. From 1861 to 1870, 72.3 percent of the husbands who wrote wills naming executors (34 / 47) named their wives executors; this was up from the roughly 55 percent of the earlier period. As for fee simple inheritance, half of the wives who had children were granted some property in fee simple (16 / 32), while 28.1 percent (9 / 32) received their entire legacy in fee simple. These figures compare with 55.8 percent and 34.9 percent respectively for the period 1831 to 1860.

22. "Petition for Mr. Davis' Release," *Southern Historical Society Papers*, XXIV (1896), 240–42; William Henry Tappey Squires, comp., *Petersburg, Va., A Collection of Virginiana*, p. 54, Virginia State Library.

23. Undated pamphlet, Baxter Family Papers, University of Virginia.

Index

slaves *(continued)*
  see also emancipation of slaves
Sleppy, Adeline V., 181, 192
Smith, Catherine P., 82–83
Smith, Daniel Scott, 49–53
Smith, Mrs. George J., 191
Smith, William, 109–10
Snelson, Nathaniel, 65
Solomon, Mrs., 191
Somerville, Elizabeth Ann, 122–23
Somerville, John, 122–23
Sons of Temperance, 229
South-Side Democrat, 12, 93, 109–10, 165–66, 167, 180, 190, 227, 242–43
Spaulding, Henry, 25
Spaulding, Kate, 138–39
Spencer, Eliza, 176, 195–96, 199
spinsters, *see* single women
Spruce, Polly, 105
status, women's:
  before and after Civil War, 239, 247–49
  feminism and, 240, 248–49
  of free blacks vs. whites, 90
  historical controversy on, 48–53, 148–49, 196–97
  impact of racial opression on, 90
  property reforms and, 84–86
  separate estates and, 56, 57–58, 79, 84–86
  women's organizations and, 196–97, 232–36
Stephens, Ann, 107
Stevens, Alexander, 87
Stevens, Elizabeth, 47–48
Stevens, Samuel, 47
Stevens, Sarah Ann, 48
Steward, Jane, 191
Stewart, John, 75, 79–80
Strange, Mary, 124

Swail, Ann, 73–74
Swail, Elizabeth, 169
Swan, Amelia A. E., 98
Syme, Jean, 160

Tabb, Thomas, 114
tavern and innkeepers, women, 178
Taylor, Elizabeth, 128
Taylor, George, 109, 206
Taylor, Jane, 173–74, 206, 207
teachers, women, 172–76
  male teachers vs., 172, 175–76
Tenain, Elizabeth Ann, 186
Thomas, Lydia, 75
Thomas Cooke Paul Female Orphan Asylum, 228
Toole, Sarah J., 181, 192
Tract Distribution Society, 218
Trokes, Martha, 45
Trotter, Elizabeth, 68
Trotter, James G., 68
true womanhood, cult of, 49, 50, 143–44
Tucker, Margaret, 212
Tucker, Thomas, 93
Turner, Nat, 92
Turner, Susan, 241

Union Agricultural Society, 229
unmarried women, *see* single women
Updike, Lucretia, 167

Vaughan, James, 107
Vaughan, John, 107
Vaughan, Nancy, 75
Vaughan, Sarah, 107
Virginia (Glasgow), 146–47
Virginia Conductor, 229
Virginia Evangelical and Literary Magazine, 226
Vizonneau, André Thomas, 80